Balderdash & Piffle

One sandwich short of a dog's dinner

Balderdash & Piffle

One sandwich short of a dog's dinner

Alex Games

BOOKS

takeaway media

This book is published to accompany the second series of *Balderdash & Piffle*, produced by Takeaway Media Ltd, and first broadcast on BBC2 in 2007.

Executive producer: Archie Baron Series producer: Caroline Ross Pirie

10 9 8 7 6 5 4 3 2 1

Published in 2007 by BBC Books, an imprint of Ebury Publishing.
Ebury Publishing is a division of the Random House Group.

Text copyright © Alex Games 2007
Illustrations copyright © Andy Davey 2007

Alex Games has asserted his right to be identified as the author of this Work
in accordance with the Copyright, Designs and Patents Act 1988.

The Random House Group Limited Reg. No. 954009
Addresses for companies within the Random House Group can be found at
www.randomhouse.co.uk

A CIP catalogue record for this book is available from the British Library.

ISBN 978 1 846 07235 2

The Random House Group Limited makes every effort to ensure that the papers
used in our books are made from trees that have been legally sourced from
well-managed and credibly certified forests. Our paper procurement policy can
be found at www.randomhouse.co.uk

Commissioning editor: Martin Redfern Project editor: Patricia Burgess
Designer: Linda Blakemore Cartoonist: Andy Davey
Indexer: Helen Snaith Production controller: Antony Heller

Printed in the UK by CPI Mackays, Chatham, ME5 8TD

Contents

Foreword 7

One One sandwich short 11

Two Fashionistas 33

Three Who were they? 61

Four Man's best friend 85

Five Dodgy dealings 107

Six Put-downs and insults 133

Seven Spend a penny 155

Eight X-rated 183

Endword 207

Further reading 227
Index 229
Acknowledgements 240

Note: Words and phrases discussed and/or defined in the text appear in **bold** type and are all listed in the index. Foreign words appear in *italic* type.

This book is dedicated to anyone who works in a bookshop. You are an incredible bunch of people who do an amazing job.

And would you mind putting a big pile of these near the till, please?

Foreword

After the first series of *Balderdash & Piffle* (and thanks to the sterling work of amateur detectives all over the country, who helped us to investigate the history of words and phrases), forty-three changes were made to *The Oxford English Dictionary* (*OED*). Why are we so proud of that?

It's partly because the English language is our greatest national treasure, and there is a pure satisfaction in recording it correctly. If you are the kind of person who enjoys the neatness of a finished crossword, the solving of a riddle, or the clear explanation at the end of a Sherlock Holmes mystery, you will know immediately why we yearn to make sure that the dictionary's entries and dates are completely accurate.

But there is more to it than a geeky desire for properly ordered facts. The history of our language unlocks the history of our culture. Those dictionary changes that our wordhunters helped to make after the first series included ante-datings for the words 'balti', 'cocktail' and 'cool', as well as the phrases 'chattering classes', 'on the pull' and 'smart casual'. In tracing the first entry of these terms into the English language, we discover when we first started to act, speak, eat, drink or think in certain ways. They are little souvenirs along the path of social change.

Group words into themes, and we can learn even more. Consider 'bung', 'swindle' and 'Glasgow kiss'. Why do we use such jolly alternatives to 'bribe', 'defraud' and 'head-butt'? Having one cute, colourful term for a violent or criminal act is a linguistic quirk. Having three begins to tell us something about ourselves. Our love of this colourful slang is connected to our fondness for

TV characters such as Del Boy, Arthur Daley, the Mitchell brothers and Norman Stanley Fletcher. Why are we so ready to enjoy the lighter side of crime?

The English language is equally full of light-hearted terms for madness: 'bonkers', 'bananas', 'one sandwich short of a picnic'. Such phrases sound rather old-fashioned these days alongside the trend for more serious jargon inherited from America: 'bipolar', 'therapy', 'post-traumatic stress'. Tracing a dateline for the demise of one lingo and the rise of the other reveals the genesis of a more sombre and sympathetic society. For better or worse? That is surely not for the amateur lexicographer to say.

Delving into the history of comical phrases, such as 'spend a penny' or 'kick the bucket', we can think about when and why the concept of euphemism took hold. Or rather, when and why it changed; the ancient Greeks used *euphemismos* to avoid ill omens. We do it to be socially 'nice'. Were we never able to discuss sex, death and bodily functions frankly? Or was there a particular moment in our history when, like Adam and Eve after eating the apple, we suddenly felt ashamed and started draping everything in fig leaves? If we can discover the exact dates when these fig-leaf phrases were born, we will know more about the history of human behaviour.

If you ask me, the most delightful words from our second Wordhunt are those that are (unfortunately) put-downs: 'wally', 'pillock, 'plonker' and 'prat'. Looking at them all together, enjoying their humorous sound, inspires one to wonder why there is so much more linguistic pleasure to be had from insulting people than praising them. It isn't just TV and restaurant critics who find this to be true; it's everybody. Are we all awful? (At least it was the Germans, and not we, who coined a special word for 'malicious enjoyment of the misfortunes of others' – *schadenfreude.*)

And there may be no better way to demonstrate how wordhunting unlocks our cultural history than by tracing the language of sexuality. The *OED* currently traces the word 'kinky' (in the sense of adventurous sexual practices) back to 1959. If that was indeed the year that experimental sex reached the conversational mainstream, thus requiring its own adjective, then we can almost hear the liberation of the 1960s banging at the door. But if our wordhunters can help us to push it back earlier, that will force us to look again at the 1950s, or even the 1940s. It would mean that, in those supposedly grey decades, people didn't talk exclusively of rationing and the weather.

When did the dark, technical term 'sadomasochism' become the everyday shorthand 'S&M'? If you think about it, there must have been a moment when people started talking about this tendency so often that they needed to say it more quickly. The linguistic change signifies a notable shift in moral outlook and social conversation. The date of that shift can tell us a lot about our parents – or grandparents.

I'll be honest: as we set out on a new series of *Balderdash & Piffle*, I am hoping not to spend too much time thinking about the possibility of my grandparents' dark sexuality. Nevertheless, I am excited about embarking on a whole new adventure, unlocking the secrets of our language to find out more about the people we are, and the people we have historically been.

Victoria Coren

Chapter One

idiot Cretin Moron Barmy Doolally Shell sho
Bonkers Off your trolley Losing your marble
Basket case On ~~sa~~ short Out to lunc
Nuts Cuckoo Durr-brain Idiot Cretin Moro
Barmy Doolally Shell shock Bonkers Off you
~~ey Losi~~ ~~ce~~ ~~ne san~~
~~ort Out to lun~~ ~~us Cuckoo Durr-brain Id~~
~~etin Moron Barmy~~ Doolally Shell shock Bor
~~ff your trolle~~ ~~arbles Basket c~~
One sandwich ~~ort Out to lunch Nuts Cucko~~
urr-brain Idiot Cretin Moron Barmy Doola
hell shock Bonkers Off your trolley :osing yo

One sandwich short

*T*alking about the condition popularly known as 'madness' is a delicate subject these days because, quite rightly, we are hesitant about offending people who are mentally disturbed – or their families, friends and employers. And yet those deemed mad have always been around us. In pre-Victorian London they were herded into a place called the Hospital of St Mary of Bethlehem, later shortened to **Bedlam**, which was located on three sites around central London between 1247 and 1815. Viewing the inmates cost a penny every first Tuesday of the month, and many and varied must have been the unkind expressions aimed at the wretched residents.

These days, we don't queue to stare at the lunatics in the asylum. Rather, we use language to distance ourselves from people undergoing mental turmoil. Some of us don't know whether to laugh or sympathize, which goes some way to explaining the bewildering variety of terms used to describe it. Quite clearly 'mad' people – however inexactly that term is used – worry us. They threaten our sense of normality and remind us of what we might be. And, as with Shakespeare's Fool, they sometimes tell us things we'd rather not know because they see around corners where we'd rather not look.

The variety of words used is pretty dazzling, and it represents just about every shade of linguistic influence that the English language has ever undergone. Everyone, it seems, wants to get in on the madness-naming game. So of course we find the classical languages involved at an early stage. **Mania** and **psychosis** are Greek; **insanity**, **dementia** and **lunacy** are Latin. Lunacy comes from *luna*, the Latin word for 'moon'. Folkloric wisdom has it that the moon's waxing and waning affects the minds of those afflicted by mental turbulence. Howling at the moon is one symptom of these phases. The word **lunatic** dates from the thirteenth century, while its shortened form **loony** is from the late Victorian period. Since then the studied casualization of our attitude to lunacy in areas such as media and fashion have led to, for example, the cartoon craziness of *Looney Tunes* (from 1930) and the surreally wide flares known as **loons**, which date from 1971. Let us pray that this is one form of licensed insanity not about to make a comeback.

Of course the trousered loons should not be confused with the fifteenth-century **loon**, which means 'scamp' or 'rogue', but which is descended by a different route, possibly from the Old Norse *lúenn*, which means 'beaten' or 'benumbed'.

As for the word **mad**, that has an impressively long record. It is probably descended from the Middle English *amad*, meaning 'demented' or 'distracted', or, to use the modern terminology, 'mad', and disappeared from English around 1315. *Amad* itself seems to have emerged from the Old English *gemæd*, which came from the Gothic word *gamaid(s)*, meaning 'bruised', and it's not hard to see how bruised on the skin might lead to bruised in the head.

Various other meanings of 'mad' have evolved over time, such as 'extravagantly foolish' or 'wild with desire'. And the African-American use of 'mad' the adverb, as in 'mad scared', sounds contemporary, but is in fact at least five centuries old. It's an intriguing thought that the phrase 'mad drunk' could just as easily have been uttered in a twenty-first-century nightclub as by Sir Thomas Lodge – of whom more later.

This chapter discusses some other ways in which we've labelled mad people or their movements, from mildly odd to downright schizoid, and from children's taunts to in-jokes revolving around sandwiches and picnics.

Idiot

Incredibly, words such as **cretin**, **imbecile**, **idiot** and **moron** were once used as diagnostic terms in the early stages of psychiatry, and have all gone on to be terms of abuse, which is why all of them– apart from 'idiot' – are pretty much taboo in polite society.

'Idiot' now means 'a stupid person', but in previous centuries there was a fair bit of jostling as to its precise definition. In New Testament Greek an idiot is an uneducated person, but around the fourteenth century it could also mean (according to the *OED*) a clown, a layman or a private individual. But the definition that's stuck – perhaps because it was so specific, or because there was a lot of it about – reads: 'A person so deficient in mental or intellectual faculty as to be incapable of ordinary acts of reasoning or rational conduct' – and therefore to be distinguished from someone who was merely temporarily insane, or having lucid intervals.

Idiot is Greek, in origin. It comes from the noun *idiotes*, which really meant 'a private person or an individual'. It was a rude term then, but not in today's sense. In ancient Athens it meant someone not prepared to take part in the Greek democratic process because they were too preoccupied with their private concerns. It certainly adds a layer of meaning to the phrase 'You'd be mad to vote for them'.

Up until the late nineteenth century an idiot could be a 'natural fool' or half-wit: it was all but a legal term, in fact, meaning a person on the very bottom rung of the intellectual ladder, an adult with a mental age of two, incapable of looking after himself or of being trusted not to hurt himself. When IQ tests came along the idiot score was given as twenty or under.

Cretin

The term **cretin** is more recent than idiot, and much more specific. It was coined to describe mentally retarded individuals – perhaps we should use a more sensitive phrase, such as 'intellectually challenged' – who were found mainly in the Swiss Alps. It defines a person of severely stunted physical and mental growth, and some amazingly colourful descriptions of those afflicted in this way appeared in the February 1858 edition of the *Atlantic Monthly*. The Hartford physician Linus P. Brockett wrote:

> By the roadside, basking in the sun, he beholds beings whose appearance seems such a caricature upon humanity, that he is at a loss to know whether to assign them a place among the human or the brute creation. Unable to walk, – usually deaf and dumb, – with bleared eyes, and head of disproportionate size, – brown, flabby, and leprous skin, – a huge goitre descending from the throat and resting upon the breast, – an abdomen enormously distended – the lower limbs crooked, weak, and ill-shaped, – without the power of utterance, or thoughts to utter, – and generally incapable of seeing, not from defect of the visual organs, but from want of capacity to fix the eye upon any object, – the cretin seems beyond the reach of human sympathy or aid. In intelligence he is far below the horse, the dog, the monkey, or even the swine; the only instincts of his nature are hunger and lust, and even these are fitful and irregular.

That, then, was the first, pitiful sighting of a cretin, and it is impossible to avoid feeling the shock of the writer as he happens upon these miserable individuals. The reason for the very specific citing of cretins in parts of Switzerland seems to have been

'All I meant was, you look like you come from Crete…'

caused perhaps by insanitary water and lack of iodine in the diet. But as the modern world became more sanitary, the symptoms began to recede. Eventually, as the nineteenth century wore on, you no longer needed to have a huge goitre descending from your throat to be called a cretin. As the novelist James Joyce wrote in a letter in 1933, 'The crétin of a concierge … has misdirected half my mail.' Cretinism is no longer a general medical term as it was in the nineteenth and early twentieth centuries, though it does still, amazingly, refer to a condition known as congenital hypothyroidism, which impedes physical and mental growth. But even if that's the diagnosis, the word isn't used in front of patients.

Where does 'cretin' derive from? It may have come from the French word *Chrétien*, meaning 'Christian', as if the very name were a plea for these afflicted people to be accepted as God's children. Nonetheless, cretin persists as a term of abuse.

Two other possible routes for the word have been advanced. Could the ghostly pallor of cretins' faces have inspired a link to the Latin word *creta*, which means 'chalk' (as in the white earth of Crete)? There is also an alpine French word *cretira* (from the Latin *creatus*), which means 'creature' – as if alluding in a somewhat sentimental way to the fact that, whatever our intellectual level, we are all God's creatures. Sadly, or happily, none of these derivations is fixed with any certainty.

Moron

Another word with distant roots, **moron** meant 'foolish' or 'stupid' in ancient Greek, and the American psychologist Henry Goddard (1886–1957) propagated it in 1910. In his report to the *Journal of Psycho-asthenics* about his work for the American Association for the Study of the Feeble-minded, he argued for the adoption of 'the Greek word *moron*', which he defined as 'one who is lacking in intelligence, one who is deficient in judgement or sense'. At first it was taken to apply to an adult with a mental age of between eight and twelve – pretty sharp, in my experience. The American humorist Robert Benchley (1889–1945) picked up on it seven years later, writing in the magazine *Vanity Fair* that 'A person entering one of these drawing-rooms and talking in connected sentences … would have been looked upon as a high-class moron'.

Moron, as noted above, has not made its way that frequently into high literature, though it did feature in one of the Sex Pistols' most notorious songs – 'God Save the Queen' (1977) – as well as in the 1978 one-off hit and anthem of *punk pathétique* 'Gordon

Is a Moron' by Jilted John, the onetime persona of Graham Fellows, the comedic genius who gave the world the northern saddo John Shuttleworth. All together now: 'Gordon is a moron, Gordon is a moron, Gordon is a moron, Gordon is a moron.' It sounds better with the music.

The Latin word *imbecillus*, meaning 'feeble in body or mind', led to the word **imbecile**, first noted in 1549, when it tended towards meaning weakness of the body. The mental version of imbecile was defined in Dr Samuel Johnson's 1755 *Dictionary* as 'weak; feeble; wanting strength of either mind or body'. The Latin verb *imbecillare* (to weaken) led some early lexicographers to maintain that this word lay at the root of the verb 'embezzle', though it's now known that it came into English via the fourteenth- or fifteenth-century Anglo-French verb *enbesiler*, meaning 'to make away with, cause to disappear, fraudulently destroy'. Since the Victorian age, an imbecile has meant someone who is inane or stupid. It used to mean a state of mental retardation, but not so great as idiocy, and not inherited. As with the other terms for madness, this word has slipped from the medical text books. You won't hear it in a lot of playgrounds either, as it's quite fancy. These days you'll find it used more often as a form of self-laceration by, among and against middle-ranking business executives.

Most of the words mentioned earlier have lost their medical connotations and are just emphatic terms for 'stupid', but it's interesting how they once defined different, subtle degrees of mental retardation. We now prefer to use more clinical terms, which don't really tell anyone (unless they're a specialist) what they mean. But is this helpful? If a forklift truck were labelled 'Not to be operated by idiots, cretins or morons', would that not be clearer, easier to understand and generally safer than 'Not to be operated by anyone with developmental disabilities, ranging from congenital hypothyroidism to severe or profound mental retardation'?

We may no longer regard lunatic asylums as tourist destinations or sources of amusement, but neither have we become more comfortable with the idea of madness and incapacity.

Barmy

Another word for generally crazy is **barmy**. If you're going to be called mad, or any variant thereof, barmy is probably the one to go for: indeed, it must be one of the most genial insults to be thrown around in any language. The title of David Lodge's novel *Ginger You're Barmy* (1962) comes from a song that was popular in the 1950s:

> *Ginger, you're barmy,*
> *You'll never join the Army,*
> *You'll never be a scout,*
> *With your shirt hanging out...*

Barmy is a formation from the earlier word *barm*, a northern European word, similar to the Swedish *barma* and the Danish (and modern German) *bärme*, which is a type of froth found on the top of fermenting malt liquors. This word came to mean 'yeast' or 'leaven'. The ancient verb **to barm** (*c.* 950) meant 'to leaven or ferment', or 'to mix with yeast' (*OED*). The verb was last spotted in John Galt's 1822 Scots-tinged novel *The Provost* – 'It set men's minds a barming and working' – by which time it had come to mean something more like the process of frothing and fermentation. Not surprisingly, then, the verb first spotted in the year 950 referred to the froth of fermenting liquor. Given its use as a fermenting agent, the adjective 'barmy', as in 'good barmy ale' (1535), means 'covered with barm' or 'frothing'. By the year 1602 barmy could also mean 'excited or jumpy'.

But the next evolutionary stage in this word's journey introduces us to a confusion. How many times have you said 'barmy' and meant **balmy**? Are you sure you could tell a barmy army from a balmy afternoon? To clear up any confusion, we must set our sights on balm and its progeny, and follow that back and forth. **Balm** is an aromatic, resinous substance, a fragrant oil for anointing, as well as being the stuff applied to dead bodies, or for healing wounds. It first oozed on to the page around the year 1200. Sir Thomas Lodge (1558–1625), Lord Mayor of London, wrote many works, including a collection of humorous verses called *A Fig for Momus* (1595), which contained the words: 'To guide the Sages of balme-breathing East'.

Deliciously soft, or fragrant, or mild – 'balmy' had all these meanings between the seventeenth and eighteenth centuries, when it was used by writers from John Milton to William Shakespeare – the latter, in particular, using the word in all its meanings. But then, in 1857, Henry Mayhew (1812–87), the co-founder of *Punch* magazine, and a man who kept his ear closer to the ground than was considered aurally hygienic by polite Victorian society, records the use of 'balmy' on the lips of London's cockney rebels as meaning 'insane'. An 1892 cutting from the *Daily News* refers to 'balmy' criminals, the quote marks around the word perhaps suggesting that the confusion with 'barmy' was still under discussion. By the time the word had entered the twentieth century, its meaning as slightly mad had become widely accepted, and the slippage is clearly from the 'soft' of balm to a more metaphorical weak-minded or idiotic.

The *Westminster Gazette* noted the crossover in 1896: 'Should not "balmy" be "barmy"?' it wondered. 'I have known a person of weak intellect called "Barmy Billy"... The prisoner ... meant to simulate semi-idiocy, or "barminess", not "balminess".'

In the 1980s the term **barmy army** became a term of abuse coined to describe the hard-left rump of the Labour party, which its then leaders, such as Neil Kinnock, were trying so hard to restrain. Then, in the 1990s, it became synonymous with a certain type of jingoistic English football fan. Within a few years it had also come to embrace that squad of raucous, mainly good-natured, largely drunken but surprisingly knowledgeable band of loyal supporters who follow the England cricket team around the world from one sporting disaster to another.

Doolally

War has made many mad over the years, and a climate of war is conducive to the creation of many colourful phrases to express madness, either on civvy street or among those in uniform. Some of these phrases are sympathetic; others, as the military campaign presses on and the longed-for peace seems ever more unattainable, merely cynical.

In India during the Raj (the period of British rule), British troops who were waiting to return to Britain by sea were sent to an army camp at Deolali, 100 miles northeast of Bombay. And there, an awful long way from Tipperary and other home comforts, they waited. And waited. And, in some cases, waited for so long that they came down with what became known as **doolally tap** – English being no respecter of foreign spelling. 'Tap', Persian in origin, is a nineteenth-century word for a malarial fever. 'Doolally tap' was noted first in 1925, and is still in demand as a non-medical synonym for madness, as in 'I went completely doolally with the woman in the call centre when I was complaining about my gas bill'. And since the call centre may recently have been relocated to somewhere around Bangalore, it's nice to think that the phrase is, in some way, going home.

Shell shock

During the First World War, soldiers who had seen too much action on the front line in northern France were said to be suffering from a condition that was first discussed in the *British Medical Journal* in 1915, the second year of the war, and described as **shell shock**. They were invalided out, treated with as rudimentary psychiatric care as was then felt appropriate, and shipped back into the war zone, either to suffer the fate they so dreaded, or to see their colleagues suffer it for them. Shell shock is a horrid and wretched condition, that state of psychological exhaustion produced by exposure to near-constant shellfire. The classic symptoms are exhaustion, indecisiveness and confusion over simple tasks. There could also be nausea, shaking and sweating, bed-wetting, suicidal thoughts, aggressive behaviour… In other words, pretty much any sign of disturbed mental activity.

After that terrible war, psychiatrists were allowed greater access to the army. The term 'shell shock' was seen as one of the many unwelcome hangovers of the 1914–18 war. Sadly, the symptoms that it so accurately described were anything but alien to Second World War soldiers, even though trench warfare was less of a factor. *Soldier and Sailor Words and Phrases* by Edward Fraser and John Gibbons, first published in 1925, claims that the army preferred to latch on to the nineteenth-century and the more medical-sounding term 'psycho-neurosis'.

By 1943, although 'shell shock' was still very much in use among the soldiers themselves (including Spike Milligan, who was struck down with it in Italy and, arguably, never recovered), other terms, such as **combat fatigue** or **war neurosis**, were preferred by the authorities. In more recent years, especially since the Vietnam War, the terms have become ever more psychological. In that war, soldiers on both sides suffered horrendous psychological shock, and that's without even mentioning the Vietnamese civilian casualties. In the 1980s the term **post-traumatic stress disorder** was adopted. But the cruder the terms, the longer their postwar shelf-life. Consequently, 'shell shock' is still very much in use today, although more likely to be used when describing the effect of getting a rocket from the boss than to describe the symptoms of a soldier serving in Iraq.

Being shell shocked on civvy street is more akin to surprise than trauma.

Bonkers

Another term for 'mad', popularized in the early years of the Second World War but altogether less intimidating, is the word **bonkers**. This can be taken in two ways. Eric Partridge included it in his *Dictionary of Forces Slang* (1948), with the meaning 'light in the head', but it gradually evolved to mean 'mad'. The *OED*'s first reference to the word in this context comes from 1957, but a *Balderdash* wordhunter has unearthed a cutting from a 1945 edition of the *Daily Mirror* in which a British soldier writing from India laughingly confesses his fear of going 'bonkers' (see also 'doolally', page 21). The *OED* doesn't commit itself on the origin of 'bonkers', but Partridge hazards a guess: 'Perhaps from **bonk**, a blow or punch on the **bonce** or head.' 'Bonce' takes us off in the direction, first of an 1862 word for 'marble', and, by 1889, the head itself. Why head? Possibly because it's similar-sounding to **bounce**, which is what we prefer not to happen to our heads.

Off your trolley

Who remembers Care in the Community, the mental health policy formulated by the Thatcher government in the 1980s? In theory, it meant releasing people from Victorian-style institutions and allowing them to receive better treatment at home. In practice, it led to some extremely disturbed people in bobble hats wandering around shopping centres. It proved to be a short step from 'There should be a reorientation in the mental health

services away from institutional care towards care in the community' (official report, 1977) to 'I have already heard my daughter and her friends refer to a scruffy-looking boy as "He looks a bit **care-in-the-community**"' (*Daily Telegraph*, February 1995).

As our attitudes to mental health change, we seem to be releasing more of these words into the community, with mixed results. Often they become terms of abuse, or excuses for comedic digs. The phrase **off your trolley**, for example, means to be a bit simple, or not all there. It meant something similar to **tuppence short of a shilling** (from the days of old money, when there were twelve pennies in a shilling, so being two short meant you were worth only tenpence). It belongs in the category 'Strange Ways of Describing Strange Situations', but the trolley word, perhaps appropriately for a wheeled object, has launched off in several other directions.

The derivation of **trolley** is a bit of a puzzle. The word means the kind of low-sided cart that you'd recognize from any railway station forecourt or yard. One of its possible origins is an Old French verb *troller*, meaning 'to quest, to go in quest of game, without purpose'. There is a fine irony in this, since the trolley that we still associate with manly work is linked closely to the verb **to troll**, which has come, since the early twentieth century, to mean 'cruising for gay sex'.

The American journalist and humorist George Ade (1866–1944) first used trolley in the context of madness in his 1896 play *Artie*: 'Anyone that's got his head full o' the girl proposition's liable to go off his trolley at the first curve'. The phrase is still going strong a century later: in 1983 *The Times* (of London) reported that 'The London college gym mistress who is suing her former lover for libel in the High Court heard a lawyer say yesterday that she had "gone off her trolley" about the affair'.

Fans of the London punk rock band the Clash will recall with a wistful sigh the song 'Lost in the Supermarket' from their breakthrough double album *London Calling* (1979). The phrase certainly seemed of its time: how many of us, pushing our wire trolleys up and down aisles packed with food and other products that we don't really need, begin to feel slightly unhinged? The first **supermarket trolleys** were wheeled out in around 1937, since when they have spread to almost every green- or brownfield site in Europe.

My initial problem with 'off your trolley' was that I couldn't see the picture. How can you *be off* a trolley? You might fall off a trolley, if you'd been waiting for several hours in an under-funded NHS hospital corridor, but that's not what the words say.

Of course, it takes a moment to realize that when George Ade talked of going off his trolley, he was referring to a **trolley-car** (what we'd call a tram), a mode of transport introduced in the first half of the nineteenth century, not wheeling what Americans call a 'cart' around Costco. The transport sort of trolley can have very dangerous results when out of control.

Losing your marbles

Another way to go mad is to **lose your marbles**, but whose marbles were they and how and when were they mislaid? It's certainly a phrase with which many dictionary-minded people have had a great deal of fun. Nigel Rees – the inventor of Radio 4's hallowed but hoary *Quote … Unquote* word quiz – runs through the main theories in his book *A Word in Your Shell-like* (2004), including the so-good-it-can't-possibly-be-true one that it's a reference to Lord Elgin and the troublesome Parthenon marbles, whose removal to the British Museum in 1816 so enraged the Greeks that it drove them **round the bend**. Nice idea but unsubstantiated, sadly.

More respectable is the cross-Channel connection with the French word *meubles* (furniture). Marbles was a playful swap for *meubles* in mid-Victorian England in what would now be called mockney parlance. In his novel *Claverings* (1867), the author Anthony Trollope (1815–82) used it to mean 'cash': 'She won't get any money from me, unless I get the marbles for it'. But can losing your furniture turn your head? Rees notes some northern expressions, such as 'He's got all his chairs at home', to denote mental stability. He goes on: 'If someone is a bit lacking in the head, we say that they haven't got all their furniture at home.' But the *OED* puts all further claims to shame with a citation from a

North American writer, G.V. Hobart, in 1902: 'I see-sawed back and forth between Clara J. and the smoke-holder like a man who is shy some of his marbles.' This was followed, in 1927, by a citation in a journal called *American Speech*: 'There goes a man who doesn't have all his marbles.' And it's been that way ever since.

Basket case

Depending on how ambitious your trip to the supermarket is, you'll either be loading up your trolley or your basket. A basket-holder could, with impunity, join the 'Five items or fewer' queue, whereas the trolley pusher has to stand in one of the longer lines. So who's crazier: the **basket case** or the person who is off their trolley? Surely a basket case is more disturbed, and here's why: there is a cutting from 1919 about 'basket cases' in US military hospitals, but this wasn't substantiated until 1944, in a journal called *Yank*: 'Maj. Gen. Norman T. Kirk, Surgeon General, says there is nothing to rumors of so-called "basket cases" – cases of men with both legs and both arms amputated.' Ouch.

Naturally enough, the phrase soon acquired metaphorical dimensions: 'Kwame Nkrumah [President of Ghana, 1960–6] should not be written off as a political basket case,' wrote the *American Saturday Review* in 1967. Whether you had a profound physical disability or were in a politically vegetative state, being a basket case was clearly not an enviable position to be in.

One sandwich short …

Among other expressions to denote madness or eccentricity is **one sandwich short of a picnic**. Perhaps not surprisingly, the phrase began life down under. There is something about

Australian national culture – one thinks of Barry Humphries' inspired creation Sir Les Patterson – which is attracted, magpie-like, to glittery verbal expressions. And, indeed, the Australian National University's National Dictionary Centre has a detailed entry on this expression. They agree that to be 'a sandwich short' means 'not very bright', or 'just not with it', which has the additional meaning of being 'somewhat confused'. As well as thoroughly Aussie expressions for madness, such as **to have kangaroos in the top paddock** and the downright bewildering **as mad as a gum tree full of galahs**, they also list **a stubbie short of a sixpack**. This has probably been common knowledge in Australia for several decades, but it was not granted access to the *OED* until June 2005.

The sandwich expression first emerged in print in a book called *Travellers: Voices of the New-Age Nomads* (1993) by Richard Lowe and William Shaw. It's a book about unconventional lifestyles, and, appropriately, includes the sentence: 'I thought either I had something very wrong with me physically, or I was two sandwiches short of a picnic'. Since then, the lunacy threshold has shrunk from two sandwiches to just one.

Out to lunch

Clearly, the madder a situation or person, the greater the temptation to coin a pithy description, especially one that can be muttered under the breath, and that sympathizers might understand more quickly than the person it describes. And, talking of food, we shouldn't overlook **out to lunch**, the first recorded instance of which dates from a 1955 edition of the American monthly magazine *Science Digest*: '"Out to lunch" refers to someone who, in other years, just wasn't "there" – and he is told immediately to "Get with it!"' Its meaning has hardened over the years, but it can still mean anything from a little bit lost to bordering on insane.

Nuts

There are certain words that seem to fall naturally into madness. **Nutty** is one: we can't quite say how 'nutty' went from meaning 'studded with nuts' to meaning 'mad or crazy', but perhaps it happened like this. When the Elizabethan writers Francis Beaumont and John Fletcher were writing their comedies and tragedies around 1625, the adjective 'nuts' could mean something pleasurable or delightful. If, therefore, you did something 'for nuts', it was merely for fun. Being 'nuts' sounds very twentieth century, but it was in use in the eighteenth and nineteenth centuries, mainly in Britain, to describe matters of the heart: you could be **nuts on** (or **upon**) someone. If you were **nutty** about someone in 1825, you were probably in love. And then an American came up with **nutty as a fruitcake**, a nonsensical food simile used to suggest the craziness that accompanied being infatuated with someone. By the very early twentieth century, and largely in the USA, **to be nuts** meant to be really wild about someone or something, so much so that you had virtually lost your senses.

Cuckoo

Other words have slid into insanity in different ways. It may be true, for example, that a bird does not have a large brain, so a person who is **bird-brained** (first spotted in 1922) is generally defined as **not the sharpest knife** in that ubiquitous picnic box. The idea of birds and madness is suggested by expressions such as **strictly for the birds**, but this dates from only the mid-1950s and is American. Maybe we should plunge back into Greek history and consult the works of the playwright Aristophanes, whose play *The Birds* (414 BC) gave us the sublimely perfect world known as *Nephelokokkugia*, literally Cloud-cuckoo-land. This wonderful phrase has survived, hale, hearty and nutty as a fruitcake, into the twenty-first century from 2500 years ago.

The fascinating thing about the **cuckoo** is that it has the temerity to lay its eggs in other birds' nests to avoid the chore of looking after them. This may – the *OED* says 'must' – have given rise to that unhappy word for the husband of an unfaithful wife, a **cuckold**. There is, in fact, no better possible derivation. And since when did being a cuckold not drive certain men towards a state of madness? This is probably also the root of the expression **to be cuckoo**, which means 'not all there in the head'.

Early writers in English, from the mid-sixteenth century onwards, heard the bird's monotonous call – it really isn't that hard to copy – and this seemed to make the poor cuckold's life even more difficult. If the man, like the bird's call, could be so easily substituted, there must be something simple about him. By the late sixteenth century the word had come to mean 'fool'.

Durr-brain

There is no *OED* entry for the sarcastic interjection **durr**. (If you look that up, it suggests, not that helpfully, 'door'.) Nor does it have an entry for **derr**. Other, more reactive dictionaries define 'derr' as **special needs**. The *OED* does, however, list **duh** ('imitative', it explains), first used in 1948 and expressing 'inarticulacy or incomprehension'. This naggingly appropriate expression has gone from being on the lips of the 'stupid' to being said by the clever person in mocking imitation of the 'stupid'. 'Duh' survives today, as have the more emphatic 'durr' or 'derr' (spell it how you will), and thanks to them both, we have the thoroughly pitiless **durr-brain**, which means someone who is, basically, **thick**. Brits, it seems, are condemned to put people down by questioning their sanity. Do Americans do the same? Maybe not quite so much.

Chapter Two

Fashionistas

You can never keep up with **fashion**. The world of fashion is fickle and vain. But the *word* of fashion is much more complicated than hair-raisingly expensive handbags and impossibly skimpy miniskirts might suggest. Ideas that come and go are said to be **in fashion** one minute and **out of fashion** the next. To be **fashionable** could be used as an insult or as a term of praise since the first years of the seventeenth century. *Balderdash* word-hunters have even noted the uniquely awful phrase **on trend**, as if even the fashionable word for 'fashionable' is subject to the whims of fashion. It seems appropriate for the world of fashion that many words to do with being, becoming or appearing fashionable have come and gone and not quite caught on, including **fashionative** (1584), **fashionate** (1593), **fashion-monging** (1599), **fashionly** (1613), **fashionist** (1616) and **fashional** (1617).

It's as though the language was trying on new clothes and forever queuing up at the returns counter to ask for a refund – or, perhaps more accurately, a credit note, since they were traded in for something else. Take that example above from 1616: someone who followed fashion could have been called a 'fashionist'. Add one letter and reach forward over 350 years and you find **fashionista**, first spotted in *Thing of Beauty: The Tragedy of Supermodel Gia* by Stephen Fried (1993). The Gia in question was Gia Carangi (1960–86), the model who became a drug addict and was one of the first celebrity victims of Aids.[1] The term 'fashionista' can be used with greater or lesser degrees of ridicule, whether you're in the industry or not. It's defined as 'a devotee of the fashion industry' or 'a wearer of high-fashion clothing'. The rather fabulous '-ista' ending is an homage to the

---

[1] Read more about her life, addiction and legacy at
www.thegiacarangiproject.com

heady days of Sandinistas (1928), Peronistas (1945), Senderistas (1982) and so on, as if these fashion icons become political radicals merely by putting on a T-shirt. It's, like, ironic?

Fashion has given so many looks to the world, and so many words, especially in the twentieth century. The **fashion industry** has been around since at least 1968; people have been **fashion-conscious** (i.e. fashion-aware) since 1951, and **fashion journals** (magazines about fashion) were first noted in 1905.

In this chapter we are going to perform a striptease[2] by reaching into our fashion wardrobe and trying on – and then removing – a number of items of clothing. These objects reveal a variety of different influences. Culled from all over the world, many are refugees from different cultures. Some are more or less insults, others are compliments. Some items of clothing have been extended to include whole sections of society; others have become different types of metaphor, far removed from their original clothing-based sense. Others are, to put it mildly, mutton dressed as lamb. In this spring collection of well-wrapped words we'll start from the outside of the word and make our way to the middle: and we'll also start with the outer layers first, and work our way down to the skimpiest possible undergarments.

Balaclava

The **balaclava** was named after the village of the same name near Sebastopol in the Crimea (now Ukraine). During the Crimean War (1854–6), knitted balaclavas were sent from Britain to protect the soldiers' faces against the bitter cold. The helmet-type

---

2 A word first noted by *Variety* magazine in 1930, originally in the form 'Girls have the strip and tease down to a science'.

hat can be worn around the head only, or hijab-style, covering the mouth and even the nose, depending on the weather or the amount of stealth required. The men wearing them must have been a fearsome sight, and it's no wonder that an 1892 article on mountaineering referred to the hat as the 'Balaclava (Templar) cap' since the wearer does somewhat resemble one of the Knights Templar. There are no references to the balaclava contemporary with the Crimean campaign: the first is from 1881, a quarter of a century later.

The switch from military to civilian use seems to have been spotted first by *Queen* magazine in an article from 1901. Balaclavas went to war again in 1914, resurfacing in a 1929 copy of *Blackwell's* magazine, when they were restyled for the men's military look together with a woolly muffler. Fashion on civvy street, in other words.

Parka

The *OED* defines a **parka** as 'a long hooded jacket made of skins and sometimes trimmed with fur, worn by the people of the Arctic'. The first written record of it comes from 1625, in a work by Samuel Purchas (?1577–1626). (Purchas's accounts of his intrepid journeys to exotic foreign courts were said to be among the inspirations for Samuel Taylor Coleridge's poem 'Kubla Khan'.) The word 'parka' has an intriguing origin: it is in fact a Nenets word, Nenets being a language of one of the Arctic peoples. It turns out that parka is not the only word that Nenets has given to the English language. There are two more: Nenets itself and an alternative word for Nenets – Nganasan. Not, perhaps, as impressive a list as one might have hoped for. In fact, Nenets is part of a language cluster centred around Finland and the Ural mountain range in Russia. The family name for these languages and their peoples is Samoyed: Russian for 'self-eater' or 'cannibal'. To the Russians, these were obviously just a wild and uncivilized people who lived far away.

The Samoyeds are a Mongolian race, from Siberia. A very helpful Nenets language website suggests that Nenets is spoken by 27,273 people, 26,730 of whom are native speakers. Presumably the other 543 just find it useful for business purposes.[3]

So the parka, that item of clothing no self-respecting Mod would be seen without in the 1960s, and that is currently enjoying a resurgence as high fashion, has its roots in a style of life first reported by one of our most intrepid travellers.

Anorak

You could be forgiven for thinking that the **anorak** and parka are from roughly the same vintage, but they're not. 'Anorak' is a Greenland Eskimo word, defined in the *OED* as 'a weatherproof jacket of skin or cloth, with hood attached … a similar garment in countries other than Greenland'. In fact, we should stop right there because, as a BBC language website[4] points out, the word 'Eskimo' is neither polite nor accurate. It is, they argue, rather like calling a Scotsman 'a Jock', or a German 'a Kraut'. It's also a bit like calling an Australian 'a Kiwi', or a New Zealander 'an Aussie' – and you know how they feel about getting those terms the

---

3 Actually, this is a very serious matter. This author passionately supports the survival of these tiny, highly localized language groups that are threatened by big business, pitiless governments and worsening atmospheric conditions. Long live Nenets! Long live the Samoyedic people!
4 www.bbc.co.uk/dna/h2g2/A616268

wrong way round. The BBC suggests that the word 'Eskimo' may be a corrupted form of a French word for someone who eats raw fish. Best not to linger over these details: we shall in future use a more appropriate term, such as Inuit.

In any event, the first *OED* citation of 'anorak' is from 1924, so since parka goes all the way back to 1625, lexicographically speaking, they're 300 years apart.

In design terms, an anorak – according to the excitingly unregulated Wikipedia know-all website – 'is a waterproof jacket with a hood and drawstrings at the waist and cuffs, while a parka is a knee-length cold-weather jacket or coat, typically stuffed with down or very warm synthetic fibre, and having a fur-lined hood'. It also specifies that an anorak should be a pull-over jacket without a zipper, but that 'this distinction is now largely lost, and many garments with a full-length front opening are now described as anoraks'.

In its early days, the anorak was a 'gay beaded' item worn by Greenland women or brides in the 1930s. It was also given the rather splendid appellation of 'glacier smock' by the writer E.A.M. Wedderburn in 1937. At the beginning of the 1950s it was made of nylon, and by 1959 it had become so much a fashion item that it had been noticed by *Vogue* and was made of poplin.

But then came the 1980s.

A 1984 copy of the *Observer* seems to have been the first to transfer the label 'anorak' from the clothing to the people who wore it: 'At weekends boatloads of Dutch "anoraks" – pirate radio fans – come out to cheer on their latest hero.' From this point onwards 'anorak' became the term of choice for – according to *The Dictionary of Contemporary Slang* (edited by Tony Thorne) – 'one of those boring gits who sit at the front of every lecture with their Pringle jumpers asking the lecturer their clever questions'. Perhaps that was a little too participatory or outgoing. In any event, **anoraks** are obsessive characters, who have rightly become identical in the public mind with trainspotters.

Hoodie

When David Cameron, the leader of Britain's Conservative Party, asked, in effect, that we all **hug a hoodie**, he clearly did not have in mind the hooded or royston crow (*Corvus cornix*). That bird became the first **hoodie**, or hoody, in print (1789), in lines written by the Scots poet David Davidson: 'Upon an ash above the lin/A hoody has her nest'. The next rustle in the linguistic undergrowth came in 1990, when the Irish author Roddy Doyle mentioned in passing a new item of clothing that was gaining popularity in urban Britain: the hoodie. Fifteen years later, journalist Lesley Thomas, writing in the *Daily Telegraph* in July 2005, described her life in Brixton, south London, an area where 'It's jolly cutting-edge to live cheek by jowl with crack whores'. She noted of Brixton's younger population that 'Members of this demographic wear the dodginess of their surroundings as a badge of honour on their Marks & Spencer hoodies'.

One of urbandictionary.com's community of self-appointed lexicographers defines 'hoodie' as a 'sweatshirt with a hood and a very large pocket in front, capable of carrying, but not limited to, Walkman and headphones, candy being smuggled into movie theatres, pencil and notebook, pet snake that your parents don't know about, and certain less-legal substances that you don't want people finding'. Thanks, guys.

The hoodie has come to define the person inside it in the same way that anorak does and the negligee (see page 53) doesn't. Certain items of clothing, it seems, come value-laden.

No one ever *was* a leather jacket or a Stetson. Today, the wearers of hoodies are a defining symbol of every school, youth club, shopping centre, fast-food joint and concert in every town, city, village, field or beach in the country. They don't define themselves as hoodies, of course, but that doesn't stop us designating them as such, and even banning them from places where they make us feel threatened.

The word **hood** has meant a covering for the head and neck ever since the year 700, and probably since some time before then. In fact, the two other senses of the noun 'hood' play very well in the mind of any self-respecting hoodie: it's a shorter form of **hoodlum**, as well as a shortened form of **neighbourhood**, as in the 1991 film *Boyz N the Hood*, taken from the song of the same name (see page 122). But back in 1871 in Cincinnati a 'hood' was 'a youthful street rowdy'. Either of these senses could still come within the cultural arc of today's hoodies.

It might be asking us a bit much to hug a hoodie, but if you're confronted by one of these strange creatures, why not try and *bug* a hoodie by pointing out to him that the word 'hoodie' is an example of a metonym? As you stare into the blank depths of his eyes, you could point out hastily, but with growing confidence, that a metonym is a way of referring to something by one of its attributes. So when we say 'hoodie', we mean 'a sweatshirt with a hood and also the person who wears it'. The same goes for 'suits', which is a metonym for 'men in suits', while 'skirts' is a metonym for 'women (who wear skirts)'. By now the hoodie might be desperately texting his mates, seeking reinforcements. Alternatively, it might have been a positive learning experience for you both.

Swaggering, dodgy, preoccupied with sex, unlikely to win the best attendance record at school … how far we have travelled from an earlier 'hoodie', the folk hero **Robin Hood**. Bear in mind Robin's ethos of 'Steal from the rich, give to the poor'. That's sort of how hoodies see it too, especially in Robin's native Nottingham, a city that in 2005 had one of the worst criminal records in the country, at 115.5 crimes per 1000 people.

Jumper

Before we start unravelling the etymology of knitwear, it's worth mentioning that **knitting** is related to **knotting**, and our lexicographical top brass reckon that both derive from the very old Dutch verb *knutten*, which is very similar to the Old English *cnyttan*, to knot. Like knotting, knitting is all about making knots, or just connections. In the USA groups that gather to knit and gossip are known as 'stitch and bitch' sessions, and it's catching on in the UK too. After all, 'knit happens', as it says on the website www.bust.com.

The names of our favourite items of knitwear all have ancient and fascinating verbal histories. **Jumper** is a good jumping-off point, since we need to know what the verb **to jump** came from, and why the action of springing into the air has anything to do with a woollen item that is lowered over the head.

Jumpers were originally worn by rowers or athletes in the nineteenth century when doing exercise, and the garment was defined as a 'loose outer jacket or shirt reaching to the hips'. It seems to come from the earlier noun **jump**, a short coat worn by men in the seventeenth and eighteenth centuries. It may have been formed as a corruption of *juppe*, the medieval French word for 'jacket' (see also 'gyp', page 126). Over the years *juppe* lost a 'p', sank to the hips and in modern French became *jupe*, meaning 'skirt'.

There have been other types of jumper. The term was also applied around 1760 to Welsh Methodists, who used to jump about while they prayed. At around the same time, there were also Quakers, a Christian sect who 'rejected sacraments, ritual and formal ministry' (*Collins Concise Dictionary*) and concentrated on more important things, such as making porridge oats and quaking when the spirit moved them.

Pullover

We all know that a driver will **pull over** to the side of the road at the behest of a police officer, but what could possibly be the connection between that activity and another item of knitwear? Well, add a hyphen if you wish (or close up the gap later) and you will find four pullovers: and not one, but two of them, refer to items of clothing.

The most interesting of the earlier references is a dialect usage, an eastern counties phrase from an 1883 copy of the *Lincoln Chronicle*: 'The sea swept over the **pull-over** at Sutton'. This is not some poignant tale of the discovery of a lost child's abandoned article of clothing. A pull-over, then, and there, was defined as 'a gap in the coast sand-hills where vehicles can be pulled over to the beach; a cart-road over a sea-bank'.

In 1875 a **pullover** was a hat that you pulled over your head. (Perhaps this was an early name for the balaclava? The *OED* doesn't say.) In 1907 the first mention is made of the pullover (in its current sense of a woolly jumper) as one of the few items of clothing to get its name from an instruction for putting it on. This is the fashion equivalent of the picture on a tin of chick-peas showing a serving suggestion – a picture of some chick-peas in a bowl.

Cardigan

James Brudenell, 7th Earl of **Cardigan** (1797–1868), was one of the commanders of the Charge of the Light Brigade at the aforementioned Battle of Balaclava. The item of knitwear to which he gave his name is 'a knitted woollen over-waistcoat with or without sleeves'. The testament to his military prowess is the very first line of the *OED* entry: 'Named from the Earl of Cardigan, distinguished in the Crimean war (1855)'. The presence of Lord Cardigan at Balaclava was one of the last times in British military history when two really great trends in knitwear came together, although with calamitous consequences: by some estimates, Lord Cardigan lost 110 men out of the 674 under his command. Tragic for the men, but at least it put cardigans and balaclavas on the map.

'Right, men, we're going in. Cardigans on!'

Muffin top

The entertainment 'industry' manufactures a huge number of
new words and expressions. Many of these phrases are particularly expressive of a certain type of fashion tragedy, and they
spare little in the way of tact. Unlike the expressions we have
encountered so far, very few describe actual items of apparel:
rather, they shine a merciless light on the lengths many of us are
prepared to go to in order to cram our increasingly unsylph-like
figures into clothes that fail to flatter.

In the hands of comedy scriptwriters, the joke is not so
much about what we wear, as why we wear it, and why on earth
we don't get serious and slip on something more appropriate to
our age, weight and looks. In fact, they don't bother to name
clothes: their wit is reserved for those who wear inappropriate
ones. Scriptwriters, a tribe that doesn't generally give a toss about
dressing in 'this year's black', excel at observing the quirks of the
fashion industry – quirks that renew themselves every season.
(Just for the record, the *OED* first lists the phrase **the new black**
from a 1986 copy of the *New York Times*. In those days it was
'gray'.) The fashion commentators write drooling copy, while the
scriptwriters behave as if they are the only people in the room
to notice that the king is completely naked, or that he's wearing
ridiculous clothes. Respect, then, to Australian ABC's comedy
series *Kath & Kim*, which seems to have popularized the
expression **muffin top**. This may not yet be gracing the online
pages of the *OED*, but when Maggie Alderson in the *Sydney
Morning Herald* defines it as 'the perfect way to describe that
small waterfall of midriff fat that cascades over the top of your
low-cut bootleg jeans', it's enough to make a good many readers
swallow uncomfortably and disdain a second helping of trifle.

There have been **muffins** since the early years of the eighteenth century, but this new use of 'muffin' as a fashion term is very much a twenty-first-century development. Other phrases from the *Sydney Morning Herald* survey of 19 March 2005 are even less flattering. The first is **camel toe**, which seems to have entered the language from the USA. This term, which has also not yet made an impact on *The Oxford English Dictionary*, could be defined as a more intimate version of **visible panty line**, in which, so sharp-eyed claimants maintain, 'a lady's too-tight trousers unfortunately bifurcate her private parts'. The similarity to a camel's toe is, well, unfortunate, but for a male version the reader is directed to **moose knuckle**, which, allegedly, describes a similar phenomenon. And since we're in the region, we might also tick the box marked **hanging gardens of Babylon**, which refers to – can you believe this? – 'wayward pubic hair emerging from swimwear'. All right, that's quite enough of that: let's move on.

Sequins

Perhaps concealing your muffin top (if you like a bit of glitz) you might have a top decorated with shiny coloured discs known as **sequins**. This word conceals an exotic tale, beginning with the Persian or Arabic word *sicca*. Trying to catalogue all that word's linguistic twists and turns takes us on a journey through Renaissance Italy's narrow, bustling streets and into British trading history, but let's start with the Arabic verb *sakka*, meaning 'to lock or bolt' (a door) and 'to mint or coin' (money). The coins produced were known as *siccas*, and you don't see a lot of them these days. They're certainly nothing to do with the Latin adjective *siccus* (dry), which we find in words such as 'desiccated'.

The **sicca rupee** was a traded coin, much used by the East India Company as British influence was expanding into the subcontinent during the seventeenth century. In addition, the government of Bengal referred to new coins, which were not smoothed or tarnished by frequent use, as 'sicca rupees' from 1793 to 1836.

But what has this to do with shiny metal discs on clothing? Here's the next clue. *Sicca* passed into Italian as *zecca*, and into Spanish as *ceca* or *seca*, depending on which dictionary you consult. In both cases it means 'the mint'. In seventeenth-century Venice there was a gold coin called a *zecchino*, which passed into English, via French, as **sequin**. This sequin was worth a mint: in 1788 the writer Thomas Jefferson estimated its worth at £27,000. (The name was also used during the years of the Ottoman Empire to refer to a Turkish gold coin called a *sultanin*, though this was worth only about eight shillings [40p], so obviously it was handy to know what sort of sequins you were dealing with.)

Clearly, no Venetian man or woman was going to be very popular at home if they ventured out on to the streets carrying a coin worth £27,000 and returned without it. (It's amazing that such valuable coins existed in those days, especially when the highest denomination these days is worth only £2.) If such a coin had slipped from their fingers, or through a hole in their bag, it might not have been worth their while to go home at all, so measures were adopted to safeguard it. These days, we hear a lot about tying up money in investment funds and so on. It could be said that the inhabitants of eighteenth-century Venice did this quite literally, since the custom arose of sewing the coin into a headdress or gown to keep it safe. Eventually, sequin values dropped, but not before the sewing of coins to garments had become a decorative feature. By the late nineteenth century, at least in Britain, the sequin was more fashionable than monetary. 'Never before, probably,' wrote the *Daily News* in 1882, 'have dress trimmings been more artistic than they are now. Sequins are the newest.'

Well heeled

Some phrases enter the language appearing to be connected with fashion, but then go on to tell a very different story. Take the phrase **well heeled**. We all pretty much know what it means. *Chambers Dictionary* defines it as 'comfortably supplied with money' and states that it comes from the word **heeled**, meaning 'provided with a heel'. At first glance – even at second glance – this seems a little odd. Why should the state of your heels be a

useful indication of your wealth? Most of the time heels are the last thing observers see, and to get a good look you would either have to be standing behind someone and crouching on the floor, or peering at them from, say, the slats in some stairs. A pretty inferior position, in other words.

'Heeled' could also mean 'loaded', in the sense of 'armed with a revolver'. Mark Twain, in his collection *Letters from Hawaii* (1866), wrote that 'In Virginia City, in former times, the insulted party … would lay his hand gently on his six-shooter and say, "Are you heeled?"' Earlier still, in 1862, it meant to be furnished with a **set of heels** (guns), and the person carrying them would be described as **long-heeled**. The *OED* does not anywhere define 'well heeled' as meaning 'well dressed'. They date it back to 1880, when it meant well-off in terms of money, and cite it from an American journal. But eminent word-sleuth Michael Quinion says that originally it had no connection with wealth or even dress sense. His source – though not acknowledged by the *OED* – was cockfighting.

Cockfighting was – and still is where it continues – a nasty sport, with much blood and flying of feathers, particularly since the cockerel combatants were equipped with sharpened spurs to add potency to their blows. When conducted without these extra weapons, it is called **naked-heel** fighting, and is an even more drawn-out business. So, the theory goes, if you attached a spur or heel to your cockerel, you were at an advantage, though there can surely not have been a game in which both birds were not equally equipped. From this practice, at any rate, comes the expression 'well heeled', first spotted in print in a story – again by Mark Twain – from 1866. Nowadays someone described as well heeled can be either 'well off' or 'well dressed', and few people are aware of the phrase's bloody origins.

Stiletto

As we continue our progress down the body, we come to something that has, at different times, been the epitome of **style**: the **stiletto**. In fact, the two words are connected. The word 'stiletto' is a diminutive of the Italian *stilo*, which means 'dagger'. *Stilo* is descended from the word *stylus*, which itself comes from the word *style,* both of which mean 'pin' or 'stalk'. It's easy to see how *stylus* came to be applied to the needle on record players. It's also easy to understand how, between 1300 and 1600, 'pin' took on the meaning of 'knife'.

The *OED* lists twenty-eight meanings for the small but perfectly formed 'style'. At first it was a physical object that had a pointy end for inscribing and a flat end for erasing what one had written on a tablet (1387 and onwards). But at the same time

(1300 and after) 'style' also meant a manner of writing: later (by 1587) it meant the manner of speaking too. And during the fifteenth century it grew from a way of speaking into a whole way of being.

So when you stick the stiletto in, you're not digging the pointy heel of your shoe into something (or someone): you're actually puncturing them with a small knife. The first printed record of a 'little sharpe dagger called a stiletto' dates from 1611. Thereafter it wasn't always used literally as a dagger, but even when being used metaphorically, it always retained the sense of a knife. The **stiletto heel** was first described in the *New Statesman* magazine in 1959: 'She came ... smooching forward, her walk made lopsided by the absence of one heel of the stilettos.'

Mules

Having kicked off our stilettos, we might feel like slipping on something more comfortable, such as a pair of **mules**. But what are mules and where do they come from? Ask at any good shoe shop these days and you will be shown an array of backless shoes, high- or low-heeled, usually for women, but not exclusively. If you get chatting to the staff they might know that Marilyn Monroe made them popular in the 1950s. In fact, mules go back way beyond Marilyn to the *mulleus calceus*, a reddish or purple-coloured shoe worn only by the three highest magistrates in ancient Rome.

Language plays tricks on us all. Who would have thought that in French *mules* referred not to fancy footwear but to chilblains, that itching or swelling you get in the hands and feet from having poor circulation. It sounds like a schoolroom joke, but when it

first surfaced in English via the French word for chilblains about 700 years ago, 'mules' meant exactly that. The word limped on with this meaning until the mid-twentieth century, albeit in regional dialects. Meanwhile, its application to 'slippers' crept into use during 1562, although it was then spelt **moyles**. (Is this where Radio One DJ Chris Moyles gets his name from?)

Mules, as in chillblains, used to refer to sores on a horse's pastern (between the hoof and the fetlock). But how nice it is to see that the other mules, the ones with four legs, get a revised reputation from the Oxford lexicographers. In *The Concise Oxford Dictionary* this amounts to a definition of the mule as 'beast of draught and burden and undeservedly noted for obstinacy'.

Pumps

So there are mules and mules. But there are also pumps and pumps. The *OED*'s main entry for **pump** describes the item that is useful for getting bilge out of ships and other places that we'd rather not contemplate. But the derivation of **pumps** – the sort of low-cut shoes worn by dancers and acrobats – remains a mystery. Is it an 'echoic' word deriving from the sound they make when smacking more lightly against the ground than big heavy shoes? It seems that all offers are open on this, but they've been around since at least 1555. There are possible links with the word **pomp** (as in circumstance), but these are too tenuous to expound. At times like these the dictionary compilers have to hold up their hands and admit defeat. And not just defeat: de hands, de legs and sometimes de arms too.

Flip-flops

Who would have thought that **flip-flop** is such a variable word? It can mean anything from 'a flighty woman' to 'a football move', the latter devised by the 1970s' Brazilian player Roberto Rivelino. This manoeuvre, also known as the 'Elastico', involves the player moving to play the ball one way and then, bafflingly, flicking it in the opposite direction, leaving the other player for dead. Nor let us forget the 1970s' word for sandals that flap up and down at the back as you walk. These **flip-flops** have moved from cheap and cheerful rubber beach shoes to high fashion statements in recent years. Just to confuse us, Australians refer to them as **thongs** (see page 57).

Within the last few years 'flip-flop' has been dragged into the political world, and in February 2006 Tony Blair and David

Cameron were accusing each other of **flip-flopping** (changing their minds) over policy. The origin of this term is nothing to do with footwear, and everything to do with the acrobatic flip-flop or **flip-flap** (in use since 1902), suggesting that a politician is flipping first one way and then another. In fact, it was an American term, first applied in 2004 to John Kerry, the Massachusetts senator and Democratic presidential candidate. Throughout his campaign he was accused by opponents of going back on his word, especially on the wisdom or otherwise of military action in Iraq. It's a good way to describe how politicians adjust their views to suit the prevailing mood, much as fashion is said to reflect the times in which it is created.

Negligee

In Eric Partridge's edition of one of the great works of English lexicography, *A Classical Dictionary of the Vulgar Tongue* by Captain Francis Grose, the word **negligee** is listed as 'a woman's undressed gown, vulgarly termed a neggledigee'. There is abundant evidence here of the Englishman's reluctance to tackle French at its most intractable, while nonetheless being alert to the erotic possibilities offered by the French language.

I don't think I'm reading too much back into the word when I say that the interplay of vowels and consonants in the word 'negligee' implies an article of clothing that was intended not so much to be put on as to be taken off shortly afterwards. Indeed, wearing a negligee at all seems somehow to be missing the point. A negligee fulfils its destiny by lying in a crumpled heap on the floor while its owner gets down to it on the nearby bed.

Negligee was an adjective before it became a noun. Its first surviving appearance in print – meaning 'dressed informally' –

'Is that a dictionary of etymology in your pocket
or are you just pleased to see me?'

is in a comic play by John Durant Breval (*c*.1680–1738) called
The Play Is the Plot (1718), which underlines its sexy credentials:
'Never more like an Angel than at this instant … thus negligee
as you are, if I would not take you before a Dutchess'. In
eighteenth-century America it was also the word for 'a loose
gown worn by women' (or sometimes men), and in the nineteenth century it was, says the *OED*, 'a necklace or girdle of
(usually irregularly set) beads, pearls, etc.'.

The Latin verbs *neglegere* or *negligere* can mean either
'to make light of' or 'to not care for'. Both meanings suggest a
degree of carelessness, which is embodied in the flimsy item
of nightwear, found in an 1862 edition of *Harper's Magazine*
in what the *OED* defines as 'a woman's light dressing-gown,

especially one made of flimsy, semi-transparent fabric trimmed with ruffles, lace, etc.'. The word is almost a joke on its properties. It seems to be saying: 'What, this? Oh, it's nothing,' whereas it's definitely something that conveys a mystical allure to the person looking at it.

The *Encyclopaedia Britannica* states that the French root of negligee means 'careless or negligent', and it's certainly meant to imply this, but the negligee has a more complex history than its ruffled translucence might suggest. In that first citation from 1718, it meant 'informally dressed'; the come-hither quality came later. In mid-eighteenth-century America, a negligee was a loose gown worn by women. In fact, according to the *OED*, it has also been 'a type of man's wig fashionable in or shortly before the early 1750s'.

Pants

Now our verbal striptease is really getting down to basics. Whether big pants or flimsy smalls are your preferred option, we'll get to the bottom of them here.

How do you want to be remembered? My guess is that, of all the inscriptions to go on your headstone, the one you'd least like would read, 'Here lies so-and-so: everything he or she did was utter pants'. The word **pants** seems to draw the vigour of its offensiveness from its utter limpness. It is the equivalent of being smacked around the face by a wet fish. If you suggested to a clutch of politicians that their government's policy on Iraq was flawed or dangerous, or even self-destructive, they might debate with you, and even do you the honour of getting steamed up in their own defence. If you told them you thought the government's policies were **total pants**, they might well try to punch you. It's the smack of dismissiveness that makes 'pants' so hurtful.

British pants and American pants went off in different directions during the nineteenth century. Over here they became an undercover matter, while to the Americans they more or less retained their sense of trouserness. In 1904 the British meaning was described sniffily by *The New English Dictionary* (the forerunner of the present-day *OED*) as 'colloquial and shoppy'. The resultant trail of confusion has led many a visiting American comedian to score a few easy laughs on their first gigs in this country. The same goes for British comedians over there. But why do we wear pants, or **panties**, and what have they to do with the heavy breathing that marks the end of a marathon (or just one flight of stairs) or a brief moment of passion or excitement?

Chambers Dictionary cites the French verb *pantoiser* (to tremble), which is what you do when you're out of breath, and which explains **panting**, but it has nothing to do with pants, the underwear item. And if the sound of *pantoiser* reminds you of 'fantasy', you're not dreaming. The Greek verb *phantasoun* means 'to bring images before the mind'. This suggests that Greeks panted more out of passion than they did from physical exertion, which might sound strange coming from the birthplace of the marathon.

'Pants' are descended from a different line altogether. In French **pantomime** the *pantalon* (pantaloon) character was 'an absurd old man, the butt of the clown's tricks' (*Collins*). This character was descended from a fourth-century Venetian saint, Pantalone, which was a popular name in Venice at the time. The Pantaloon character, on which the English harlequin was based, was defined by the **pantaloons** he wore. These ranged from a garment that covered the entire body to a type of breeches or trousers. Pantaloon himself came to represent authority, and was frequently taken to be a bit of a fool.

The use of 'pants' as a put-down seems to have been popularized by yet another (now former) Radio One disc jockey, Simon Mayo. 'It's a **pile of pants**!' was touted as his catchphrase by the *Guardian* in September 1994. A pile of pants: it doesn't strike one as particularly offensive, does it? Amazing what regular airplay can do.

Obviously, pants come into play in other areas of social embarrassment, an experience well captured by the phrase **to be caught with one's pants down**. In fact, it's not as old as you might have thought. This sublimely British phrase owes its genesis to that other well-known popularizer of twentieth-century catchphrases, the Irish writer James Joyce, who first hit upon it in his iconoclastic 1922 novel *Ulysses*: 'Must be careful about women. Catch them once with their pants down. Never forgive you after.' It's not often you get the chance to leap from Simon Mayo to James Joyce.

Thong

Given that any discussion of **thong** these days brings to mind images of near-naked women on beaches, you might have thought that the word was a relative newcomer to the dictionary. You might have placed it in the same vintage as the **G-string**, both clothing and musical versions of which were first spotted – but only just – towards the end of the nineteenth century.

The G-string's origins are hard to locate, unlike the area that it's meant to be concealing. (The **G-spot** would be easier: that's named after a German-born gynaecologist called Ernst Gräfenberg [1881–1957], who pretty much put his finger on the most

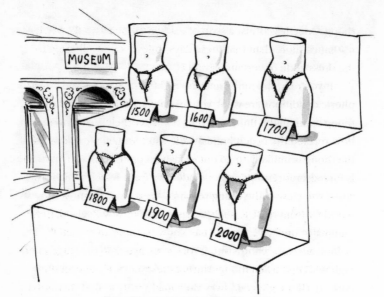

'The Thong Remains the Same.'

erogenous area of a woman's body.) 'G-string', first cited in print in the USA in 1878, is baffling, though. Could the G stand for 'girdle'? Or is it because the G-string itself resembles the letter G? We don't know, but if you had to guess on which came first between thong and G-string, I imagine most people would say they were roughly contemporary.

Well, you'd be thwong. In fact the thong has been around since long before records began. Check out the fashion manuals of the year 950, back in the days when we had the perfect clothes for global warming, but lacked the climate – whereas these days it's the other way round. The thong was there, even then, descended from the even Older English **thwang**, and related in some way to the rather nastier **twinge**, which is, I suppose, understandable if you've just executed a hurried turn in your thong. Once it was just a strip of leather. Come to think of it, it's not much more than that these days, unless you're adhering to the dress code of certain private clubs.

If you're in the mood and the night is still young, and atmospheric conditions are right, you might well enjoy wearing just a thong at midnight. But most of us don't get the chance, no matter how relaxed the beach holiday. Still, whether you wear it or not, the thong is unlikely to go out of fashion quite yet. As a result, one is forced, unforgivably, to conclude that, from which whichever angle you view it, the thong remains the same. In parts of the world far from the UK, such as Australia and New Zealand, these minimalist underwear items have now become an essential fashion accessory, and visiting rock stars may find the stage piled high with discarded thongs during the course of a successful concert. (If the gig goes awry, they might instead find themselves pelted with the other type of thongs – see page 52.)

Proof of thong's early origins can be found in the Lindisfarne Gospels, now dated at AD 710–20, in a line from the Book of John (1.27): 'Ic ne am wyre ætte ic undoe his uong scoes' (I am not worthy to undo the thong of his shoes). This clearly shows thong's original meaning as 'a narrow strip of hide or leather, for use as a lace, cord, band, strap, or the like'.

Chapter Three

Gordon Bennett Bloody Mary Jack the lad Sweet
Bob's your uncle Hobson's choice Take the Mickey
Gordon Bennett Bloody Mary Jack the
Sweet F. A. Bob's your uncle Hobson's choice Take
Mickey Round Robin Gordon Bennett Bloody Ma
the lad Sweet F. A. Bob's your uncle Hobson's choi
ake the Mickey Round Robin Gordon Bennett Blo
ary Jack the lad Sweet F. A. Bob's your uncle Hobs

Who were they?

We are told that we live in an era of people power, but this is not a recent phenomenon. Phrases that have names attached carry an extra punch: they're more colourful. We could, for example, just say **the real thing**, but many of us prefer to say **the real McCoy**. But what or who was McCoy? The trouble is that we don't always keep full records during someone's lifetime, so speculation has centred around a railway locomotive engineer called Elijah McCoy, a rum-smuggling Bill McCoy in Prohibition-era America, and the pure heroin that came from a misspelling of Macao. The truth is that it's most likely to be a mishearing of MacKay, the name of an Edinburgh firm of whisky distillers in 1870.

Every named phrase has a different origin. You might have done something very fast, or for added colour you might say that you did it **as quickly as Jack Robinson**. Jack who? Of the many theories, the most likely seems to be that Jack Robinson was the officer commanding the Tower of London between 1660 and 1679, so the speed alluded to was connected with the downward swing of the hangman's axe. The bloodier the story, the more likely it is to stick.

You might be feeling happy, or very happy, but if you say that you're **as happy as Larry**, that gives your happiness a particular identity. Ah, say the wordhunters among us, but who was Larry? Could it have been a boxer called Larry Foley (1847–1914)? Or was it simply a shortening of the Australian word **larrikin**, meaning 'a rough or hooligan' (see page 120), or 'generally happy-go-lucky individual'. We'd prefer the former, but we'll probably have to stick with the latter.

This chapter offers a selection of first names, surnames, whole names and nicknames that embrace English history stretching all the way back to Tudor times, and coming more up to date with the founder of the world's most respected air-ballooning race and the nephew of one of our most distinguished prime ministers. The honours board of phrase-naming is shared equally by a former English monarch with a taste for persecuting Protestants and an otherwise blameless little girl who was simply playing in the street when she made an unwelcome appointment with fate.

With today's world so fixated on celebrities, we wonder if any will go down in naming history. Will people involved in gruesome or sensational murder trials, such as Myra Hindley, Peter Sutcliffe or even O.J. Simpson, one day suffer the fate of finding their names woven into the fabric of a phrase? The surest way to be immortalized used to be through playground chants ('Lizzie Borden took an axe/And gave her mother forty whacks'). Let's just hope not too many British schools outlaw skipping ropes on health and safety grounds, since that would inevitably reduce the ways in which sing-song references enter the language.

Let's make a few predictions. We predict a new adverb of emphasis: not just **plug ugly** but **Rooney ugly**. Or how about a new scale of beauty, with Wayne at one end and George Clooney at the other? 'Give me the whole thing, from Rooney to Clooney.' We'd like to see a new noun, as in 'to talk utter **Jade**', which means to speak without engaging the brain. How would you like to be remembered? Perhaps, given some of the stories contained here, it would be safer simply to slip away unnoticed.

Gordon Bennett

Some phrases that have names attached to them seem to have existed for ever, as if they appeared from out of the linguistic ether. Others have a shortlist of possible claimants, and one such is the slightly dated oath '**Gordon Bennett**', which is uttered at moments of high surprise. It's easy to see where its appeal lies: you can hear the sound of God – extended to the more expressive Gawd, as in **Gorblimey** or **Gawd Almighty** – in the word 'Gordon', so it's clear that the Lord's name is being invoked via someone else's name.

Gordon Bennett appeared as a cartoon character in the *Beano* comic, though only as recently as 1999. But was that name based on a real character? If so, the main contender to claim this honour is the scion of a famous publishing dynasty. His father, Gordon Bennett (1795–1872), was a newspaperman. Born in Scotland, he moved to America, where he founded the *New York Herald* (1835) and worked his way up from humble beginnings to achieve wealth and fame. But James Gordon Bennett (1841–1918), always known as 'Gordon', threw his money around with unseemly gusto and became one of the most colourful and talked-about characters of his day, a bit like Paris Hilton, except without the leaked Internet sex scenes.

Bennett junior was brought up in France. In 1869 he shrewdly invested some of his father's thousands by sponsoring Henry Stanley's trip to present-day Tanzania. Stanley's famous greeting to the only other white man for hundreds of miles – 'Dr Livingstone, I presume?'[1] – was a masterpiece of understatement, glaringly at odds with the overblown lifestyle of his newspaper sponsor – and, according to a new biography of Stanley,[2] very possibly made up by Stanley after the event. Still, it was a cracking line.

The younger Bennett certainly had a nose for a story: or rather, for a publishing machine that printed stories. He founded

----

[1] Henry Stanley found Livingstone at Ujiji, near Lake Tanganyika, on 10 November 1871.
[2] *Stanley: The Impossible Life of Africa's Greatest Explorer* by Tim Jeal (Faber & Faber, 2007).

the *International Herald Tribune* in Paris in 1887, and he led a lavish and at times dissolute lifestyle that included having his own railway carriages (nineteenth-century-speak for 'private jet'), plus yachts and mansions (nineteenth-century-speak for 'yachts and mansions'). Maybe it was his extravagant behaviour that led to the uttering of his name – frequently accompanied by a despairing shake of the head – becoming synonymous with expressions of amazement or disbelief. In fact, muttering 'Gordon Bennett' could be said to be the quintessential British exclamation, in that it can be used to express either jubilation or extreme disappointment.

Famously, Bennett junior blew his engagement to the New York socialite Caroline May by urinating, when drunk, into a fireplace in front of her family on New Year's Eve 1877. The family was not amused, and before long Bennett was on a ship bound for France, where attitudes to urinating in public were more enlightened. Bennett's drunken feat was recognized by *The Guinness Book of Records* as the 'Greatest Engagement Faux Pas', something that could also be described as the 'Most Spurious Entry for a Guinness Book Record'.

Given the prevalence of Gordon Bennett's name, it's interesting that the exclamation is not recorded earlier in the popular books and journals of the day. The first example, in fact, is from a 1962 episode of the TV sitcom *Steptoe & Son* called 'The Bird'. The exact wording is: 'Gordon Bennett, if you don't know that after all these years'. To a scriptwriter in postwar Britain, the opportunity to sneak in a concealed reference to God was irresistible.

Balderdash wordhunters may be aware of other theories as to the phrase's origins, though none is likely to receive the royal nod from the *OED*. One story refers to the Australian lieutenant-

general Henry Gordon Bennett (1887–1962), who was bomb-
arded with criticism on the grounds that after he surrendered to
Japanese forces in Singapore in February 1942, he then managed
to escape, leaving his men behind. The troops probably aimed a
few choice expressions at his departing rear, but would they have
included the words 'Gordon Bennett'? Wordhunter correspondents claim that an entire generation of Australian schoolchildren
used to call their sports shoes **Gordon Bennetts** because that
was what they wore to run away.

Another story comes from the north of England, and concerns
a Gordon Bennett who led a foxhunt in the early years of the
twentieth century. His name, it is claimed, was shouted to gee up
the other hunters. It's a great-if-true story, but so far the documentary evidence has been a bit thin on the ground. The same
goes for Gordon Bennett, a hanging judge in Victorian London.
The names of these individuals may have been real enough, but
we can't prove that anyone uttered their name as an oath.

Returning to our first Gordon Bennett, some readers may
have heard about his sponsorship of motor racing, as well as a
prestigious air-balloon race that started in 1906 in Paris. Anecdotal
evidence has it that a number of wealthy race-goers were lured
by Bennett's fame and reputation to travel to County Kildare in
Ireland, where the 1903 Gordon Bennett Cup for automobile
racing was to be held. Local café and bar owners duly raised their
prices, at which point oral history asserts that the locals were
moved to exclaim 'Gordon Bennett!' as the price of a pint of
stout shot up to reflect the spending power of the visitors.
If someone had written their exclamation on the back of a
suitably re-priced menu, we would have the vital evidence we
need. But, frustratingly, no contemporary evidence exists for
this attractive story.

Bloody Mary

A splash of vodka, a squirt of tomato juice and **bob's your uncle** (see page 74) – there's your **Bloody Mary**. Worcestershire sauce? Oh, why not. The Bloody Mary has been propping up people who prop up bars for over sixty years, thanks to the antics of one of the heroes of the early cinema, the actor George Jessel (1898–1981). His latest idea to make a party swing was recorded in a December 1939 edition of the *New York Herald Tribune*, in a cutting that was dug up by a *Balderdash* wordhunter and is included in the June 2005 Draft Revision of the *OED Online*: 'George Jessel's newest pick-me-up which is receiving attention from the town's paragraphers is called a Bloody Mary: half tomato juice, half vodka.' That quotation appears in the entry for **paragraphers**, which was the vogue term for journalists, i.e. those who write in paragraphs. Not a word about optional extras, such as celery, horseradish, cayenne pepper – still less beef consommé, for goodness' sake.

In fact, there are two mysteries about the Bloody Mary: who mixed it first and who it's named after. The second question might be easier to answer. Queen Mary I of England (1516–58) was a woman of strong views. Fourth and penultimate in the line of Tudor monarchs, her stated aim was to shout 'Time, please!' to the tide of Protestantism that Henry VIII had introduced to England during the Reformation. She reigned for a brief five years, but kept busy by executing 300 religious dissenters on charges of heresy – more than twice the number killed during the previous 150 years.

As if that isn't dark enough, there was another Bloody Mary, notorious in folklore and children's street life of the Victorian period. Bloody Mary was the name of a witch invoked during children's games. Sometimes she had a full name, such as Mary Worth, at other times she was just Mary, but always Bloody. Bloody Mary was a real bogey figure. She would appear in a bathroom mirror if you stood in the dark and shouted her name three times, or spun around and rubbed your eyes, or lit a candle. The inspiration for this Bloody Mary may have been a child murderer, and the redness of the tomato juice in a glass of Bloody Mary is clearly reminiscent of the blood of her victims, but was it inspired by the monarch, and – furthermore – was the story of the witch related to Bloody Mary the monarch?

The trouble is we still don't know, which is annoying, but after a Bloody Mary or two, dissatisfaction begins to soften into mere curiosity. So let's try to find out who mixed the first such drink. One popular theory is that it's all down to the barman of Harry's New York Bar in Paris during the 1920s, Fernand Pétiôt. In fact, the owner of Harry's Bar, Harry Macelhone, later claimed to have served the first Bloody Mary to Ernest Hemingway, possibly in 1919, though Hemingway, who wrote most things down, didn't record the event. Hemingway later boasted, in a letter dated 1947, that he was responsible for introducing the drink to Hong Kong in 1941, where it 'did more than any single factor except the Japanese Army to precipitate the fall of that Crown Colony'.

Pétiôt moved to New York in 1934 to become head bartender at the Regis, where he tried to call the drink a Red Snapper, but the name wasn't popular, and the New Yorkers wanted a bit more flavour. He experimented, and this must have paid off because he made the following claim in an interview with the *New Yorker* in July 1954:

> George Jessel said he created it, but it was really nothing but vodka and tomato juice when I took it over. I cover the bottom of

the shaker with four large dashes of salt, two dashes of
black pepper, two dashes of cayenne pepper, and a layer of
Worcestershire sauce; I then add a dash of lemon juice and some
cracked ice, put in two ounces of vodka and two ounces of thick
tomato juice, shake, strain, and pour.

And even he didn't say anything about beef consommé.

As for the name, Pétiôt claimed that 'one of the boys
suggested we call the drink "Bloody Mary" because it reminded
him of the Bucket of Blood Club in Chicago, and a girl there
named Mary'. Elsewhere, it's claimed that the drink was inspired
by Bloody Mary, a character in James A. Michener's *Tales of the
South Pacific* (1946), the book that inspired the musical *South
Pacific*. Bloody Mary was so called because her teeth were stained
red from chewing betel nuts.

Quite where the truth lies in this swirl of twentieth-century
intoxication is not that clear, but the thread of historical logic
seems to connect George Jessel and Mary I, so let's stick there for
the time being while we poke around at the bottom of our glass
with a celery stick – a refinement invented at the Pump Room in
Chicago, according to Joseph Scott and Donald Bain, authors of
The World's Best Bartenders' Guide (1998).

Jack the lad

If you look up the name **Jack** in Eric Partridge's wonderful
Dictionary of Slang and Unconventional English (1948), you'd
better not have a taxi meter running. There are six columns of
closely written type, and it's no wonder why. There is something
irrepressible about the very letters of the name, which suggest
optimism and a hint of cheek. 'Jack' has had its snappy reputation

right from the start of its life as a 'familiar' form of the more formal John. Ever since, it has worn its reputation for flippancy with a definite swagger: it's a man-of-the-people type of name. Hence the plethora of references, from **Jack in the water** ('a handy man at a boat-house or landing stage') to **Jack Weight** ('a fat man').

The *OED* has a reference to the phrase that seems to have been the direct predecessor of **jack the lad**. It's not quite the same – it's **Jack's the lad**, from a song containing the lines 'For if ever fellow took delight in swigging, gigging, kissing, drinking, fighting,/ Damme I'll be bold to say that Jack's the lad'. That song achieved a certain prominence around 1840, but when did we go from 'Jack's the lad' to the simpler 'jack the lad'? At the time of writing, 'jack the lad' doesn't appear in print until a June 1981 edition of *New Society* magazine, by which time the phrase has been shortened, and 'jack the lad' is described as a bit of a chancer – but also a bit of a loser: 'I was always Jack the Lad – the one everyone liked but nobody wanted to know.'

In fact, there may well have been one such Jack, and we even have his dates: 4 March 1702 to 16 November 1724. **Jack Sheppard** was an English robber, burglar and thief, and therefore highly dodgy (see page 109). His parents named him John, but we are told that he was known variously as John, 'Gentleman Jack' and even 'Jack the Lad'. Sheppard's career in crime, including five successful clink breakouts in his *annus criminalis mirabilis* of 1724, lasted only two years before he was hanged at Tyburn. However, his escapades, especially his ability to elude the authorities, gave him an awesome reputation among the poor, similar to that of Robin Hood, though without the same principles of wealth distribution. Plenty has been written about Jack 'the Lad' Sheppard, though, as yet, physical evidence of the nickname 'jack the lad' still eludes wordhunters.

That's one problem with the name 'Jack'. We all love it dearly, but it's a bit of a mongrel. If you survey the columns of Jacks in Partridge's dictionary, from **Jack Muck** (a seaman) to **Jack Shilloo** (a boaster), you wouldn't expect a real Jack to spring up and claim to have given the term its original meaning. Similarly with jack the lad: he can't be a real person, can he?

Jack the lad, then, suggests a certain jauntiness, especially combined with the recent but quintessentially British sense of 'lad'. Lad had a busy time of it in the late 1980s and early 1990s when, depending on your point of view, it either came to represent the acceptable face of post-politically correct sassiness, or merely a sly way by which sexist blokes could say words like 'tits' in public. But it hasn't always been roses for Jack. Its very accessibility as a name meant that when searching for someone to typify selfishness, complacency or a certain dog-in-the-manger attitude (see page 94), the phrase **I'm all right Jack**, first used in 1919, seemed to fit. The famous 1959 film of the same name, starring Peter Sellers as a particularly nit-picking trade union official, has set the pattern for 'I'm all right Jack' ever since.

Nevertheless, we can't believe that there is no printed evidence for 'jack the lad' prior to 1981. Maybe the *Balderdash* wordhunters will come upon buried treasure.

Sweet FA

These days, **Sweet FA** is short for 'Sweet fuck all' and means 'precisely nothing'. It is uttered in a despairing, throw-away tone, as in, 'I paid £25 for that computer manual and what use was it? Sweet FA.' The initials appear first in a 1944 volume of *Penguin New Writing*: 'Bread – that's about what we got as kids. Bread, and sweet FA.' The expression 'fuck all' was pretty strong language for the first half of the twentieth century, so it was common to commute it to a name: Fanny Adams. The first written reference to Sweet Fanny Adams is from a volume called *Digger Dialects*, written by W.H. Downing in 1919. Fanny Adams sounds like a predictable way of bowdlerizing the letters FA to avoid causing offence, and yet there is cast-iron historical evidence to prove that there was a real Fanny Adams, and it was the horrific story of her excruciating death – still more what happened to her dead body – that led to the phrase's familiarity. Be warned, though: it really doesn't make for pleasant reading.

The gruesome details are contained within the Curtis Museum at Alton in Hampshire, not far from the home of George and Harriet Adams on Tan House Lane in the same village. The date was Saturday, 24 August 1867, and their daughter Fanny, aged eight, and her seven-year-old sister Lizzie were playing with their friend Minnie Warner, also eight, near Flood Meadow, when they were approached by a man.

In a sequence of events chillingly familiar to modern readers, the stranger offered Minnie and Lizzie three halfpence to go off and play, and then offered Fanny a halfpenny to walk with him along a road called The Hollow towards the village of Shalden. Fanny seems to have been uncertain about taking the money, whereupon the stranger carried her into a nearby hop-field. Her two friends went off to play, unaware of the unspeakable act that was taking place near by.

The state in which her body was found, later that very day, is shocking even by today's lurid tabloid standards. Fanny had been murdered, mutilated and then dismembered. Parts of the poor child's body were scattered over a wide area. If you really want to read all the gory details, log on to the website of the Curtis

Museum,[3] but be warned: it's pretty gruesome stuff.

The prime suspect was a twenty-nine-year-old solicitor's clerk called Frederick Baker, who had been seen emerging from The Hollow at about five o'clock. Yet he had appeared calm when he was questioned by police. Amazingly, he even went for a drink with a colleague from work that evening, though by now the story was out that a girl had disappeared. When he was arrested later, blood was found on his clothes. Then a stone was found in the hop-field. It had blood on it, together with pieces of flesh and strands of long hair. Baker loudly protested his innocence. The trouble was, he had rather shot himself in the foot because police found his diary entry for that day: '24th August, Saturday – killed a young girl. It was fine and hot.' If *The Guinness Book of Records* had a category for 'Most Incriminating Diary Entry Relating to a Murder', that surely would win the prize by several lengths. After fifteen minutes' deliberation, the jury returned a guilty verdict and Frederick Baker was hanged before a crowd of 5000 – mostly women – on Christmas Eve 1867.

The spectacular and frenzied nature of the attack led to a succession of grim jokes, the most famous of which was in circulation among sailors. In 1869, as a particularly tasteless tribute to the mutilated state of Fanny's sliced and diced body, a consignment of tinned mutton that turned out to taste even more putrid than normal was dubbed 'Sweet Fanny Adams' by the **jack tars** (the name for common sailors since 1781). Fanny Adams was defined in Albert Barrère and Charles Leland's 1889 *Dictionary of Slang, Jargon and Cant* as '(preserved mutton) brought from the ship' and it retained this meaning in W. Granville's 1962 *Dictionary of Sailors' Slang*: 'General nautical slang for stew or

---

3 www.hants.gov.uk/museum/curtis/fannyadams/index.html

hash'. Sometimes just repeating a name, a word or an idea that has horrible connotations can deaden its potency. Not that this would have been of any help to Fanny's family, of course.

Meanwhile, on the other side of the world, our Australian cousins, with their well-known fondness for colourful expressions, enthusiastically invested FA, Fanny Adams or Sweet Fanny Adams with the sense of 'nothing'. This was noted in 1919, and is its principal meaning today. The combination 'Sweet FA' is first noted in 1930, and is nowadays a handy newspaper headline, especially whenever the papers want to bash an organization that is luckless enough to share those same initials, such as 'The Football Association admits it knows Sweet FA about when Wembley Stadium will be open for business'.

Bob's your uncle

When we say **bob's your uncle**, we are saying 'simple', 'easy', 'no problem' or 'job done'. But how many of us pause for a moment to ask which Bob/bob we are invoking and why? While the meaning of phrase may be 'easy' or 'straightforward', bob's journey to phrasehood is not at all easy or straightforward to work out. It is beset with complications, in fact, and the *OED* has refused to wade into the battle, merely marking it as slang. Eric Partridge's *Dictionary of Slang* recorded it first in 1937, dating it back to *c.* 1890 and giving a snatch of conversation as an example: 'You go and ask for the job – and he remembers your name – and Bob's your uncle.' Partridge makes no further comment, but how telling is it that someone remembers a person's name?

'Bob' has been a pet form of the name Robert since 1721, but the *OED* has ten entries for it, the meanings ranging from

*'This government will end cronyism, and my brother's
just the man for the job!'*

'a bouquet of flowers' to 'a manoeuvre popular with bell-ringers'. Few of them, though, are relevant to our present investigation. Alongside bob's your uncle, it's worth noting that Partridge quotes **bobby's job**, defining it as an 'easy job', though again we're not told exactly why, nor whether it's connected to Bob and his uncle.

It has been suggested that the Bob in our phrase was a reference to Sir Robert Peel, the man who started the Metropolitan Police Force in 1828, when he was merely Mr Peel the home secretary, and whose police officers were known as **bobbies** from at least as far back as 1844. And yet, can this really be taken seriously? Grateful though Londoners must have been to have a new force keeping the streets safe, there seems no likely reason why they should have transferred their loyalties so far as to think of these police officers as their uncles, no matter how efficient they might have been at apprehending criminals.

In Captain Francis Grose's 1785 *Dictionary of the Vulgar Tongue* – a major early contributor to the field of lexicology – we find the phrase **all is bob**, that word 'bob' being a slang term also cited in the *OED* from 1721 as 'lively' or 'nice'. But, again, it's the word 'uncle' that brings us up short. As a result, we have no option but to draw upon the political career of Lord Salisbury (1830–1903). Also known as Robert Arthur Talbot Gascoyne-Cecil, 3rd Marquess of Salisbury, trading under the name Lord Robert Cecil before 1865 and Viscount Cranborne from 1865 until 1868, he was the last British prime minister to hold that position while still being a member of the House of Lords. For his first two terms in office he rotated the job so frequently with William Gladstone (1809–98) that they must at times have met in the middle. The third time round he was succeeded by Arthur Balfour (1848–1930), who happened to be his own nephew.

In fact, Balfour had been made Chief Secretary of Ireland by his uncle in 1886, a move that provoked a certain amount of muttering on the red and green benches of the Palace of Westminster, in the days before the Ireland job became something of a poisoned chalice. Balfour had also served as president of the Local Government Board and Secretary for Scotland: top jobs. Clearly, then, Uncle Bob had a pretty high opinion of Arthur. Naturally, suspicions arose. Had young Balfour netted these jobs on his own merits or with a little help from his uncle? If, as was widely felt at the time, it was the latter, the charge of nepotism could be applied.

Nepotism, as any classically trained schoolboy would have known in those days, comes from the Latin word *nepos*, which means … 'nephew'? Well, not in classical Latin, where it means 'grandson'. But in post-classical Latin it *does* mean nephew: it's not Latin out of the top drawer, but close enough for the joke to be made by those waggish Victorians. The charge of nepotism can be laid, then, with the mildly waspish 'bob's your uncle', or so the story goes. Unfortunately, none of those waggish Victorians thought to write the remark down in their waggish diaries; nor were any contemporary journalists obliging enough to transcribe it so that we can see the phrase bedding down. This is all very frustrating. Unlike the obliging Frederick Baker, whose diary proved so useful (see page 71), no one wrote down the words 'bob's your uncle' until all the main parties had popped their clogs (see page 166).

Hobson's choice

There are an awful lot of choices around these days, but they don't all get the recognition they deserve. Often they are wrongly labelled. What, for example, would you call a choice between two equally unattractive options? Whatever you call it, don't confuse it with having to make a decision, which appears to be a free choice, but is actually between something and nothing. The origins of the term for this latter choice are both colourful and historically attested, and they relate to a man with a keen eye for a swift shilling, and a stable full of horses of varying speeds. His name was Thomas Hobson (c.1544–1630), and the choice he offered came, in his own lifetime, to be called **Hobson's choice**.

It happened as follows. Hobson was a stagecoach proprietor who ran a mail-carrier company situated outside the gates of St Catherine's College, Cambridge. His horses plied a route between Cambridge and London. When they weren't needed to ferry mail bundles back and forth, they were hired out to the town's students and university staff. Obviously, the faster the horse, the more in demand it was, but Hobson was fearful that his best horses would be run into the ground, so he developed the system for which he became famous. Horses were rented out in strict rotation to allow the swifter ones time to recover, so the would-be rider simply had to take whichever horse was the next one in the queue at the stable entrance. These days it's called the taxi-rank principle; Hobson referred to it as 'this one or none'.

This phrase for a choice between something and nothing is enshrined in *The Oxford English Dictionary* in a quotation from a 1660 work by the Quaker Samuel Fisher: 'If in this Case there be no other (as the Proverb is) then Hobson's choice … which is, chuse whether you will have this or none'. Alternatives could be **take it or leave it**, or – if you are holding a large mug of tea and sporting a beard like Noel Edmonds – **deal or no deal**.

Hobson achieved a fair amount of fame in his own life. The great English poet John Milton (1608–74) liked him so much that he wrote not one, but two epitaphs after his death, giving people a very unHobson-like choice.

In fact, lack of choice wasn't all that Hobson was famous for. He also built the pipe, known as Hobson's Conduit, that in 1614 delivered clear drinking water to Cambridge. The conduit head is still standing, though it has been moved slightly from its original position, and is now just out of town, past the Fitzwilliam Museum.

The first full-length account of 'Hobson's choice' was recorded in the *Spectator* magazine,[4] a literary but gossipy

---

4 In print for two years, 1711–12. Not to be confused with the present-day *Spectator* magazine (founded in 1828), though the modern version was, in part at least, a tribute to the original.

journal founded by Joseph Addison and Sir Richard Steele. On
Tuesday, 14 October 1712 Steele wrote:

> Mr Hobson kept a Stable of forty good Cattle, always ready and fit
> for travelling; but when a Man came for a Horse, he was led into
> the Stable, where there was great Choice, but he obliged him to
> take the Horse which stood next to the Stable-Door; so that every
> Customer was alike well served according to his Chance, and
> every Horse ridden with the same Justice.

Steele's pithy conclusion of the practice was that 'From whence
it became a Proverb, when what ought to be your Election was
forced upon you, to say, *Hobson's Choice.*' In 1688 another writer,
Thomas Ward, wrote a poem called 'England's Reformation', in
which he noted that 'Where to elect there is but one, 'tis Hobson's
choice – take that, or none'.

Take the mickey

Teasing or having fun at someone else's expense is often referred
to as **taking the mickey**. The *OED* defines it as 'to behave or
speak satirically or mockingly; to make fun of, satirize, or debunk
(a person or thing)'. Inevitably, there has been a good deal of
discussion over the identity of mickey. One popular theory that
has made it into the *OED* claims that it is an offshoot of **taking
a mickey bliss**, the name being rhyming slang for a 'piss'; and
'taking the piss', of course, means mocking someone or something. The identity of Mick(e)y Bliss has never been seriously
proposed, though the phrase is more recent than one might think.

The *OED* records that the words 'mick' and 'mickey' were
both nineteenth-century Australian slang for 'a wild bull' (and

therefore a testosterone-fuelled male), as well as Irish slang for 'a penis'. 'Taking the mickey' is first quoted by Joseph Alexander Baron in *From the City, from the Plough* (1948), a British working-class view of the First World War: 'Higgsy,' said the sergeant, 'they think I'm taking the mickey.'

In 1945, buoyed up on hopes of victory in Europe, spirits among Penguin New Writing authors were running high, and there was little room for reverence. 'The corporal ... sat back in his corner looking a little offended,' reads one entry. 'He thought I was taking the piss.'

The variation **to take the mike out of** was in use between the 1930s and the 1970s, and the first recorded instance we have appears in *Mint* (1935), the posthumous memoirs of T.E. Lawrence (of Arabia): 'But, mate, you let the flight down, when he takes the mike out of you every time.' Other variations include the mock-gentrified **extracting or taking the Michael**, the first instance of which comes from Harold Pinter's 1959 play *The Birthday Party*. 'They won't come. Someone's taking the Michael ... It's a false alarm.'

One corking theory is all wrapped up with male pride. The story goes that if a man has a very full bladder, it causes him to have an erection or 'stand proud'. This became known as 'piss proud' – a bit like 'morning glory' – because one's 'pride' is not a macho badge of honour (and where would you wear it anyway?) but is merely to do with an overfull bladder. If you **took the micturate**, or **took the piss**, you dented the person's pride and restored them to normality. So 'taking the mickey' might be a shortened form for the more refined act of micturition (or the less refined act of pissing), though this may be a *post hoc* etymological explanation. In other words, first we started taking the piss, or the mickey, and then someone saw the connection between 'mickey' and 'micturate,' and the link was too good to refuse, so on that occasion Bob was your uncle.

Meanwhile, a *Balderdash* correspondent in the United States suggests that **taking the mick** arose from a derogatory term for Irish people (micks), and the fact that they were mocked because people ignorantly assumed that they were insufficiently mentally alert to understand the rudeness of remarks being made around them. This sounds fanciful, however, as well as downright rude. Let's hope our *Balderdash* wordhunter is making his own plans for St Patrick's Day.

The popular historian Adam Hart-Davis is something of an expert in the field, having written a book called *Taking the Piss: The Potted History of Pee* in 2005. He has a very imaginative explanation for the phrase, based on the vast amounts of urine that were used in the wool-dyeing process. He records how huge quantities needed to be transported in barrels, which were loaded on to boats and then shipped from London to Humberside. To spice things up, he adds that the captain used to claim that he was carrying wine, but that when the truth came out, it was acknowledged that, actually, he was only **taking the piss**. And so a phrase grew, though to date we don't have much more than Hart-Davis's word to go on, not that there's anything wrong with that.

Round robin

'This has been a difficult year for us, what with Abigail not quite managing to get an A* in her maths GCSE and our beloved Mr Fluffy finally departing for the great hamster wheel in the sky. On a happier note, however, we had a lovely family holiday in August, returning once again to Fuengirola. Our fifth visit in seven years:

some of the locals are even getting to recognize us!' These days,
the **round robin** is a pretty derided form of communication,
consisting of information about which we care little, emanating
from people whom we hardly see. Email has contributed greatly
to the alarming proliferation of the medium. The result is that,
more than ever, being on the receiving end of a round robin is
tantamount to accepting that your friends would rather tell you
what they've been up to than see you.

The round robin, though, was not always the confirmation of
this social relegation. In fact, at the start of its life, in jarring
contrast to the apparent merriness of that shared initial R, putting
your name to a round robin could be a way of avoiding the lash
of the cat-o'-nine-tails on a ship. Here is a definition from the
Weekly Journal, January 1730:'A Round Robin is a Name given by

Seamen, to an Instrument on which they sign their Names round a Circle, to prevent the Ring-leader being discover'd by it, if found'. So it was meant to conceal the identity not of the signatory, but of the *first* signatory, who must be the force behind the petition.

Why **robin**? Perhaps because it's a corruption of the French *ruban*, meaning 'ribbon', since the letter goes round in a circle like a ribbon. But why should the names be laid out in this way? A year after the explanation given above the *Gentlemen's Magazine* yielded a further clue: the names go in a circle when the crew mutiny. Little wonder that no single individual was ready to put his hand up first. Was someone called Robin one of the first signatories of that letter of protest? We don't know. It would be nice to think that there was such a person on board. Could this Robin have been a trifle podgy around the waist, hence the play on round Robin? That would fit even better, but until a miraculous discovery puts it beyond doubt, we can only speculate.

The writer Samuel Taylor Coleridge (1772–1834) used the phrase as a metaphor in 1816, referring to 'a round robin of mere lies', but it wasn't until the end of that century that the next evolution in the phrase's meaning took place when the sport of tennis conducted its own mini-mutiny. It arose in the United States, where the *Official Lawn Tennis Bulletin* reported in January 1895 that 'The so-called **round-robin tournament**, where each man plays every other, furnishes the best possible test of tennis skill'. Here it was being taken well beyond its 1731 definition of men 'signing their names in an orbicular manner'.

The sporting round robin exploded the term to the point where – though we don't know exactly when – today's round robin is defined not by the number of people sending the message, but by the number of people receiving it. Who first wrote this meaning in print is still far from clear, but sporting tournaments – tennis, for example – have recently attempted to revive that original round robin method of play in which every player plays everyone else at least once. The formula for calculating the number of possible results for such a competition can be presented as $s(n)\in\emptyset(4^n n - \frac{1}{2})$, where, if your maths is up to it, n is the number of competitors, s is the number of wins scored by a competitor and $\emptyset$ (theta) signifies an asymptotically tight bound. And if that last mathematical expression is giving you a headache, you're not alone because it frightens us too. Those in need of a simpler explanation should think of the s as Maria Sharapova, n as the grunting noise she makes when hitting the ball, the € symbol as the amount in euros that the spectators paid for their seats, and the $\emptyset$ sign as representing the number of times they'd like to throttle her. Word has it that traditionally organized round robin tennis tournaments are haemorrhaging audiences, but the evidence for that is still anecdotal.

Finally, the delightful and vastly entertaining but not always absolutely reliable urbandictionary.com offers a few extra meanings for 'round robin', from 'double penetration of the vagina and anus' to 'a sexual act which entails a person becoming dizzy (by any means) and then defecating on their partner's body'. Whatever happened to curling up in front of the telly with a pizza and a bottle of wine?

Chapter Four

Man's best friend

Dog Hound To dog Dogged Doggerel Sleep
gs Going to the dogs Dog eat dog Dog's d
haggy dog story Doggy style Shaggy dog s
g's b nd T
gea Doggerel Sleeping dogs Going to the
Dog eat dog Dog' dinner Shaggy dog sto
Doggy style D gy business D
gerel Sleeping dogs Going to the dogs Dog
ggy style Dog's bollocks Doggy business Do
Hound To dog Dogged Doggerel Sleeping a

The word **dog** has made quite a bed for itself in the English language. Altogether the entry for the noun 'dog' takes up a monster 11,000-odd words in the *OED*, running to twenty-two pages. **Hound**, on the other hand, has a mere 1700 words spread across four pages, yet if English behaved anything like most of its linguistic cousins in northern Europe, we would be talking about hounds, not dogs. Quite why remains a mystery, though it's one of the subjects we'll discuss, without, we hope, making too much of a **dog's dinner** of it. And if we can't solve it, we'll just put it aside and say we're **going to see a man about a dog**.

Once you start looking for them, you notice that doggy phrases are strewn all over the English language. That must be one of the positive side effects of being **man's best friend**.

'Man's best friend's best man.'

We have imputed many of our moods and actions to dogs so that we can see them better in a dog's skin. **Every dog has its day**, of course, and almost every doggy phrase gets a walk in this category, though we couldn't possibly attend to them all because it would by then be **raining cats and dogs** with doggy expressions.

The English national animal, for good or bad, is a British bulldog. This fierce creature was originally used for baiting bulls. Nowadays, the bulldog might have to be restrained on a lead, as its sometimes aggressive behaviour can illustrate the less likeable aspects of the British **bulldog spirit**, but – **good dog** or **bad dog** – it only serves to emphasize that dogs are essential to how the British see the world. Some have even slipped off the lead and gone out on their own. If you describe someone as a dog, it's plainly not a compliment, no matter how well disposed you feel towards dogs. And when the word **dog-house** comes to mind, you probably think 'someone's in trouble' more than 'a kennel in which a dog sleeps'.

We have, of course, worked hard – **like a dog**, in fact – to get this selection of words into tip-top shape. We hope there's more than a **dog's chance** that you'll finish this chapter. In fact, we're confident that you'll find it all absolutely **top dog**, or even **the dog's bollocks**.

Dog

When is a **dog** a dog? Or, to put it another way, why is a dog not a **hound**? The first, perhaps the greatest, mystery about the word 'dog' is how it came to represent man's best friend in the first place, because in other European countries dog isn't man's best friend: hound is. So what does a dog have that a hound doesn't? European languages have that word, but not in our sense. Danes have *dogge*, the Swedes have *dogg*, Italians have *dogo*, but these all mean a type of dog, not just dog in itself. 'Dog' seems to have gone walkies in continental Europe, starting with the Netherlands in the late sixteenth century, but it always had a label around its neck, such as '*een dogghe … canis anglicus* [English dog]'. It wasn't just the Dutch. The Germans referred to an '*englische Dock*' in the sixteenth to seventeenth centuries, while the French talked of '*le généreux dogue anglais*'. The dog these titles all referred to was – and is – a specific type of dog: the mastiff. Was 'dog', linguistically at least, the runt of the litter?

It didn't used to be that way. The Old English word for a dog was *docga*, which sounds fairly close to today's word. The roots of this word are hard to trace. We know they're somewhere, but we just can't find them: it's like a bone that we buried and now we can't remember where. In Britain the word *docga* replaced the term *hund*, which remained common across the rest of northern Europe. The *OED* says that 'dog' used to be 'the name of a powerful breed or race of dogs'. Was this dog a bit of a pit-bull terrier, scaring off the hound? We don't know, but we could speculate on the brutish dog word snapping at the heels of the more playful hound until it turned into a **dog-fight**, and dog won.

'Hound' has always been a better European than 'dog'. You will find it or its puppies in old German, Swedish and Danish, even Greek and Lithuanian. In fact, if you go as far back as Sanskrit you'll find the word *çwan*, and if you're an etymologist, you can easily persuade yourself that the two are more or less directly related. The *OED* has tracked 'dog' closely and discovered that its pedigree is extensive: there's almost no field of human activity that dogs haven't poked their noses into.

The *OED* defines 'dog' as 'a quadruped of the genus *Canis*'. A hound, on the other hand, is defined as 'a dog, generally'. In other words, 'dog' is such boiled-down English that you can use it to define 'hound'. As words go, 'dog' really is man's best friend, and pretty much has been since its first written citation in the year 1050. The word has a familiarity to it: if one of our pre-Norman forebears returned to chat to us, amid the embarrassed silence as we thumbed through the dictionary to try to reduce the linguistic gap, 'dog' would be a welcome refuge. On one level, it means exactly the same now as it did then: it does, you could say, exactly what it says on the label.

'Dog' is ur-English – pretty much as old as you get. 'Hound' takes a bit more explaining. The very first reference to 'dog' is by the Spanish-born poet Aurelius Prudentius Clemens, or just Prudentius for short. Sections of his work (in Latin) appeared 600 years after his death, around 1050. We don't know if Prudentius was a dog-lover, but the Latin word *canum* (meaning 'of the dogs') is translated as *docgena*.

'A gentyll hounde … hath lesse fleshe than a dogge and shorter heere and more thynne,' wrote John of Trevisa in 1398 in an early attempt to differentiate between the two, as if they were different species. There was also the word **cur**, first seen around 1225, but that too is defined in the *OED* as 'a dog' – and is always meant in a 'depreciative or contemptuous' sense, despite a 1530 definition of 'dogge' as 'a mischievous curre'. Evidently not a dog-lover, that man.

The same John of Trevisa (?1340–1402) obviously thought of dogs as hunting animals – 'Brockes [badgers] … [have] ben huntyd and chassyd wyth hunters dogges' – and there was obviously plenty of evidence from around the country that badgers were indeed being hunted and chased with hunters' dogs. But it was William Shakespeare who upped the metaphorical ante to include the phrase the **dogs of war** in his play *Julius Caesar* from 1601.

'Dog' has been used as a term of insult ('Dogge, ther thou ly!' – Dog, there you lie) since around 1325. But the use of 'dog' to suggest something mediocre or bad can be dated to 1936, when a song described as a dog meant something 'that's kicked around'. It hasn't always been kicks and insults, though. 'Dog' has also been used as a term of affection, as in a letter from Queen Anne to Lord Buckingham: 'My kind Dog…'

Hound

If you go back far enough in Greek and Latin, the words for 'dog' – Greek *kuon* and Latin *canis* – can be seen edging towards each other to the point where they are virtually sniffing each other's bottoms. The word **hound** comes from quite different etymological roots, and in English usage refers specifically to a hunting dog. (Doesn't **riding to hounds** suggest something much more vigorous than 'riding alongside a dog'?) Thus we have fox*hounds* but sheep*dogs*. In German the sheepdog breed is known as Schäferhund, but other dogs used for herding sheep are called Hirtenhund. Both terms use the word *hund*, and for a while so did English, but this eventually stopped and 'dog' took over as the main word.

So closely is the fate of the words 'hound' and 'hunt' intertwined that you could be forgiven for thinking they share a common linguistic ancestor. This is not the case: the very, very Old English verb *huntian* comes from *hentan*, meaning 'to seize'. Hound's etymological roots are equally ancient, though: Old English and Old Saxon both have *hund*, and, since we're in the area, let's greet Old Norwegian (*hundr*) and Gothic (*hunds*).

A later hound that pretty well encapsulated the creature's fearsome qualities was *The Hound of the Baskervilles*, Sir Arthur

Conan Doyle's (still scary) Sherlock Holmes novel, originally published in monthly parts in *The Strand* magazine from August 1901 to April 1902. The fact is, however, that 'hound' has been pretty much replaced by 'dog', and is now restricted mainly to archaic or poetic or high literary forms. The 'Baskerville Dog', for example, would not sound nearly as impressive.

Nonetheless, 'hound' crops up in some unlikely places. **Houndsditch**, for example, is the name of a street in the City of London. The original ditch was built by the Romans as a defensive trough, and then again by the Danes. The name Houndsditch first appears in the thirteenth century, and alludes to the waste that was dumped in it: dung, household rubbish, old clothes, and a huge, huge number of dead dogs.

To dog

'Dog' really is the most obliging of words – always ready to go for a run. And it's territorial too: it likes to mark its page in the dictionary, and does it in a variety of ways. We have barely sniffed the dog's bottom, but it's time to sink our teeth in a bit deeper.

To dog someone, says the *OED*, means 'to follow like a dog; to follow pertinaciously or closely; to pursue, track (a person, his footsteps, etc.), *especially* with hostile intent'. The first recorded use is from a book called *Vulgaria* (1519) by William Horman (*c.* 1458–1535), an Oxford scholar who went on to become headmaster of both Winchester and Eton, two of the topmost jobs in education at the time. The book consisted of handy Latin phrases or aphorisms, such as *a tergo instabat*, which he trans-lates as 'our ennemyes **dogged** us at the backe'. **Dogging** was not always by people set on physical assault. A character in *The Plain-Dealer* (1676), the last play to be written by William Wycherley (1641–1715), complains that 'The Bayliffs dog'd us hither to the very door'.

Dr Johnson was perhaps the first to lament being pursued by the paparazzi of his day, in a 1750 edition of *The Rambler* magazine: 'Eleven painters are now dogging me, for they know that he who can get my face first will make his fortune'. Over a hundred years later, in 1872, William Dixon (1821–79) wrote a study of the life of William Penn in which he noted that 'Spies and informers dogged his footsteps'.

Dogged

How was the dog viewed by our ancestors? With extreme scepticism, it seems. To have **a dogged harte** in 1540 meant 'to rejoyce in another mans mysfortune' according to the humanist and diplomat Sir Richard Morison (c.1510–56). It didn't end there. 'Ill-tempered, surly, sullen, morose' is how the *OED* summarizes a rash of bad press for dogs from 1400 to 1852. **Dogged** also shares a sense with the adjective 'crabbed', which dates from the same period and has meant disagreeable, perverse, churlish, irritable and so on. The designation arose in German too, according to the brothers Grimm (great etymologists, as well as compilers of folk tales), apparently 'because these animals are malicious and do not easily let go what they have seized'.

'Crabbed' or 'crabby' are still very far from being compliments, but 'dogged' has turned a corner and now has a much more positive sense. That doggy tenacity is what eventually swung it for the canines, and this rise in the fortunes of 'dogged' must have coincided with an improvement in relations between man and dog. It starts with Dr Johnson commending one of the Dukes of Devonshire for 'a dogged veracity' in 1779, takes a slight dip in 1818 thanks to Sir Walter Scott, in his adventure tale *Rob Roy*, describing 'an air of stupid impenetrability, which might arise either from conscious innocence or from dogged resolution', and then slowly claws its way, paw by paw, to near-respectability thanks to positive dog talk in books such as Charles Kingsley's *Water Babies* (1863): 'He was such a little dogged, hard, gnarly, foursquare brick of an English boy'.

To be dogged is to be persistent, tenacious and to some extent just as cussed and perverse as in the bad old days, but it's won a new respectability through all that hard work. In some hands it even became a national trait. Hilaire Belloc (1870–1953), the writer of cautionary verses, wrote in 1902 of a time when British people started to romanticize Britain's '**dogged determination**, bull-dog pluck, the stubborn spirit of the island race, and so forth'. The phrase 'dogged determination' has become a bit of a cliché. In fact, so closely associated are the two words that using them together is regarded almost as a tautology.

When **doggedness** was less admired, that churlishness also prompted a phrase that recalls one of Aesop's fables. This was the one about the dog who went to sleep in a manger, surrounded by hay. When he was awoken by some of the other animals on the farm, he was so crotchety that he prevented the ox and the horse from coming anywhere near the hay to eat it. The ox was heard to mutter, 'People often begrudge others what they cannot enjoy themselves,' and that was the beginning of the expression **dog in the manger**. The fable was first cited in English in a work by the physician William Bullein called *A Dialogue against the fever pestilence* (1564), where he wrote: 'Like unto cruell Dogges lyng in a Manger, neither eating the Haye themselves nor sufferyng the Horse to feed thereof hymself.'

Doggerel

Dogs are many things to many people, but they are not poets, nor should they claim to be. **Doggerel** is a description applied to 'comic verse, usually irregular in measure' (*Collins*). 'Worthless verses' adds *Chambers*. Pretty compelling evidence, it seems, and once again, who's at the centre of it all? The dog.

The word 'dog' has long been used in a contemptuous sense in certain contexts. We have had **dog-rimes** (it's not a compliment) by the writer and translator John Florio in 1611. And in the nineteenth century many writers were very rude about people writing in **dog-Latin** or **dog-Greek**, which was a sort of public school shorthand for 'not very good'.

In a slightly more elegant way, Geoffrey Chaucer (*c.* 1343– 1400) mocked **rym doggerel** in 1386, and George Puttenham

(?1529–91), the reputed author of *The Arte of English Poesie,* and a man, therefore, who could be said to know a thing or two about verse, scoffed that 'A rymer that will be tyed to no rules at all … such maner of Poesie is called in our vulgar, ryme dogrell'. The main criticism of such verses, from early times to the nineteenth century, was that their rhythm was irregular; the carping about their contents came later.

John Taylor (?1578–1653), who came from a humble background to achieve a reputation as 'the water-poet' of London's waterways, may have been as honest as his own verses deserved when he wrote: 'In doggrell Rimes my Lines are writ/As for a Dogge I thought it fit'. All sorts of unflattering descriptions attached themselves to doggerel in later years, from 'bastard' (sixteenth century) to 'bad or trivial' (seventeenth century). The *OED* isn't sure exactly why doggerel comes from dog, but the nineteenth definition of the word 'dog' is 'bad, spurious, bastard, mongrel'. This is the sense that lies behind doggerel, whose mongrel status is underlined by the fact that it can also be spelt 'dogerel, doggerell, doggrell, dogrell, doggril and dogrel'.

This contemptuous sense of dog has, sadly, dogged dog's reputation for years. Somehow the associations with dog are mostly either comical or pathetic. The discarded tip of a spent cigarette, filtered or not, which you'd have to be pretty desperate to try to relight, has been called a **dog-end** since 1935, when Hippo Neville immortalized it in his book *Sneak Thief on the Road*: '"Dog-ends," said Yank. "Dust, funny mixings, ten a pennies, cigarette ends out of the gutter."'

If you don't take proper care of this book, and don't mind it falling into some pretty dodgy company (see Chapter 5), it will end up with crumpled corners, and thus will merit the description **dog-eared**. This rather poetic phrase was first used by

William Cowper (1731–1800) in a volume of verses produced in 1784. The reference runs as follows: 'Let reverend churls his ignorance rebuke,/Who starve upon a dog's-ear'd Pentateuch'. **To dog-ear** a book was originally regarded as an act of conscious vandalism, a grave offence first described in around 1659 by the Hon. Mrs Sarah Osborn: 'To ruffle, dogs-ear, and contaminate by base Language and spurious censures the choicest leaves of a book'. The shameful practice of **dog-earing**, i.e. making an impromptu bookmark by folding down the corner of a page, persists to the present day.

Sleeping dogs

Why are we told to **let sleeping dogs lie**? The phrase is the inverse of the phrase **to wake a sleeping dog**, written first in 1562 in a book of proverbs and epigrams by John Heywood (?1497–?1580): 'It is ill wakyng of a sleapyng dogge'. The *OED* defines that rather laboriously as 'some person or influence which is for the present quiet, but if aroused will create disturbance'. However proverbial that first entry was, it came into sharper, more practical application in 1607 in a statement of Edward Topsell (*c.*1572–1625), who can lay some claim to having been the David Attenborough of his day. His love of animals featured in several volumes, including *The History of Four-footed Beasts* (1607).

Topsell also wrote *The History of Serpents* (1608), which, by pure coincidence, included the line, 'It is good therefore if you have a Wife, that is … unquiet and contentious, to let her alone, not to wake an angry Dog'. As the phrase moved into the nineteenth century, it was suffused with the deeply dignified joking of the era, as seen in *Frederick the Great* (1864), the last major work by Thomas Carlyle (1795-1881). This includes the remark, 'Friedrich is not the man to awaken Parliamentary **sleeping-dogs**'. Sleeping dogs were, by now, irreversibly metaphorical.

Going to the dogs

There is, perhaps inevitably, a UK blog called **Going to the Dogs**, in which the author gives the government a good roasting every few days. The phrase 'going to the dogs' can mean to wend one's way to a greyhound race meeting, of course, but the proverbial use of 'to the dogs' means 'to destruction or ruin' as in **to go, send or throw to the dogs**.

The phrase is first noted in one of the great early works of British pedantry, the Latin–English *Thesaurus* of Thomas Cooper (*c.*1517-94). This majestic book, an early draft of which was accidentally thrown in the fire by Mrs Cooper and then pains-takingly rewritten, includes the entry: '*Addicere aliquem canibus*, to bequeath hym to dogs'. The idea of someone or something being thrown to dogs was equivalent to tossing a piece of meat at them: the person or thing was as expendable. Shakespeare made use of this in *As You Like It* (1600), in an ill-tempered exchange between Celia and her cousin Rosalind. Celia asks, 'Why Cosen, why Rosalind: Cupid have mercie, Not a word?' Rosalind replies, 'Not one to throw at a dog.' Celia comes back with, 'No, thy words are too precious to be cast away upon curs.' But this testy use of throwing something to the dogs has influenced all similar expressions since.

The first use of the phrase **gone to the dogs** came in a sermon given in 1619 by Robert Harris (1580-1658), when he preached upon the causes and dangers of drunkenness: 'One is coloured, another is foxt [drunk], a third is gone to the dogs'.

The American writer Washington Irving (1783–1859) gave the phrase a further literary twist when, in his book *A History of New-York from the Beginning of the World to the End of the Dutch Dynasty* (1809), he described the behaviour of Peter Stuyvesant, the founder of New York. Angered by the Yankees' constant sniping 'his wrath was terrible. He … threw diplomacy to the dogs … giving them their choice of sincere and honest peace, or open and iron war.' Irving, the Bill Bryson of his day, was feeling so playful with this book that he wrote the work under the pen-name Diedrich Knickerbocker, from which all subsequent knickerbockers derive. From Cooper's hands to Irving's, the phrase has evolved from meaning 'to actively consign something to ruin or destruction' to a more internal, systemic form of decay.

Dog eat dog

It may have been a dog's dinner of a meal, but everyone knows it's a jungle out there, and no creature knows that better than a dog. Really? Well, that seems to be the general view, as the poet Charles Gray put it in a letter in 1858: 'I cannot promise any special instruction, and shall take no fee. "**Dog does not eat dog**" is the saying, you know.'

Gray was paraphrasing Marcus Terentius Varro (116–27 BC), who was considered by some contemporaries to have been the greatest Roman scholar of them all. Certainly he was a tireless collector of proverbs, and something of a whiz as a bee-keeper too. One of the most famous sayings he collected was Canis caninam non est (**A dog does not eat a dog's flesh**). Brewer's Dictionary of Phrase and Fable (1923) lists '**Dog don't eat dog**' and compares it to 'There's honour among thieves'.

This is, of course, undoubtedly true. Cannibalism is unknown among dogs, and yet the phrase **dog eat dog** has arisen, maybe to emphasize just how mad and bad a world it really is, and the sorts of pressure it puts people under to behave in an uncharacteristic way. Our first sniff of it comes from *The Milk and Honey Route; A Handbook for Hobos* by Dean Stiff (real name Nels Anderson) published in 1931: 'He knows and lives the justice of the jungle as well as he knows and lives the dog-eat-dog code of the main stem.' Evidently, this is one hobo who knows his Varro. The phrase was certainly on the streets by then.

The phrase has also been used ironically, first in the novel *Taxi!* (1963) by Maurice Levinson: 'No woman can call herself weak if she is prepared to throw herself pell-mell into the "dog-eat-dog" kind of driving that goes on in the West End'.

CHOMP
CHOMP

Dog's dinner

In 1934, or perhaps we should say between then and 1954, if you wanted to give someone a mild or slightly backhanded compliment about their appearance, you would probably have said, 'You look like the **dog's dinner**'. The phrase is first cited in C.L. Anthony's play *Touch Wood*, first performed in 1934: 'Why have you got those roses in your hair? You look like the dog's dinner.' This was praise to a woman, as was a sentence from a 1945 edition of Penguin New Writing: 'A dizzy blonde all dressed up like a dog's dinner'. But the tough-guy novelist J.S. Curtis applied it to an overdressed man in his 1936 work *The Gilt Kid*: 'The geezer … was dolled up like a dog's dinner with a white tie and all.'

This usage continued until 1954. What happened then is a slight mystery, but for some reason this use of 'dog's dinner' was sent to the dog-house until it emerged in a different form seventeen years later, by when it had been flipped on its head. Perhaps this lukewarm praise had reached a sort of dead end: maybe we decided to get real. At any rate, when a character in John Wainwright's *The Last Buccaneer* (1971) refers to the north of England as 'a dog's dinner of hovels, dives and drinking dens' there is no longer any ambiguity about whether the phrase is complimentary or not.

In fact there are parallels with another phrase, less used now, but popular in its day. Partridge, in his *Dictionary of Slang*, dates **dog's breakfast** from 1937 and defines it as 'a mess'. The first mainstream quotation is from *The Times* in 1959: 'He can't make head or tail of it … It's a complete dog's breakfast.' As construed then, it's not aimed at a person, but an idea. Or here again from *The Times* in 1963, notably only eighteen years after the cessation of Allied operations in Europe: 'The warders … are very angry and have rejected the latest War Office offer as totally unacceptable. They feel the offer is a bit of a dog's breakfast.'

It may have been the popularity of 'dog's breakfast' that caused 'dog's dinner' to be rehoused under the general heading 'total mess'. Was it accidental, or was dog's dinner mark one originally confined to novels, while dog's dinner mark two was the preferred terminology of newspapers? We're still chewing that one over.

Shaggy dog story

David Low, in the *New York Times Magazine* in 1940, wrote an essay on 'The logical lunacy of "Shaggy Dog"', which may be our first printed reference to that term. The *Penguin Dictionary of Literary Terms* defines it thus: 'An improbable kind of yarn, often long and spun out, which, as a rule, does *not* have a witty or surprise ending; but comes, rather, to a deflating and quasi-humorous conclusion'. Exactly. It's the sense of inevitable disappointment that one finds so dispiriting about **shaggy dog stories**: it's hard not to walk away from them feeling that your time has been wasted and that you would really quite like those five minutes of your life back again. And yet you curse yourself because you couldn't guess where that stupid and, only in retrospect, predictable twist could have come from.

Doggy style

What springs to mind when you see the words **doggy** (or **doggie**) **style**? There is of course the style of swimming (better known as **doggy paddle**) in which the body remains more or less vertical in the water and is propelled forward by paddling with the hands and feet. But there is another sense of 'doggy style' that demands attention.

The *OED*'s only recognition of the phrase is a quotation from 1981 by the late, great rock journalist Lester Bangs, quoted in *Psychotic Reactions*: 'They did it **doggie-style** and rocked so mighty they damn near broke the bedposts', which gives you a fair idea of the intensity of the manoeuvre involved, but not of the nuts and bolts of the technique. However, if you have ever observed two dogs copulating, you will be aware that doggy style is a classic rear-entry position. To put it a little more bluntly, it's a style of sexual intercourse in which the man crouches behind his chosen partner and effects an entrance therefrom. 'Doggy' underlines the difference between this and the face-to-face, human-to-human 'missionary position'. Doggy style is animalistic:

'Just try it for a change – you might like it!'

the adjective **doggish**, now obsolete, meant 'brutish, bestial, sensual' in 1594. No wonder that the phrase **coming from behind** has such a high snigger factor.

The almost acceptable face of 'doggy style' is the rapper Snoop Doggy Dogg (real name, or the closest we'll get to a real name, Calvin Cordozar Broadus Jr), whose first solo album was entitled *Doggystyle*. In *The Kama Sutra* 'doggy style' is upgraded to the position known as 'the congress of the cow', which is high praise indeed, given the esteem in which cows are held in the Hindu religion. The doggy-style position is not designed for chatting. In fact, the person in front, woman or man, can't even get a good view of their partner without craning their neck, though having a face-to-face chat may not be uppermost in one's mind at the time.

Dog's bollocks

In a society built on aspirations to tabloid excellence, the **dog's bollocks** really is the last word in praise. The generally held view is that it was given to the world by *Viz* magazine in 1989. A strapline on the front cover claimed it was the dog's bollocks, i.e. the best of issues. *Viz* may not have coined the expression, but it has always been such a skilled adapter of whatever was out there on the street – or the pavement – that it's no wonder it picked this one up.

Other theories abound. The eminently respectable Eric Partridge, in his *Dictionary of Slang* has a plethora of expressions to do with dogs, including **dog's ballocks** – note the 'a' rather than 'o' – which is defined as 'the typographical colon-dash' (:-). Partridge also notes the term **dog's prick** for that favourite of women's magazines, the exclamation mark (!).

'Dog's bollocks' outshines, out-booms and generally outsmarts the more sedate **cat's whiskers** or **bee's knees** (both 1923) or **cat's pyjamas** (1925) by a country mile. The *OED* defines 'dog's bollocks' as 'the very best, the acme of excellence', but doesn't venture into the matter of how this came to be, though it's hard not to agree with the assessment of a contributor to urban-dictionary.com that 'It refers to the fact that a dog can lick his own balls, which seems to be an ideal situation for any single dog'.

There is a crucial difference between 'the dog's bollocks' and just 'bollocks' or 'ballocks' – first cited in 'For God's sake, don't talk ballocks, Johnson', from *Mister Johnson* (1939) by Joyce Cary. **Bollocks** were first spotted in 1744, being a playful variation of the older – by about 750 years – **ballocks**, which also meant testicles. It's amazing what a vowel change can achieve. Bollocks still haven't been around for as long as ballocks, but bollocks are everywhere today, while the humble ballocks has retired to lick its wounds.

'Bollocks' is a word you can almost say in front of very small children without feeling that you have **dropped a bollock** (first used in 1970 by Peter Laurie in his book *Scotland Yard: A Personal Inquiry*), or **getting a bollocking** (first seen in literature in the 1950 novel *To the Victors the Spoils* by Colin MacInnes). 'Bollocks' basically means 'rubbish' or 'pants' (see page 55), but **the bollocks** is a term of high praise – and it's a confusion that films such as *The 51st State* (2001) have capitalized on.

So from 'the bollocks' (meaning 'very good') to 'the dog's bollocks' (meaning 'very good to the power of ten'). That juxta-position of 'bollocks' with the doggy element is a sublime com-bination. Maybe we like it because dogs are so marvellously unabashed about the amount of time they're prepared to devote – in public – to trying to swallow their own genitalia, an activity that most men would – perhaps literally, perhaps not – give their right arm for.

The only other part of its body that a dog takes as much interest in – and this goes for bitches too – is the tail. No wonder, then, that the postwar twentieth century also gave us the phrase **like a dog with two tails** to express utter joy, the theory being that, given how much dogs enjoy chasing their tails, one-tailed happiness is great, but only half as good as twin-tailed ecstasy.

Doggy business

Dogs are marvellously versatile. Take a phrase such as **dog knot**: in engineering terms, 'dog knot' refers to a section of rod or pipe that enlarges so that it doesn't come out of the hole in which it's inserted. However, the term also applies in doggy love to what is known as 'the inflation of the *carpus cavernosum* of a dog's penis during intercourse'. The truth of this entry is not super-reliable, and some older or less patient readers should fast-forward to the next section, but the source for this definition (the extra-ordinary urbandictionary.com) is worth pursuing since its list of words is, frankly, the dog's bollocks, besides speaking with illiterate, zit-faced articulacy about our continuing love affair with dogs.

As most of urbandictionary.com's contributors seem to be college kids, and American college kids at that, most entries are self-defining, and some, frankly, are a little juvenile. The great majority bring us back time and time again to sex. **To dog nose**, for example, means that 'a male urinates and then wipes his wet cold penis on his partner'. Have you ever tried **dog tubbing**? It means 'attempting to insert one's testicles into a female's ass during sex. So named because it is as difficult to keep the nuts in the butt as it is to keep an unwilling dog in a bath tub.' Doesn't it make you nostalgic for those college days?

Some entries tell us about the beguiling and inviting – is that sarcastic enough? – state of youth culture, as in the apparently inoffensive **dog people**, which actually means 'lads that do piss themselves at parties like raves and punk festivals that do go on all night'. Others betoken a swipe at relations with authority, such as the mysterious **dog roza**, defined as 'a police officer in charge of a police dog'. Others are radiantly inventive. **Dog perch**, for example, is another term for 'beer belly', and an English one at that to judge from the example: 'Have you seen the size of that bloke's dog perch?'

But urbandictionary.com isn't obsessed only with sex, oh no. The other thing for which dogs are famous is excretion, and this subject receives copious attention too. For example, **dog poo sandwich** means 'something that is absolutely rubbish'. Loving (if that's the right word) attention is paid to various types of dog poo: **dog oogie** is defined as 'bright reddy brown dog turds with an orange/yellow center, similar to an onion bahjee', while **dog leg** is – I should have guessed – 'a large turd that sticks up out of the water'. **Dog skidder**, anyone? 'The quarter size … smeared poop dot left by a dog wiping its ass on your carpet.' Verily, all human life, and doggy faeces, is there.

And there are, of course, so many more demure doggy expressions, from **doggone it** and **dogsbody** to **lying doggo** and **hair of the dog**. But for now we must toss this particular bone aside and go chase some other rabbits. Well, actually, there is one other doggy word that we touch upon later. That's the reasonably recent sexual proclivity known as **dogging** (see page 201). Look at if you must, but don't blame us if you're shocked. And don't, for Dog's sake, say we didn't warn you.

Chapter Five

Dodgy dealings

*T*here is a lot to be said for reading the 2007 edition of *Archbold: Criminal Pleading, Evidence and Practice* if you need a law book. But *Balderdash & Piffle* is no law book, so we're not going to be dealing with the language of formal criminality. The police, the courts, the whole 'Do you find this person guilty or not guilty?' experience relies on a language all its own. We prefer to inveigle ourselves in among the slightly uneasy-looking types hanging around the back of the court, who might be popping out every now and then to squawk on their mobiles, or to light up a Lambert & Butler. These people have their own sub-language, a vocabulary in which crime is condoned more than condemned. It is a colourfully amoral world of slang and phrase-making, the kind of thing you find in the pub, in the press or in the police notebook – but rarely in the court record.

The devil, as we are constantly told, has all the best tunes. The forces of law and order, on the other hand, do not have all the best words. There is, as someone very clever once put it, a morality to geometry. Straight is good because it connects two points directly: a straight line has no wiggles. Euclid, the father of European geometry, defined a line as 'breadthless length', and a straight line as a line that 'lies evenly with the points on itself'. These straight lines are moral entities: they are described just as you would someone's good behaviour, or their determination to make a new start and clean up their act. There is, as a result, something effortlessly charismatic about badly behaved language. It has verbal charisma far in excess of the action – be it a street mugging or a corporate scam – and the consequences that it describes. The fact is that when you deviate from the true and rightful path, you are, literally, swerving into trouble.

To be **dodgy** or to hold dodgy goods is not a capital offence. It is, though, a deviation from the path of straightforwardness.

The language framework of right and wrong is coloured in these terms. If someone is 'straight' or 'direct', he or she is also 'good'. Divert from this and, you're in a different terrain altogether. Dodgy sits alongside **bent** (either numismatic or uniformed), **shifty**, **perverted**, **off the straight and narrow**. Dodgy words are dodgy because they are not sticking to the path of rightness: they wobble, jump and wriggle off the leash. But dodgy still has enough of a connection to the original path to be potentially a detour, not an actual abandonment of the true way. And that's why we sometimes find it endearing, not downright evil. It's bending the law, not snapping it like a twig.

So far, so dodgy. But the language of dodginess creates another set of opposites. It is unashamedly tribalist, even racist. Words and phrases that have their linguistic roots in English, such as 'jack the lad' (see page 69) have a cheerful, almost playful innocence about them – unless you come home to find them rifling through your drawers. But these words clash with the much less flattering connotations of terms related to foreigners – **Jew**, **Welsh**, **Turk**, **gyp** and **thug** – whose shiftiness almost always used to be linked to their racial background. Nowadays, anti-immigrant feeling can express itself in different ways, but there is less of a tendency for the name of a specific ethnic group to be used as a byword for dodgy behaviour.

Dodgy

The adjective **dodgy** means 'risky, difficult or dangerous' (*Collins*). If you've ever bought a **dodgy motor** or **felt a bit dodgy**, you'll know that the word also means 'shifty, iffy, a bit strange'. But the word itself has played fast and loose with dictionary compilers over the years. 'Dodgy' is not included in

Francis Grose's *Dictionary of the Vulgar Tongue*, which contains all the dodgiest lingo from 1785, but Eric Partridge defines **dodge** as 'a shrewd and artful expedient, an ingenious contrivance', and quotes some lines from Charles Dickens's *Pickwick Papers* (1837): 'It was all false, of course?' 'All, sir,' replied Mr Weller, 'reg'lar do, sir; artful dodge.' Dickens, of course, should know: he gave us Oliver Twist's friend the **Artful Dodger.**

The origins of 'dodgy' are suitably arcane. Our first sight of it is from an 1861 book by Andrew Wynter with the unlikely title of *Our Social Bees: or Pictures of Town and Country Life*. The context, curiously, is nothing to do with bees: 'Beggars divide themselves in several classes: the humorous, the poetical, the sentimental, the dodgey [sic], and the sneaking'.

The other words, such as 'humorous' and 'sentimental', are all in the mix too. A **dodgy geezer** will not kill you, but he might not hesitate for too long before separating you from the contents of your wallet if you're silly enough to leave it lying around. 'Dodgy' is a halfway house between good and evil. We tolerate, even admire, **dodginess**, finding expressions such as 'It fell off the back of a lorry' so much sweeter than 'I stole it'. It's the behaviour of a chancer, but not of a hardened felon.

'Dodgy' was in the news in a big way in 2003, when various broadcasters, including Channel 4 and the BBC, discovered that one of the documents underpinning the Blair government's justification for invading Iraq had been 'plagiarized' from an article by the scholar Ibrahim al-Marashi, written for the September 2002 issue of the *Middle East Review of International Affairs*. The discovery led to the item being labelled the **dodgy dossier**, which was as direct a rebuke as you could get. The dossier was dodgy because it had been 'ripped off' (see page 114). In fact, once the war had begun, we discovered that the dossier was just plain wrong because Iraq had no weapons of mass destruction capable of being fired at Britain, let alone WMD that would give us only forty-five minutes to prepare. 'Dodgy', it turns out, was inadequate to the task of describing the level to which we had all been duped. The dossier had, in fact, been **sexed up**.

That term was an Americanism first spotted in 1942 and it meant, fairly obviously, to put a little va-va voom into something, 'giving something a sexual flavour'. In those days it was literally sex, but in 1958 the *Observer* was reporting about 'the business of "sexing up" the titles of foreign films'.

By the way, **dossier** had a slightly dodgy past too, and very different from its ultra-professional image. The French word *dossier*, anglicized in 1880, refers to a bundle of papers bulging so much that it looks like someone's back, for which the French is *dos*. That word gives all sorts of *dos*-related words, such as the late eighteenth-century **doss** and the early nineteenth-century **doss-house**, which was where you rested your **dodgy back** if you didn't have a lot of money.

Underhand

The word **underhand** is a bit of a gent compared to the sort of company kept by other words in this section. *Chambers Dictionary* defines it as 'surreptitious', adding 'with the hand below the elbow or shoulder'. It doesn't say why, but this meaning stretches back to 1592. In terms of the geometry of honesty, if a straight line is totally upfront and pukka, 'underhand' represents a kink, a sudden dive to below the table while your eye is distracted by what's happening above. With reference to people, 'underhand' – defined simply as 'not straightforward' – has been dated to 1842. But its roots lie in a most surprising area:

archery. 'Thus the underhande [shaft] must have a small breste, to go cleane awaye oute of the bowe,' wrote Roger Ascham (?1515–68), one of Britain's finest toxophilites or archery lovers. 'To shoot underhand' was a common enough archery term, though it could also mean, as it still does, 'to keep one's hands below the body when doing a certain activity'.

But during the sixteenth century, 'underhand' went three ways: one part carried on working with the sense of 'quietly' or 'behind the scenes'; another part went 'secretive but above-board' (to borrow a seventeenth-century phrase from card play); while a third became 'shady'. We have plenty of evidence from the sixteenth century to support all three of these activities, but it seems that the covert and stealthy underhand snatched the limelight. The Tudor diplomat and scholar Sir Thomas Elyot (c.1490–1546) equated underhand with stealing in a 1538 edition of his dictionary. In truth, underhand still has that sense today.

Underhand cricket (i.e. cricket played underarm) was first noted in 1850. These days, underarm bowling is rare, but not unprecedented, and certainly not much loved. Ask any New Zealander about underarm bowling and you may have to take a few steps back because Kiwi memories are still fresh from 1 February 1981, when the Australian captain, Greg Chappell, ordered his brother, Trevor, to bowl the last ball of the match underarm. Chappell, T. bowled a daisy-cutter, right along the ground, which prevented the New Zealand batsman Brian McKechnie from clouting the six runs his side needed to tie the third of five games in the final round of the Benson & Hedges World Cup Series at Melbourne. Very underhand, and pretty dodgy too.

Swindler

The German word *schwindler* means 'giddy-minded person or cheat', especially, we are told, 'in money matters'. It stands behind the English word **swindler**, which means to cheat someone of money or in some other way defraud them. The *OED* tells us that the word arrived in England via a boat full of German-Jewish immigrants hoping to make a new life for themselves and maybe introduce some of their own words to their new homeland.

In fact, the main waves of Jewish immigration from the Continent were in the nineteenth century, but the date 'swindler' arrived is stamped at 1762, which is very early indeed. It was regarded as a **cant** word, 'cant' being a secret language spoken by a distinct group of people, whether beggars, thieves or those belonging to particular religions. (They were, if you like, outcasts, reacting to respectable society that had said to them, 'You can't come in.' Can't, cant: oh, never mind …)

In medieval England the occupations of Jews were regulated by the Crown, while Christians endured certain restrictions imposed by canon law. One pursuit open to Jews but not to Christians (at least not in public) was money-lending. Thus – in the careful wording of the *OED* – 'the name of Jew came to be associated in the popular mind with usury and any extortionate practices that might be supposed to accompany it, and gained an opprobrious sense'.

Lots of rude references to 'grasping Jews' continued for centuries. The *OED*'s most recent reference to the verb **to jew** is from *Harper's Magazine* in May 1972: 'Jew the fruitman down for his last Christmas tree'. In that same year and month the British magazine *New Society* used the verb in the same sense of beating someone down or haggling over a price: 'I got jewed down ... over the cheap offer'. Not surprisingly, you won't find the word featured so prominently these days in *Harper's*, or at all in the now defunct *New Society*. Indeed, it is mildly surprising it had a life in respectable print as late as 1972.

Phrase books from former times contain a profusion of phrases that mention Jews, evidence of the – shall we say – lively feelings generated by them. Captain Francis Grose defines **Jew** as 'an over-reaching dealer, or hard, sharp fellow; an extortioner'. His explanation is both geographically and sociologically concise: 'the brokers behind St Clement's Church in the Strand [London] were formerly called Jews by their brethren the taylors'. This wasn't a character reference, but a job description: Jews were fulfilling their historical role as useful but unloved money brokers. Grose says this was in use from around 1600.

But as the Jewish community began to find its feet, so – as with any other community finding itself among the nouveaux riches – its standards of taste became the subject of much vulgar abuse. For example, **Jew's Rolls-Royce** is quoted by Partridge (although he doesn't reveal from where) as a 1938 expression for 'a Jaguar motor-car'. Its prominent features included 'much chromium plating and all that'. We can only guess at what 'all that' refers to.

Rip-off

A **rip-off** is a swindle. It isn't a very old word, but in its first incarnation could apply to both a person – a thief, in other words – and 'a fraud, a swindle; a racket; an instance of exploitation, especially financial'. The verb **rip** has a harshness that adds a sense of outrage to 'rip-off', suggesting that our trust has been abused. Some sweet-talking son of a con-man has been up to his tricks and we're left holding ... Well, that's just the point. He's now holding what is rightfully ours.

The word 'rip-off' first came to our attention in the pages of the *Manchester Guardian Weekly* in May 1970, when an appalled drug dealer, discussing the inhabitants of the Haight Ashbury area of San Francisco, was reported as saying, 'You have burn artists [fraudulent dope peddlers], rip-offs [thieves], and snitchers [police spies]'. But only a few months later *Melody Maker*, that other upholder of left-of-centre views, defined 'rip-off' as 'capitalist exploitation'. A good deal of fudging followed. The person who was a rip-off soon came to operate both within and outside the law. At the same time, the thing that was a rip-off soon came to operate both within the corporate and non-corporate worlds.

The rip-off is fuelled by the violence of that verb 'rip', which in this sense means, and has meant ever since William Caxton printed it around 1477, 'To cut, pull, or tear (anything) away from something else in a vigorous manner'. The *OED* says that 'rip' is 'of somewhat obscure origin and history', though there doesn't seem much mystery about the Frisian verb *rippe*, meaning 'to rip or tear', or the Flemish *rippen*, meaning 'to rip or strip off roughly'.

This verb gives us the 1967 US slang usage 'to rip off', which means 'to steal or embezzle'. In 1967 a **hustler** was described as someone who not only 'burns' people for money, but also 'rips off' goods for money. A **racketeer**, in other words. This was not an impulsive act of street crime: it was planned and organized. Over the years since, it has been applied to people embezzling within an organization, such as former vice-president Spiro Agnew (1919–96), who in 1974 was accused by the Black Panther movement of 'ripping off tax money'. More recently, the verb 'to rip off' has gone from blue collar to white collar: in the 1980s–90s, if your car had been **ripped off**, it had been stolen.

In her 1981 novel *A Death in the Faculty* Alison Cross wrote that 'Soldiers are always ripping things off, from their own outfit, from the enemy, everything.'

It has been suggested anecdotally that the noun 'rip-off' has its roots in drug culture. An unscrupulous marijuana seller (as opposed to a thoroughly principled one) selling a brick or key (kilo) of some murky substance that wasn't really the drug required would cover up his unscrupulousness by placing a small amount of genuine marijuana in a corner of the packet. The unsuspecting buyer rips open the corner, finds the real stuff and thinks all is well. Little do they know that the rest of it is actually shoe polish or some other non-narcotic.

Blackmail

There is still something swashbuckling about the sound of **blackmail**. It sounds like a cross between Black Beauty and chain mail, though that noble exterior hides a sordid truth. If you had been eavesdropping on someone and had heard some item of gossip, you might be tempted to contact the people you'd overheard and advise them that unless they made it worth your while to keep silent, you might find yourself with no alternative but to forward the embarrassing information to the last person they'd wish to know it. This is a course of action that, you could argue, puts the threatener in a worse light than the threatened.

Collins Concise Dictionary defines 'blackmail' thus: 'the act of attempting to obtain money by intimidation, as by threats to disclose discreditable information'. There are other definitions to do with putting pressure on or trying to influence people, but that first one is the classic definition. It is not, however, the beginning of the story, which is buried in heather and thistles, with a paper date of 1552 and, no doubt, an oral history long preceding that. It's defined thus by the *OED*: 'A tribute formerly exacted from farmers and small owners in the border counties of England and Scotland, and along the Highland border, by free-booting chiefs, in return for protection or immunity from plunder'.

The picture we have, then, some time in the sixteenth century, is of a big man called Jock holding a club and standing opposite a smaller man, called Jack, and demanding money in return for not hitting him. It was a threat, compliance with which led to something (i.e. violence) *not* happening. Hush money, as it's now known. But as time went on and society became a little less rugged and a little more devious – less *Braveheart*, more *Smarthead* – the threat came to be exacted in a different way, with an ever longer back-story that only began to emerge three or four centuries later.

By the time it had become a popular, if unsavoury, mainstay of twentieth-century detective stories, the picture had changed. Instead of the club, Jock now held something personal to Jack. Jack had done (or become involved with) something dodgy, whether cheating at cards or on his wife, and Jock had found out – perhaps by a spot of eavesdropping. It wasn't simply 'Pay me or I'll hit you'. It was: 'If you don't want the details of this story to emerge, you'd better give me some money', or in some other way comply with my wishes.

This form of menace is, of course, morally equivocal. It cuts both ways, and neither party wins. The initially guilty person thinks, 'Oh, no! Discovered!' But his or her next reaction is to think, 'How dare that person try to extract money with threats!' Morally, it's one of the most twisted ways in which justice can be pursued.

The word **mail** is an early Scandinavian word for 'payment or tax'. To this word were attached qualifying adjectives: either black or, much later – and this time for a good purpose – white. Blackmail can also be emotional – and it can work out more expensive in the long run. And just in case you thought you'd get ahead of the game by merging 'blackmail' with 'blogging' to produce a brilliant new word, **blogmail**, you're too late: Google already has about 83,000 (and counting) instances of that neologism.

Bung

The word **bung** used to be a mid-fifteenth-century term for a stopper to a bottle or cask; a mid-sixteenth-century purse or a pickpocket; a nineteenth-century slang word for a lie, and – as most of us know it today – a twentieth-century word for a huge bribe. Football, ever a sport with its eye on a fast buck, has more or less monopolized the lucrative bung market these days. Thanks to the soft sound of 'bung' and its sonic coincidence with other words more comical than threatening, such as 'bang', it doesn't draw a great deal of popular opprobrium. Perhaps you're more likely to think of it in relation to your bath or sink getting **bunged up**, so it seems matey and convivial. As a result, most of us probably regard it as no worse than a bit of backstreet shenanigans involving a crumpled wad of £5 notes.

The 'bung' has archetypally been located, by the media, in a brown envelope, either because it is seen – mistakenly – as a fair day's tip for a hard day's work or because the shabbiness of the enterprise is so at odds with the super-sleek image that football would like to project (see also 'dodgy dossier', page 110). In reality, the sorts of sums that have been circulating among Premiership football's top brass could not be crammed inside an envelope smaller than a large suitcase.

The 'bung' nouns have a variety of origins. **Bung-hole** comes from an early Dutch word *bonghe*, meaning 'hole'. It has nothing to do with a **football bung**, even if you likened that hole to the aperture into which a dodgy agent or manager bungs (throws) a cheque. The bung may be related to the Old English (and Frisian) *pung*, meaning 'purse'.

The bribe meaning of 'bung' is marked 'criminals' slang' and 'origin unknown' by the *OED*, but we are advised to compare it with the verb **to bung**. That arose in 1825 as a slang way of saying to throw something with a little extra force. The *Daily Chronicle* from 1903 caught the sense nicely with this lively exchange: '"We are police officers. What have you in that parcel?" Stevens replied, "I don't know; I have just had it bunged on to me."'

In March 2006 Lord Stevens of Kirkwhelpington (no relation to the dodgy Stevens just mentioned), a *News of the World* columnist and former head of the Metropolitan Police, was asked by the Football Association to sort out the mess and start issuing a number of red cards. We do not know how much he was 'bunged' – completely legally, of course – for carrying out this public duty, but in December 2006, with his inquiry not yet complete, he announced the provisional results of his examinations into the transfers of 362 professional footballers. The verdict: corruption in English football was not quite as high as had been predicted, though there remained seventeen questionable deals. More of a yellow card, as it turned out.

Hoodlum

San Francisco in the nineteenth century was not the place to be at night if you were alone, unarmed and fearful. Various words were created to describe the type of tough who used to hang out on street corners, perhaps the most evocative of which was **hoodlum**. An early definition was 'a loafing youth of mischievous proclivities'. In 1871 the correspondent of the *Cincinnati Commercial* was clearly of a mind to run for his life, so eager was he 'to escape the bullying of the San Francisco "hoodlums"'.

The Oxford English Dictionary states that 'The name originated in San Francisco about 1870–72, and began to excite attention elsewhere in the US about 1877, by which time its origin was lost, and many fictitious stories, concocted to account for it, were current in the newspapers.'

So even though the word spread across the States and beyond, its origins remain a mystery. The scholar Dr John T. Krumpelmann suggested in 1935 that it was a Germanic construction, the word

'I don't suppose any of you knew that the word "hoodlum" derives from the German Haderlumpe?

Haderlumpe being German dialect for 'rags or ragman'. A similar word is *Hudellump* or *Hodalump*, meaning 'a ragamuffin or good-for-nothing'. Perhaps hoodlum was just too mean-looking for anyone to get a straight answer out of it.

The word-sleuth Charles Earle Funk quotes various, gloriously unlikely sources to suggest that 'hoodlum' arose due to a cock-up at the printing press. A journalist reporting on a fight between two gangs became jittery that the gang leader called Muldoon would discover his name and do him over, so he changed the name to Noodlum. This name was mispelt by one of the newspaper's compositors as Hoodlum. A likely story.

The hoodlums were said to have picked on San Francisco's burgeoning population of Chinese immigrants. Albert Barrère and Charles Leland, in their far more respectable *Dictionary of*

Slang, Jargon, and Cant (1889), claim that the term can be traced to *hood lahnt,* which means 'very lazy mandarin' in pidgin English.

'Hoodlum' was shortened to the simpler **hood** by 1930, though neither word is linked to the type of hood that is a shortened form of **neighbourhood**, and emerged in the USA in the late 1960s. Nor is there any connection with Britain's own-brand hoodlum, the **hoodie** (see page 39).

Hooligan

Of all the -isms that you might want to be associated with, **hooliganism** is one of the less respectable. *Chambers English Dictionary* defines **hooligan** as 'a street rough', and our first quotation comes from an 1898 edition of the (US) *Daily News*: 'It is no wonder ... that hooligan gangs are bred in these vile, miasmatic byways'. Indeed, the *OED* brings not one, but four references from that same year, testament to the frisson that this word must have induced back then. The third extract is from the *Daily Graphic*, the first US paper to introduce illustrations, and it features a stab at the group's word origins: 'Mr. White ... stated that every Saturday and Sunday night gangs like the "Hooligan gang" came to his house, broke the windows, glass, &c., and made disturbances'. The fourth extract is from the *Westminster Gazette*, and proves not only that the word had crossed the Atlantic, but also that it was reaching over to senses beyond that of street toughs: 'The Khalifa was, after all, only a sort of Soudanese Hooligan'.

Daily newspaper law reports from the summer of 1898 suggest that 'hooligan' is 'a misunderstanding or perversion' of **Hooley's gang**, but there is 'no positive confirmation of this'.

There may also have been a rowdy Irish family at large in the 1890s, who inspired a music-hall song, possibly called 'Hooley's Gang', or that the word is named after an Irish hoodlum called **Patrick Hooligan**.

In 1921 the phrase **hooligan navy** was used by Lehmann Hisey in a book with the catchy title of *Sea Grist: A Personal Narrative of Five Months in the Merchant Marine, a Rousing Sea Tale*. It contains the exchange: 'Haven't even been in the Hooligan Navy? Just land lubbers.' Various rag-tag forces have been referred to as a hooligan navy over the years. The term combines rowdiness with a sense of order.

Trouble loves a crowd, and 'hooligan' soon begat other formations. There were the verbs **to hooligan** and **to hooliganize**, which mean 'to behave like a hooligan', and adjectives such as **hooliganesque** and the frankly unfeasible **hooliganic**. 'The avalanche of brutality,' thundered the *Daily Graphic* in 1898, '… under the name of "Hooliganism" … has cast … a dire slur on the social records of South London.'

W.S. Gilbert, one half of the musical team Gilbert and Sullivan, wrote a play called *The Hooligan*, which was inspired by the execution of Dr Crippen in 1910. Based around the prison musings of a condemned man, it is considered to be one of his most interesting works.

If you decide to throw a party at which your guest list consists of hooligans, the chances are that you will be charged with hosting a **hooley**. This has been the word for a noisy party ever since 1877, which is thoroughly confusing, since the word is 'origin unknown', but gives every suggestion of having derived from the word 'hooligan', even though that wasn't noted until 1898. How maddening.

Hornswoggle

Another, even crazier American word that means to cheat, swindle or bamboozle is the early nineteenth-century **hornswoggle**. The *OED* says its origins are 'probably fanciful', and who could disagree, but at the risk of sounding fanciful, it has been suggested that its origins lie in the combination of 'horns' and 'waggle'. That's to say, it's a gesture. If you place your fingers on either side of the head, like horns, and waggle them – probably sticking your tongue out too for good measure – you are doing or giving someone the hornswoggle. This is untested by the *OED*, which is a shame.

To be frank, it isn't the sort of word that we call on much these days, even though, to this writer's eyes, it looks as gnarled and ancient as if it had first been spoken by Dr Samuel Johnson, but clearly that isn't so. Partridge dates its life cycle as 1860–1905. In fact, the *OED*'s entry, from the Virginia Literature Museum, ante-dates that by over thirty years, taking it back to 1829, with its own definition 'to embarrass irretrievably'. It didn't always mean that, though. 'One practical working theory in advertising circles is that the ad's chief function is to hornswoggle the consumer' – prescient words from the *Boston Herald* in 1904. And in an August 2005 obituary of Lord Lane, a former lord chief justice, it was said that he accused fellow judges of 'making lazy, long-winded speeches which "hornswoggled" juries and delayed trials'. It does feel like the sort of word that only a judge could get away with saying, in Britain at least.

Welshing

It wasn't only Jews who had a reputation for swindling. How exactly, for example, did the verb **to welsh** (or **welch**) fall into common parlance during the second half of the nineteenth century as another term for 'to swindle'? The trouble seems to have broken out down at the race course. A **welsher**, according to the *OED*, arose as a term to describe a racing bookie who took money from a punter for a bet and then did a runner. 'Of obscure origin' says the *OED*. Could the editorial team have felt sheepish about coming down hard on a nation that, historically, had done nothing more controversial than dig for coal and sing like angels? It is, presumably, the same sort of neighbourly chippiness in which, viewed from the comfort of England, the Scots are tight with money and the Irish a bit slow on the uptake. In 1860 Lord William Pitt Lennox wrote a book called *Fifty Years' Biographical Reminiscences*, in which he referred to 'a gang of miscreants called Welchers, who make bets with the unwary, which they never dream of paying if they lose'.

Even in the twentieth century, 'to welsh' had only a slightly less offensive meaning – to fail to keep your word. It means as much in an early citing from 1932, and as late as 1982 in an extract from *Schindler's Ark* (filmed as *Schindler's List*) by the famously irascible Australian novelist Thomas Keneally: 'Across his desk [were] crossed copies of angry SS memoranda addressed to army officials and complaining that the army was welching on its arrangement.' The *OED* has no qualifying comment that the word 'welsh' is offensive, though it clearly is.

Turk

Between the sixteenth and very late nineteenth centuries it was common to refer to a wife-beater as a **Turk**. One states this with lots of flashing warning lights as it has now been consigned to history, but one of the *OED*'s entries for the noun 'Turk', after the various political or ethnic ones, refers to citations drawn from 1536 and defines it as 'a cruel, rigorous, or tyrannical man; any one behaving as a barbarian or savage; one who treats his wife hardly'. It adds for good measure 'a bad-tempered or unmanageable man'.

Some other countries shared this mistrust of Turks, including the Persians. In some of their dictionaries the word 'Turk' is explained as 'a beautiful youth, a barbarian, a robber' – the personification, in other words, of the exotic but dangerous and untrustworthy foreigner who will charm the pants off you and then snatch your purse. In the twentieth century the phrase **Young Turks** entered the language as the name given to a group of bright young things who were trying to modernize the Turkish or Ottoman Empire, and who were of course opposed to **Old Turks**. These days, a Young Turk is someone who tries to ring the changes in a medium that is otherwise hostile to novelty, such as David Cameron trying to persuade the Tory party to be less, well, Tory.

Gyp

Having offended the Jews, the Welsh and the Turks, are we running out of people to upset? Not when we have words like **gyp** at our disposal. It means, says *Collins Concise Dictionary*, 'to swindle, cheat or defraud'. Its first proper citation was in 1899 within the rather marvellous phrase 'Gyp this boob with a deuce', quoted in Louis E. Jackson and C.R. Hellyer's *A Vocabulary of Criminal Slang, with Some Examples of Common Usages*, published in 1914. The word 'gyp' is harsh and has truly unpleasant connotations, but the word **gypsy**, from which it derives, has a rather fascinating history. It was formed through what language specialists call aphesis,[1] a process by which the first part of the word drops away. In this case, it was the 'E' of Egyptian, since when gypsies first appeared in England in the early sixteenth century, it was assumed that they were from Egypt. Other examples of aphesis include the 'e' of esquire dropping away to leave squire, acute to cute, and escape-goat to scapegoat.

In the United States the noun 'gyp' has meant 'bitch', as in young female pup, since 1878. But there are four other definitions: 'gyp' is the name for a college servant at Cambridge and Durham universities; a nineteenth-century term for 'pain', probably from the verb **to gee up**, as quoted in *Funk's Standard Dictionary* (1893): 'To give one gyp – To make one smart for anything done'; it's also US slang for a thief; and finally 'a fraudulent action; a swindle'. The last two of these are clearly insults towards gypsies.

Third degree

Any *Balderdash* wordhunters finding themselves about to be given **the third degree** would know that they were in a spot of trouble. These days we would recognize the latent threat in 'They third-degreed Jimmy Dreek good and plenty'. This comes from the 1928 novel *The Astounding Crime on Torrington Road* by William Gillette, the American actor who perfectly embodied Sherlock Homes in the 1920s. **To be third-degreed** or **to get the third degree** means being subject to an intensive examination that, sometimes with uncomfortable literalness, leaves no stone unturned.

---

1 Aphesis is formed from the Greek preposition *apo* (from) and the fiendishly irregular verb *hiemi* (I send).

'It feels more like the thirty-third degree to me!'

Most of us probably intuit that the word 'third' indicates some greater degree of intensity, possibly the highest of all. Compared to third, the second position would, we assume, involve a very serious talking-to and a modest physical threat. For first position you could probably get away with a written questionnaire, and if you didn't tick the box 'Would you like to be tortured?', you would be on your way within a matter of minutes. But there is a deeper and darker secret behind the third degree.

Third-degree burns, which are the most severe type of skin burn, have been known about since 1866. And if you go back to the phrase's origins, you find writers such as Shakespeare employing it to imply the third or final level of intensity, even of drunkenness. Step forward, if you can, Sir Toby Belch in *Twelfth Night* (1601). Olivia says of him: 'For he's in the third degree of

drinke: he's drown'd: go looke after him.' It's clear that he
shouldn't be left in charge of heavy machinery.

But then, in the eighteenth century, the phrase acquired an
additional but crucial sense. The Freemasons, then beginning to
formalize their rituals, used it to mean the highest grade in freemasonry, known as 'master-mason'. The mysteries of Freemasonry
are a closed book to outsiders, and members can be punished with
great severity for breaching its very strict guidelines of secrecy, so
we daren't go into too much detail, but suffice it to say that a friend
whose friend's father is a member told us that the third degree is
the mystical point at which an initiate can get to use the lodge car
park between 5 p.m. and 7 p.m. on a weekday. Or something.

Thug

There are two kinds of thug: the upper-case **Thug** and the lower-
case **thug**. The former is defined by *Collins* as 'a member of an
organization of robbers and assassins in India'. According to
Chambers, they also used a poison called datura, which is
extracted from the thorn-apple genus of the potato family. Thugs
were also known as *p'hansigars*, an Urdu word for members of
'a society or cult of professional robbers and murderers who
strangled their victims', from *phasi*, the Urdu for 'noose'. Pretty
much the same as a Thug, in other words: if you were being
strangled by one, you probably wouldn't be asking if they were
a Thug or a *p'hansigar*.

The activities of India's Thugs or Thuggees were first described in the writings of the French traveller and lover of all
things exotic, Jean de Thévenot (1633–67). These serial killers
(for that's what they were) are estimated to have killed anywhere
between 50,000 and 200,000 people. From 1831 the Indian

authorities began to clamp down on the Thugs, and they were eventually brought to the point of extinction.

Under its entry for Thug, the classic *Hobson-Jobson: Glossary of Colloquial Anglo-Indian Words and Phrases* (1886) defines the word thus:

> Latterly applied to a robber and assassin of a peculiar class, who sallying forth in a gang ... and in the character of wayfarers, either on business or pilgrimage, fall in with other travellers on the road, and having gained their confidence, take a favourable opportunity of strangling them by throwing their handkerchiefs round their necks, and then plundering them and burying their bodies.

And just in case you were in any doubt, the British poet and journalist Charles Mackay (1814–89) wrote the following about their burial rites in a booklet called 'Thugs, or Phansigars':

> Their next care is to dispose of the bodies. So cautious are they to prevent detection, that they usually break all the joints to hasten decomposition. They then cut open the body to prevent it swelling in the grave and causing fissures in the soil above, by which means the jackals might be attracted to the spot, and thereby lead to discovery.

In fact, the Thugs didn't slice people up merely for fun, or profit. They were motivated to do so in order to propitiate the Hindu goddess Kali, to whom all funds were, albeit indirectly, forwarded. So it was religiously inspired gangsterism on a spectacular scale.

Nice people to do business with. The *OED* notes that 'Their suppression was rigidly prosecuted from 1831, and the system is now extinct.' True, except that where once there were Thugs, now we have thugs. This latter group was noted by British journals and newspapers between 1810 and 1897; then, while all that was going on, the term became a byword for a cut-throat or ruffian. 'Glasgow Thuggery' is a headline from Thomas Carlyle's essay on Chartism.

We still use words like **thuggery** and **thuggish**, and most of us are probably only dimly aware of the very deep roots they have. The more one reads about the Thugs, the more extraordinary their story is. We should, perhaps, be grateful that our own home-grown thugs are nowhere near as dangerous as this lot, as a further quotation from Mackay demonstrates:

> Travellers who have the misfortune to lodge in the same choultry or hostelry, as the Thugs, are often murdered during the night. It is either against their creed to destroy a sleeper, or they find a difficulty in placing the noose round the neck of a person in a recumbent position. When this is the case, the slumberer is suddenly aroused by the alarm of a snake or a scorpion. He starts to his feet, and finds the fatal sash around his neck. – He never escapes.

Chapter Six

Put-downs and insults

*S*wearing, we used to be told by our mothers, betrays a
limited vocabulary. Well, bollocks to that, because the
English language is the beneficiary of a wealth of expressive
ways in which to be extremely rude about people. Like a
migrating bird spotting a lake from afar, many languages have
touched down on British shores and found the land ideal for
breeding. From this swirl of cultures, British people have found
a plethora of ways in which to use colourful language, and one
way is to insult people or put them down. What can be
confusing to learners of English, though, is the variety of
registers – i.e. the tone of voice – of the insult or put-down.
There are significant, if subtle, differences between calling
someone a **tosser** and an **arsehole**, and these differences
frequently belie their actual meanings. Some of these words
you can get away with saying to someone's face. Others are
probably better uttered once they're out of earshot.

We're going to be looking at some of our most familiar words,
along with one or two others that have dropped off the radar.
The word **insult** itself is straight out of the Latin book. *Sulto*
meant 'I jump', and *insulto* at first meant 'I leap upon'. Only later
did it acquire a more metaphorical meaning. So too in English:
the initial meaning of 'insult', dating from 1603, was physical;
the verbal assault came a few decades later.

The verb **to put down**, by contrast, is made up from two
Old English elements, but it has to be specially tuned to achieve
its aim. You can of course **put your foot down** and insist on
something, or you can **put someone's name down** for, say, a
school or military service. However, **to put someone down** is
usually a calculated snub: it amounts to 'putting someone back
in their place', perhaps because they're getting a bit uppity. It's
usually more indirect than an insult, which tends to be just a

verbal assault. Although a put-down tends to be verbal, an insult can be conveyed by gesture.

In brief, you wouldn't want to get on the wrong side of any of these words. We're going to take a look at some of the snappiest expressions in the language, and examine why the bite went out of some of the others.

Slut

Thomas Hoccleve (?1369–1426), one of the most significant English poets of his time,[1] was famous for two main reasons: for not being as good as the slightly earlier Geoffrey Chaucer, and for describing his own mental breakdown. He gains his *Balderdash* spurs, though, for penning the first evidence we have of a particularly insulting word – **slut**, which means either 'a dirty, untidy woman' (*Chambers*) or 'an immoral woman' (*Collins*). It has German origins, coming from dialect variants such as *schlutt*, *schlutte* or *schlutz*, which mean 'dirty woman'.

These days, 'slut' is a rather direct insult when used of someone, but that hasn't always been the case. The sense as used by Thomas Hoccleve in his 1402 *Letter to Cupid* – 'The foulest slutte of al a toune' – although crude, merely means someone who didn't spend too long tidying her room. Even into the late nineteenth century, the word *could* be used as a term of abuse, but not necessarily with a sexual undertone. 'Slut' also crossed over into **slattern**, in use from 1639, which was a slightly kinder way of describing a woman who kept a similarly messy room.

----
1 Hoccleve is credited with being the first man to use the word 'talent', as in 'special skill,' though few critics now think his very long poems exhibited much of it.

In Victorian English, **slut's wool** is the evocative description for the mounds of dust that pile up in a room that rarely sees the dustpan and brush.

St Cuthbert of Lindisfarne, the island off the northeast coast of England, not the 1970s' folk-rock band, used 'slut' to refer to a kitchen maid, albeit a very lowly one, around 1450: 'The quene her toke to make a slutte, And to vile services her putt.' Here 'vile' wouldn't have the same truly odious sense it has today.

How bad was it be a slut? We have one isolated reference to it from 1460 as being merely troublesome, but even by 1450 it had the pretty heavy overtones of loose morals, though – early on, at least – these were not exclusively female. Geoffrey Chaucer, Thomas Hoccleve's hero, had men in mind when – using the adjective, not the noun – he wrote, 'Why is thy lord so **sluttish**?' in the prologue to 'The Canon's Yeoman's Tale' – one of *The*

Canterbury Tales – around 1386. But the general use of 'sluttish' to refer either to men or women didn't last beyond the late seventeenth century, and the sense of slut as a sexually promiscuous woman is now hard to shift.

And yet it could be used playfully, as when Samuel Pepys confided to his diary on 21 February 1664: 'Our little girl Susan is a most admirable slut, and pleases us mightily'. Susan was the couple's baby daughter.

The first quotation from the amazing urbandictionary.com defines 'slut' as 'a woman with the morals of a man'. The second goes into more detail: 'Someone who provides a very needed service for the community and sleeps with everyone, even the guy that has no shot at getting laid and everyone knows it'.

There are, in addition, dozens of associated entries that attempt to add detail, not always that funny, but almost all written from the viewpoint of sex-obsessed American college kids. Take **slut bagel**: an unflattering description of the shape of the genitalia of a woman who has entertained a large number of male partners.

At some point in the 1990s, 'slut' was reclaimed as a purely descriptive term by those communities that practise 'consensual non-monogamy'. Indeed, members could call themselves **ethical sluts**. A book of the same name was published in 1997, but that meaning has not yet caught up with the *OED*. The word 'slut' in modern Swedish means 'ending'. Be warned.

Pillock

If it's not sex, it's parts of the body that inspire lots of our swear words. A good example is **pillock**, an old word for 'penis'. 'Pillock' dates from 1568, when it appeared in a work by the

Scottish poet Sir David Lindsay (*c*.1486–1555). There is no mistaking the point of Lindsay's rather proud comment that 'my pillok will not ly doun'. Pillock, you see, is descended from the even older **pillicock**, which had the same meaning. Nor can there be much confusion about an earlier ballad from around 1325 that states 'My **pilkoc** pisseth on my schone [shoes]'. Just a few decades later the word had become a term of endearment in certain parts of England, with John Florio defining 'pillicocke' in his *Worlde of Wordes* (1598) as 'a darling young lad, a wanton, or a minion'.

In fact, notwithstanding the fact that 'pillock' meant 'penis', in 1608 the word **pill** was a slangy way of referring to 'testicles'. The one was, after all, closely related to the two. That same year, Shakespeare in *King Lear* (III.iv.72) had Edgar, the Earl of Gloucester's son, disguised as a character called Tom O'Bedlam (see page 12) and with a licence to behave very oddly, declare that 'Pilicock sate on **pelicocks hill**'. Etymologists, and anyone else who's had a good look at the line, have suggested that 'pelicocks hill' refers to the part of a woman's body known – with all the grandeur that Latin can bring to bear – as the *mons veneris* (mount of Venus).

'Pill' itself, incidentally, is derived from the Scandinavian word *piller*, which was a common Danish surname and who, who knows, possibly the nomenclature of a man with a lot to boast about. By the eighteenth century, therefore, the word 'pillock' triply implied the male member.

By 1719, Thomas D'Urfey – well known in his day as the creator of a country song called 'The Fart' – was writing in *Wit & Mirth* that he was 'bolt upright and ready to fight, And Pillycock he lay there all night'. The superfluity of the triple masculine overtones might reasonably be read to suggest a 'Gosh, what a man you are!' kind of fellow. This definition would also, of course, imply that the word 'pillock' can never be used as an epithet for a girl or woman, but the logic of etymology has never held an English speaker back.

The mystery remains as to how the word persisted as a predominantly masculine adjective for the next 250 years, but then, fairly rapidly, took on its mildly satirical, and much more general, contemporary meaning of 'a stupid idiot'. Perhaps it's the modern decline in masculine notions of self, or, specifically, the rise of feminism during the 1960s, but, in any event, by 1967 the annals of television history reveal a character in *Till Death Us Do Part* saying: 'What are you talking about, you great hairy **pilloch**?' (with an h). Or, in another traditionally male-on-male arena, the football magazine *FourFourTwo* clamoured in 1995: 'What a bunch of pillocks!' The damage to the male ego, let alone the male member, was well and truly complete.

The appeal of 'pillock' as a swear word is that most of us have forgotten what it originally meant. When Johnny Speight revived it in *Till Death Us Do Part*, it was even funnier that the pillock in question was hairy: a clear reference to a testicle, which nobody could deny – nor could they ban it. But in the less profane era of the 1960s, a word such as pillock was a godsend to TV comedy writers, since they could scatter it around and not face censorship from the authorities. In fact, pillock, at source, was a lot ruder than many of the words that really were on the banned list.

A former Northern Ireland secretary, the much admired Mo Mowlam (1949–2005), was in the habit of calling people 'pillocks'. She would drop the term in conversation with cabinet coll-eagues, journalists and members of the public who were wearing silly costumes or who tried to josh her as she went walkabout.

But Mowlam's freedom with the term wasn't common among all her government peers: at least, not within reach of a microphone.

Tosser

Has there ever been a better time to be a **tosser**? The earliest definition the *OED* has for this word is 'One who or that which tosses', as in 'tossers of reproaches' (1612) in a work about the Greek philosopher Proclus by the classical scholar Thomas Taylor (1758–1835). Following that, a great deal more **tossing** took place, from ticket-porters being **tossers-off of beer** (1837) to an innocent American described as a hapless **tosser-up of omelets** (1846). In Scotland, of course, people must have been **tossing the caber** since well before we have written evidence for it (1862).

At one time the word was also applied to a receptacle, as seen in a cookery book called *Hand & Heart* (1884). Cooks were advised to 'Cut the other parts in small bits, put them in a small tosser with a grate of nutmeg'. And not just food. Joan Aiken, in her children's historical novel *Black Hearts in Battersea* (1965), uses it as a consciously anachronistic word for a coin, as in 'I haven't a tosser to my kick'. ('Kick' could mean a sixpence, but it seems to refer here to trousers.)

The remarkable thing is that, until about a hundred years earlier, it had all been going so well for the verb **to toss** (origin uncertain, says the *OED*, but glancingly allied to the Norwegian and Swedish dialect word *tossa*, to spread). We start with 'Howbeit the wroughte seas tossyd and rolled us ryght grevously' in 1506, and the succeeding centuries saw plenty of activity akin to flinging, pitching or throwing, but nothing more suggestive than that. You could **toss a pancake** in 1619, or, a few centuries later,

'I'm charging you with tossing off this omelette.'

toss a drink back. You could even **toss off a book** in 1845 if you were a fast reader. And that seems to be have been where temptation reared its head.

All that flinging and jerking got too much, as in this racy couplet from an erotic Victorian magazine called *The Pearl*, which dates from 1879–80: 'I don't like to see, though at me you might scoff,/ An old woman trying to toss herself off.' That seems to have been our first reference to the masturbatory **toss off**, and the sense was obviously well established by then, though perhaps not widely throughout society. When James Joyce wrote in a 1927 letter that 'The verb "to toss off" [is] an expression for "to masturbate"', it's clear that he was still explaining its meaning – and still enjoying doing so.

'Tosser' was first spotted in an April 1977 issue of a magazine called *Zigzag*, and it was not an auspicious beginning: 'She came on in a big mac and flashed her legs like an old tosser before throwing it off'. Ever since then, it has proved a marvellously adaptable word. You could be an annoying tosser or an amiable one. But the tosser remained, in parliamentary terms, a back-bench swearword until David Cameron's revitalized Conservative party enlisted the word in an attempt to discourage people from over-reliance on their credit cards with a 'viral' media campaign urging young people to 'ignore the tosser inside you' in November 2006.

Predictably, the media were amazed that the Tories had used such a provocative word in an advert, and for days afterwards Cameron tried manfully to steer the conversation back to 'the issues'. He said it was aimed at young people and not made to offend others, but, inevitably, it was also a stick with which to beat the Tories, and one that deputy leader John Prescott seized on in the House of Commons.

Noting the opposition party's use of the word, Prescott repeated it in Parliament, adding, 'I do not know which person on the Front Bench this man is modelled on, but … I always thought that his party was full of them'. Cue laughter from one side of the House. Prescott was not cautioned by the Speaker. Indeed, Labour MPs were reported as having illustrated Prescott's remarks by making hand gestures that were unmistakably identified with the wanking theme, possibly to explain it to the more innocent members in the House.

If Prescott had referred to his opposite numbers as **wankers** or the c-word, he could no doubt have expected to spend a few painful minutes in the Speaker's office with an exercise book down the back of his trousers. But tossers was not deemed unparliamentary, and he might even have got away with calling them **berks** too, even though 'berk' is an abbreviation of Berkeley (or Berkshire) Hunt and therefore rhyming slang for the c-word – a much more offensive epithet. It is the Speaker's job to stop MPs calling each other liars, but if they are merely being called tossers, it seems he is content not to interject. Much ink has been spread since then about this latest threat to civilized society, or is it merely a recognition that even the House of Commons must, just occasionally, move with the times?

Mammet

The words 'now chiefly archaic and regional' appear at the top of the *OED*'s entry on the word **mammet**, and it's easy to see why. It was first defined as 'a false god', and used as such in the thirteenth century. In the sixteenth century it meant 'a hateful person', and in the early twentieth century it was a regional term meaning 'baby or child'. This is clearly a word that has been through several different phases.

Sir Thomas More, Lord Chancellor of England before his run-in with Henry VIII, referred in 1529 to 'The ydolles and mammettes of the paganes'. From the late sixteenth century to the early nineteenth, 'mammet' was flung about as a term of abuse by Protestant writers (and others, no doubt) to describe the images of Christ or the saints used in Catholic churches. And, more metaphorically, it was used between about 1390 and 1593 to describe a person who is the puppet of another, or has moral virtues to match – i.e. not very impressive ones. In fact, between the fifteenth and sixteenth centuries it could even mean 'fairies or pixies', as indicated in John Lyly's *Maides Metamorphosis* (1600): 'What **Mawmets** are these?/ O they be the Fayries that haunt these woods.'

Balderdash readers may have noticed that this word is being treated with unusual delicacy. They're right. The reason lies in the etymology. This is no simple word, but an Anglo-Norman word *maumet*, which was reduced from *mauhomet* and came from the twelfth-century Old French *mahomet* or *mahommet*, meaning 'an idol'. An idol? A contemporary reader would surely see something – or someone – else in it. In fact, its meaning came from the medieval Christian belief – now demonstrably proven to be false – that the prophet Muhammad was worshipped as a god. Hence the profusion of references to it in the literature of the time, and hence too the reason why you don't hear so many light-hearted allusions to it these days.

In these times of sometimes uneasy Islamo-Christian relations, though, it's interesting to pull the carpet back on an earlier time when Christians were portraying their Islamic neighbours overseas in a far from flattering light. (It's a lesson that the current pope might well have pondered more carefully before he was accused of insulting Islam in September 2006.) Nor, indeed, had they finished with it. Once again in the six-teenth century, **mammet** could mean a figure of contempt or hatred, or a weakling, or a mentally feeble person. Shakespeare talks of 'A wretched whyning foole,/A puling mammet' in *Romeo and Juliet* (1597). And in the twentieth century it still lived on, though, as the good book says, in archaic or regional uses. The poet W. H. Auden (1907–73) complained in his long poem *The Orators* (1932) that 'We're getting a little tired of boys,/ Of the ninny, the mawmet and the false alarm'. And a 1971 volume called *Twenty-Five Welsh Short Stories* contains the line 'His mouth fell open, his eyes glared under the bloody eyebrows, he shook like a mammet'. It's a word that should be used with extreme care.

Spaz

The playground is a breeding ground for terms of abuse. For their 1959 book *The Lore and Language of Schoolchildren* authors Iona and Peter Opie traipsed all over the country to record the revolting expressions children used – behaviour that these days would probably have got them into trouble with the local authority. But the fruits of their labours is endlessly fascinating, and includes childish reflections on eccentricity. Entries for the letters B, C and D alone include **bats**, **batty**, **barmy** (see page 19), **crackers**, **crackpot**, **daffy**, **dippy** and **dithering**. 'You're **daft** and dithering, wipe your chin and stop dribbling,' as they say in Cleethorpes.

One of the most effective verbal swipes among children used to be the word **spaz**, an abbreviation of **spastic**. In Britain the term 'spastic', meaning 'someone subject to muscular spasms that they can't control', dates from 1822: **spastic paralysis** was first recorded in 1877, and refers to the spasms that occur in some muscles, particularly around the neck and spine, resulting in un-predictable movements. The word 'spastic' was adopted as a term of abuse from the 1980s, though it must have been in the air long before, since the word 'spaz' was first quoted by the *New Yorker* film critic Pauline Kael in 1965, albeit with no connotation of physical disability: 'The term that American teen-agers now use as the opposite of "tough" is "spaz". A spaz is a person who is courteous to teachers, plans for a career … and believes in official values. A spaz is something like what adults still call a square.' The same goes for the related words **spacko** or **spacker** (more popular in northern England) and **spanner**. The popularity of 'spanner' may lie in its association with phrases such as **to throw a spanner in the works**, for which we may be indebted to P.G. Wodehouse's comic novel *Right Ho, Jeeves* (1934).

'Spaz', as the comment from Pauline Kael shows, was not widely known as a term of offence in the United States during the 1960s, nor is it today. When Tiger Woods, master of the plush green, lost the US Masters Tournament in April 2006, he said ruefully that although he had been at the height of his powers when he teed off, 'as soon as I got on the green I was a spaz'. There was such a rumpus in this country that his representative was forced to apologize.

Children, especially, are quick to pin unkind monikers on their contemporaries. Anyone showing signs of physical mal-coordination would, in past years, have been pounced on and called a **retard** or even a **phlid** – an extremely unkind word recalling the anti-morning sickness drug Thalidomide, which caused such dramatic growth abnormalities to arms and legs. Is it better that these terms are used about people who are not necessarily physically impaired? Not really. And it didn't help when a US company brought out a new wheelchair called the Spazz and said it was trying to reclaim the word for the wheelchair-using community. British disability campaigners were not impressed.

Joey

In 1981, the BBC TV children's programme *Blue Peter* decided to do its bit for International Year of the Disabled by focusing on Joey Deacon, who had been born with cerebral palsy in 1920 and who entered Caterham Mental Hospital aged eight. His speech was unintelligible to most people, until he had the good fortune to meet fellow inmate Ernie Roberts, who understood him perfectly. His autobiography, *Tongue Tied*, was published in 1974, and was followed by a memorable, part-dramatized episode of *Horizon*, but *Blue Peter*'s championing of him backfired slightly when schoolchildren all across the country reacted with scant sentimentality, labelling anyone showing even the slightest physical clumsiness as a **Joey**,[2] or even a **Deacon**. This, despite the fact that such behaviour was virtually guaranteed not to win them a *Blue Peter* badge.

Special needs

In today's more sensitive era, a phrase has been resurrected from the early days of the last century that health workers are hoping can be used without any unfortunate side-effects. There are all sorts of reasons why a person might have **special needs**, particularly in a physical or educational context. The *OED* contains examples of its use in official publications dated 1953 and earlier – 'the utmost care is taken to provide them with educational advantages adapted to their special needs' comes from the *Journal of Political Economy* (1913) – but this was not yet evidence of an official policy carrying that name. Its first use in the UK can be dated at 1986. It has yet to suffer the same fate that Joey did, but, as ever with children, you never know.

Plonker

Plink, **plunk** and **plonk**, apart from sounding like an animated cartoon series from Soviet-era Czechoslovakia, are all relative newcomers to the dictionary, and all descriptions of a type of sound. 'Plunk', the sound of a cork escaping a bottle, dates from

---

2 In fact, the word Joey had been a byword for 'clown', being a diminutive of the great clown Joseph Grimaldi (1779–1837) since at least 1896.

1822. The more metallic 'plink' began in 1892, while 'plonk' – a dull, thudding sound – was first noted in print in a 1904 short story by P.G. Wodehouse: 'There was a beautiful, musical *plonk*, and the ball soared to the very opposite quarter of the field,' he wrote in a collection called *Tales of St Austin's*.

In terms of etymology, these words are onomatopoeic, which means they are imitative of the sounds they describe. In the case of plonk, it's the sound made by an object going 'plonk'. This may not be a lexicological masterstroke, but it has the ring – or the plink – of truth to it. **To plonk** means 'to pluck' in a rather, well, plonky way. You could also plonk (put) something down in a casual or heavy-handed way. But the word 'plonk' has meant other things, not least as a generic term for cheap wine. The usage is helped by the assonance of plonk and *blanc*, i.e. white (wine). This rather neat play on words was first effected by Henry Williamson, author of *Tarka the Otter* and many other books. 'Nosey and Nobby shared a bottle of plinketty plonk, as *vin blanc* was called,' he wrote in his 1930 novel *The Patriot's Progress*.

From 'plonk' to **plonker** is a bigger step, but it had already come to light, in the north of England, in the mid-nineteenth century. At first it meant something abstract but significant – what further south might be called 'a whopper'. By the time of the First World War, Australians were referring to artillery shells as plonkers, but by the Second World War, it had become 'penilized' – a *Balderdash* term by which almost any word in the English language sooner or later becomes a synonym for the word 'penis'. The *OED*'s second definition for plonker is 'penis', dated from 1949. It adds 'also in extended use'. We need hardly add that it's not the penis that is extended: merely the expression.

To pull someone's plonker means 'to deceive a person humorously or playfully', and is similar to 'pulling someone's leg'.

The first recorded pulling of the plonker is as recent as 1995, in an article in *Empire* film magazine. We are confident that there must be considerable room for ante-dating this expression.

Penises being penises, by the 1960s 'plonker' came to stand for a fool or idiot. But it's fair to say that the biggest fillip that the word 'plonker' ever received was from John Sullivan, writer of the BBC TV sitcom *Only Fools and Horses.* His hero, Derek Reginald (Del Boy) Trotter, referred so often to his brother Rodney as a plonker that it fairly Araldited the word into the British consciousness. If Del Boy had simply said **prick** or **penis**, it wouldn't have been funny in that context. And if he had reused 'pillock', that wouldn't have been funny because the word 'belonged' to Alf Garnett. So Sullivan pulled 'plonker' out of relative obscurity and shot it to prominence because no one knew what it really meant.

Prat

On its first surviving appearance in print, around the year 1000, **prat** meant 'trick or prank'. In fact, in very early Middle English, around 1200, 'prat' could be an adjective meaning 'astute or cunning'. Etymologically, we have the Old English word *praett*, meaning 'guile or trick', the same word that the adjective 'pretty' is descended from. So if it comes to the worst and someone calls you a prat, you could take it as a compliment.

But the chances are it wasn't intended that way, not least because the dismissive way we use it today – as in 'Don't be such a prat' – hangs from a different linguistic thread. The *OED* lists it under 'Origin Unknown', but since 1567 it has meant 'buttocks', as proved by the following line from a comic play, *The Joviall Crew* (1641): 'First set me down here on both my **prats**.' *Both* his prats, you'll note.

'Doesn't it make you nostalgic?'

'Prat' could also mean 'a trick or a piece of cunning', but this died out in the early nineteenth century. *Chambers English Dictionary* defines it as 'a fool', and the *OED* also includes it in that sense, but this usage is far more recent than one might think. In fact, the earliest evidence the *OED* currently has for it is from the writer Melvyn Bragg in a work entitled *Without a City Wall* (1968): 'He had been looking for the exact word to describe David and now he found it: *prat*.' These days, of course, he's busy presenting arts programmes or speaking in the House of Lords, but he also has twenty-seven quotations in the *OED*, which must surely put him in the running to be the subject of one of his own *South Bank Show* specials.

A **pratfall** is 'a fall on the buttocks'. 'Don't do a pratfall in your first routine' is from *Play Parade* (1939) by Noel Coward, though we can assume that the master himself would never have been caught in such an undignifed position.

Wally

Collins defines **wally** as 'a stupid person'. *Chambers* goes for
'hopelessly inept or foolish-looking person'. Some dictionaries
make comparisons with the next word alphabetically: **wallydrag**
or **wallydraigle**, which is defined in *The English Dialect
Dictionary* as 'a feeble, ill-grown person or animal; a worthless,
slovenly person, especially a woman'. Wally is a word that, like
'plonker', was very popular in the 1970s and 1980s to describe
an idiot or a fool. It's nice to know that it isn't a codeword for
'penis', even though Partridge lists it as a cockney word for
'gherkin', in use in London's East End since the 1880s.

Where, then, is **Wally**?[3] Anecdotally (i.e. on the Internet)
there is talk of a nineteenth-century explorer called Wally
Walliams who made a bit of a prat of himself by thinking that he
had 'discovered' a new continent. As luck would have it, he had
turned up on the coast of Australia. What a wally, in other words.

A more reliable definition is that it's a diminutive form of
the name **Walter**, in the same way that Charlie – as in 'a proper
Charlie' (from 1946) – is derived from Charles.[4] The *OED* defines
'Charlie' as 'an unfashionable person; one who is foolish, inept, or
ineffectual. Also as a mild term of abuse.'

'*Wally*, out of fashion', wrote the *Daily Mirror* in 1969. The
OED's examples are culled more from newsprint than from the
pages of novels. Take this from a 1974 copy of *The Times*: 'The
successors to the flat-earthers … are at present encamped on the

---

3 The *Where's Wally?* children's books by Martin Handford first appeared
in 1987. Their US title was *Where's Waldo?*
4 The alternative spelling 'Charley' was formerly slang for a woman's
breasts, from 1874. 'Coo, look at them charlies!' comes from *The Main
Chance* by Peter Wildblood (1957).

perimeter of the great concentric stone circles … They choose to be known as the **Wallies of Wessex**, wally being a conveniently anonymous umbrella for vulnerable individuals.' In 1976 anyone dressing conventionally was a wally. The Bee Gees and Boney M were dismissed as **wally acts** during the years of punk music, and in 1979 Cuban heels were worn by wallies and John Travolta.

So which would you prefer to be called: a prat or a wally? At least prat has a rather grand – swollen, in fact – ancestry. Wally is probably just a diminutive of the personal name Walter, for no better reason than that it's a rather silly name. But is it really? Go tell that to Wally Disney, Wally Cronkite and Wally Matthau. These are major figures in Western cultural history, their greatness in no way diminished by their silly first name. And if you still disagree, maybe you'd like to take on Sir Wally Raleigh over a roll-up and a sack of potatoes.

The trouble with calling someone a wally is that it makes you sound like a bit of a plonker yourself.

Arsehole

There is surely something almost reassuring about being called – or calling someone – an **arsehole**. It isn't the rudest term of abuse ever uttered; you could probably have thought of something much worse, so it would seem that it's a grumpy put-down rather than a snarled and hateful insult. 'What an arsehole!' is marvellously evocative, though. I am an arsehole, you are an arsehole, he, she or it is an arsehole. It's a quintessentially English word, since Americans have been calling it **asshole** since at least the mid-twentieth century. Stolid, boring, workaday, **arse** has been doing the rounds since the year 1000. It feels utterly Anglo-Saxon, and certainly an Old Frisian would have known his *ers* from his elbow, though in fact it's not a million miles from the Greek word *orros*, which meant the same thing.

The word has impeccable roots. 'They say, he's valiant.' 'Valiant? so is mine arse,' comes from a 1602 play called *Poetaster* by Ben Jonson (1572–1637), a great playwright who died so poor that he was buried standing up, and not lying on his arse. **My arse** has been, ever since, a monumental expression of dignified insolence. Even on its own, 'arse' is a dismissive way of describing a stupid or contemptible person. It feels like it's been with us for ever, though it didn't really come into common parlance until well after the Second World War. But it too changed in form, from the more formal use by the Trinidadian novelist Earl Lovelace in 1968 ('Don't play the arse') to the more familiar 'A couple of stupid arses on motorbikes' by Caryl Phillips from 1986. Phillips is based in the West Indies, so did Caribbean writers pioneer its conversational use? Maybe, since if you have a Trinidadian tinge to your speaking voice, you can really add expression to the word 'arse'.

But 'arsehole', or at least 'arse hole', has been around – if you'll forgive the worthy-of-Jonson pun – for centuries. Since 1379 at least, when it clearly wasn't rude since we have the archives of Gloucester Cathedral to thank for its survival in the form 'The ers hole by egestion' (i.e. the hole from which your poo emerges) followed closely by the word 'schityng' (shitting). Assuming this wasn't some maniac coprophile priest, it seems that such words were fit for, well, a bishop at least. But arsehole's evolution has been almost balletic. When it emerged as slang, in the early 1920s, it was used to describe not people but places – and Los Angeles before all others. 'This place,' wrote the American writer and critic H.L. Mencken in 1926, on what must have been a tough trip for a native of Baltimore, 'is the one true and original arse-hole of creation. It is at least nine times as bad as I expected.'[5] Dylan Thomas (1914–53) described 'fond sad Wales' as 'This arsehole of the universe' in 1950, and from then it's been a bit of a rout, really. Feel the need to slag somewhere off? Just dust down the 'arsehole of the universe' and apply it to the place you wish to dis.

The first application of arsehole to people currently cited in the *OED* comes from an unlikely source. We have already seen the great blow for prats made by the novelist and pundit Baron Bragg of Wigton in the County of Cumbria. Among Bragg's many causes was a campaign he launched in January 2001 to prevent MPs from banning foxhunting. It didn't work, but he would have found favour with the philosopher and right-wing intellectual Roger Scruton, a man seldom seen far from a pair of tweeds. As Bragg was to prat, so Scruton is to arsehole. In 1981, a year before the publication of his book *A Short History of Modern Philosophy*, he enjoyed a foray into fiction with *Fortnight's Anger* in which he wrote: 'He is an arsehole of the first order'. Scruton is mentioned ten times overall in the *OED*. Most of his other words may be rather more uplifting – 'maenad', 'nihilist' and 'platen' to name a few – but they could scarcely be more to the point. Spare a moment, though for **podex**, first used by Ben Jonson, and meaning 'buttocks or rump'. By Scruton's time, 'podex' was mainly humorous, as in an extract from the same book, which is also noteworthy for its use of the verb 'to absterge', which means to wipe something clean: 'He made the sign of the cross … and then suddenly cried out "My God, I have forgotten to absterge the podex!"' Podex brings us back to our earlier pratfall, and better still, it can trace its origin back to the Latin verb *pedere*, meaning 'to break wind'.

----
5 Mencken's archives are housed in the Enoch Pratt (see page 149) Free Library on Cathedral Street, Baltimore.

Chapter Seven

Spend a penny

Bed Sleep Having it off Hanky panky How's
r Making love Salami Pop one's clogs Kick
g Toilet Lavatory Stool Crap Spending a p
Call of na... R...ve oneself
Powder one' nose Three sheets Cut Tired a
ed Sleep Having it off Hanky panky How's
your father ... mi Pop one's
Kick the b cket Ruling Toilet Lavatory St
ap Spending a penny Call of nature Caug
ort Relieve oneself To powder one's nose Be

*E*uphemisms – there's no nice way of putting this – say the things that, for various reasons, we don't want to say. The word 'euphemism' is Greek in origin, *eu* meaning 'well' and *phemi* meaning 'I say'. And saying things well, or at least without bluntness, is what euphemisms are all about. Sometimes, though, so anxious are we not to cause offence that they become oblique to the point of obscurity. No wonder non-native speakers have a terrible time with them.

You can refer to almost anything in an indirect way, but there are several aspects of life that have inspired an unusually large number of euphemisms. These are, traditionally, subjects where we would rather call a spade a tool for digging. We can't talk openly about death because it has always frightened us. Sex, on the other hand, is a subject about which we still have a Victorian hangover. The same goes for toilet-related matters. To these three topics we can also add drunkenness because despite the fact that some of us quite enjoy talking long-windedly about how drunk we were the other night, the rest of the world finds it distasteful. Euphemisms for drunkenness take a wry, somewhat detached view about some of the consequences of inebriation. And certain other nations, it must be said – any passing Australians, take a bow – have bent their elbows to the wheel with great enthusiasm.

Our need for euphemism arises for a variety of reasons. On one level we might feel superstitious about saying something like, 'Your auntie's just **died**', so instead we might say, 'I'm terribly sorry, but your aunt has **passed away**' (in use since the late four-teenth or early fifteenth century) to cushion the blow. At another level, the phrases **snuffed it** or **snuffed out** began to be used in the late nineteenth century. Although these don't include the word 'death', they are so terse that they could hardly be called euphemistic: they're fulfilling another function of euphemisms,

which is to demonstrate a sort of bravado in the face of the Grim Reaper.

Other euphemisms operate by concentrating fixedly on a single point, such as bed, when dealing – or not dealing – with sex. Expressions such as **going to bed with** serve to obscure the flailing limbs and grunting noises that would otherwise obtrude. Other phrases mention a non-sexual part of the body, as in **getting your leg over**, and since legs are hardly the most vital limb in the copulatory process, that gets round the thorny question of whether or not we've said something rude. But the joy of such euphemisms is that apparently innocent phrases bedevilled with sexual innuendo can rise up and bite you, as Jonathan Agnew discovered during his commentary on *Test Match Special* in 1991. His observation that Ian Botham, who had just been out Hit Wicket, 'didn't quite get his leg over' reduced him and his co-presenter Brian Johnston to whimpers of uncontrollable hysteria, and produced one of the greatest

'What the euphemistic euphemism was that?'

trophies ever in the display cabinet of euphemism.

Some euphemisms change the focus for comic effect, as in **pointing percy at the porcelain**. This was quoted by no less an organ than the *Times Literary Supplement* in 1965 as one of many 'expressive Australianisms to describe [the] prosaic function' of having a pee. Other toilet euphemisms have their roots in a grain of socio-historical truth, such as the expression **to spend a penny**, which arose from the pay-per-pee installation of the **public convenience** – and that's another euphemism, by the way.

At other times, we punningly call on bestial or animal practices as if, actually, we're all in this together with the entire animal kingdom. This leads to expressions such as **siphoning the python**, another euphemism for taking a pee, and referring to someone **going belly up** (as fish do) rather than dying. Many euphemisms have been generated either to explain certain events to children – 'Fluffy's **in heaven** now' – or in imitation of childish language, such as the inarguable 'I've done a poo'. Since most of us don't want our four-year-olds saying, 'I just shat my pants', we're happy for them to express themselves in this way. But the habit lingers on, hence pseudo-infantile expressions such as **rumpy-pumpy** (from 1968) and **hanky-panky** (see page 162).

Euphemisms contain all these inflections and more, but the crudest black-and-white division is more nuanced than the somewhat labyrinthine *OED* definition, which is 'the substitution of a word or expression of comparatively favourable implication or less unpleasant associations, instead of the harsher or more offensive one that would more precisely designate what is intended'. In fact, we're not always trying to lessen the impact of the thing itself. Sometimes the more elaborate the expression – **hiding the salami** is a popular US term for 'having sex' – the more we seem to be revelling in the act itself.

SEX

Even Casanova would have been hard put to make full use of the formidable verbal array of terms for having sex. We'll inspect as many as we can, but we can't hope to do justice to them all. Most of our examples are home-grown, but we should also delight in the Australian **spear the bearded clam**, and the Black American **bust some booty** ('booty' being a twentieth-century word for vagina or, following another line, buttocks) and **hit skins**, which, says word-sleuth Jonathon Green, is a descendant of the eighteenth-century **wriggle navels**. And that's just the start of it.

The fact is, whenever, however or wherever we talk about sex, we find it almost impossible not to use a euphemism.

The only really straight way would be to say something like 'fucking', but that doesn't always do for exploratory conversations with potential in-laws, college or job interviews, and other occasions when a measure of delicacy is required. Welcome, then, to the world of euphemism. Here, even the word **sex** stands for something more than it means. That great family-planning pioneer Marie Stopes described the **sex act** in 1918, but the word 'sex' had barely evolved since its first use in 1382, when it simply meant the gender of the species. It was the writer D.H. Lawrence (1885–1930), who in 1929 thought of combining the words 'have' and 'sex' into **have sex** – after which, of course, he thought of little else. And yet even that was a euphemism because it doesn't explicitly describe the action. In fact, the *OED* entry for the noun 'sex' consists of a mere five sections.

From the biblical expression **to know someone** to the more graphic turns of phrase that developed later, terms for sex are nearly always euphemisms. There are supposedly more technical words, such as **copulate**, which comes from the Latin *copulare* meaning 'to couple together, join or unite'. It's plainer, but it's still circumlocuting the literal truth. And there are good reasons for that.

Bed

The word **bed** may have come from an Aryan root *bhodh* by way of the Latin *fodio* (I dig), as if it were originally 'a dug-out place' or a 'lair' of beasts and men. Beds are for sleeping, of course, but we know that they have also been the scene of some lively marital and non-marital relations since around the year 1200 when documentary evidence begins, such as 'Thou hast defiled the bed of him', from William Wyclif's bible of 1382. It wasn't until the twentieth century, though, that the phrase **to go to bed** became synonymously – or rather, euphemistically – associated with sexual activity. The writer Aldous Huxley (1894–1963) seems to have got there first, in 1945: 'How much less awful the man would be … if only he sometimes lost his temper … or went to bed with his secretary,' he wrote in *Time Must Have a Stop*. From the year 1000 onwards, the verb **to bed** meant 'to put someone to bed'. Three hundred years later, it meant 'to take someone into bed', a significant shift. 'A person is said to be **in bed**, when undressed and covered with the bedclothes,' reads the *OED* definition of the noun 'bed'. Not a word about pyjamas there: what could they be hinting at?

Sleep

Both noun and verb forms of **sleep** are ancient, dating from ninth-century English. Among these are *slápan* and *slépan*, but according to the *OED*, all mean 'to take repose by the natural suspension of consciousness'. Yet by the year 900, the *OED* is defining that same word as 'implying sexual intimacy or cohabitation', as found in the book of laws of King Alfred. It's the word 'implying' that tells you the verb **to sleep with** has grown an extra skin. It may not be suggesting multi-orgasmic sex at this point, but it's clear that the word now implies more than the natural suspension of consciousness.

Having it off

There is a slightly less roundabout way of mentioning sex by not mentioning it, and that is with the common Teutonic verb form *habban*, which shook down into English as **to have**. Without beating about the bush, William Shakespeare was the first to address it sexually. When Richard Gloucester, the future Richard III, was ruminating lustfully about Lady Anne and wondering why she wasn't returning his favours (one rather glaring reason being that he had just bumped off her husband, Prince Edward), he says to himself: 'Was ever woman in this humour woo'd? Was ever woman in this humour won? I'll have her; – but I will not keep her long.'

The directness of 'to have' was not toned down until the twentieth century. In 1937 Eric Partridge noted **have it off** as used 'by a man that has contrived to seduce a girl'. There it lay for a few more years until the jazz musician George Melly – not a man to let a euphemism for sex pass by without wanting to jump on to it – completed the act of seduction: 'I derived iconoclastic pleasure from having it off in the public parks,' he wrote in *Owning-Up* (1965). The verb 'to have' continued to draw its admirers, but there was more competition now as more prepositions muscled in. Germaine Greer passed comment on another phrase in her seminal (if you'll pardon the adjective) book *The Female Eunuch*: 'The vocabulary of impersonal sex is peculiarly desolating,' she wrote in 1970. 'Who wants to … "**have it away**"?' To which the answer must be: quite a lot of people over the years.

Hanky-panky

The euphemisms for sex have become both more playful and more crude over the years. One of the funnier ones is **hanky-panky**, which came in from the rear – whoops, there we go again – since it originally meant not sex, but magic. 'Only a little

hanky-panky' was first seen in *Punch* magazine in 1841, but it didn't refer to sex. The next use, from 1847, is clearer in context: 'Necromancy, my dear Sir – the hanky-panky of the ancients' comes from a book by Albert R. Smith called *The Struggles and Adventures of Christopher Tadpole*. It could in fact refer to various types of trickery, double-dealing or underhand (see page 111) business. Hanky-panky's sexual awakening only happened in 1939, and George Bernard Shaw (1856–1950) got there first, in his play *Geneva* (1938): 'No hanky panky. I am respectable; and I mean to keep respectable.' In the case of Shaw, this was certainly true: he was one of literature's most famous celibates.

There is always something slightly innocent, or foiled, about 'hanky-panky', as if some landlady is forever hovering in the wings, waiting to stamp it out. And it survives to this day, operating at the 'sex lite' end of the erotic spectrum.

How's your father

Some euphemisms for sex are suggestive for more farcical reasons. **How's your father** is a ludicrously comical way of describing carnal activity, but it came about through the music-hall comedian Harry Tate (1872–1940). In one of his routines he was about to **get it on** (1971 is the date for that particular sexual euphemism) with a young woman when her father entered the room, whereupon he sprang up, saying, 'And how's your dear father?' It thus became a handy phrase that sprang to mind from then on as a knowing substitution for rather more athletic sexual exertions.

Making love

There's falling in love, and then there's **making love**, the latter not necessarily following on from the former. The earliest reference to **fall in love** was the rather beautiful **to be brought into love's dance**, which dates from 1423. To **make love** originally meant 'to pay amorous attention', but 'now more usually', says the *OED* (do we detect a flicker of disapproval?) '**to copulate**'. There was a lot of making love in Shakespeare's time and earlier, but no clothes were removed in the process: it was all done with tongues.[1] In a notorious passage in Jane Austen's *Emma* (1816), the unreliable narrator finds herself in a carriage with the passionate but erring Mr Elton. She had in mind to say something to him, 'but scarcely had she begun, scarcely had they passed the sweep-gate and joined the other carriage, than she found her subject cut up – her hand seized – her attention demanded, and Mr. Elton actually making violent love

---

[1] Please … no ambiguity intended!

'The Victorian Rolling Stones.'

to her'. Many is the A-level student who, on reading this passage, will have had vivid images of Jane and Mr Elton pulling at each other's clothes on the floor of the carriage. The truth was more genteel. Love-making was an oral skill[2] in those days.

Salami

There are pages and pages of euphemistic expressions for sex, whether full on (such as **hump**, a vulgar expression for sexual intercourse since 1785), or lighter – such as **slap and tickle**, a thoroughly 1920s' phrase for fairly innocent amorous fun. And the male organ, among its many derisory monikers, has been

---

2 Stop it …

referred to as a **salami** or **salam** at least since Woody Allen's film *Annie Hall* (1977), where the dialogue goes: 'We should turn out the lights and play **hide the salam**'. However, J.E. Lighter, in his *Historical Dictionary of American Slang* (1997), cites variants of the phrase going back to 1918, such as **to hide the sausage or weenie**. There is a further, post-Aids endorsement from the novel *Kicking Tomorrow* by Daniel Richler (1993): 'I'd steer clear if I was you, dude. **Slap the salami** instead, **pull the pud**, it's disease-free.' Most dictionaries define 'hiding the salami' in terms of sexual intercourse, but this author suggests, from nothing more than a close study of Richler's text, that the emphasis in that last quote is on masturbation.

DEATH

Where death and dying are concerned, our motives for tiptoeing around the subject are more understandable. While sex is something that we might not wish to discuss openly, at least we enjoy it while it's taking place. Not so our appointment with the Grim Reaper. When it comes to the d-word, it's as though if we don't say it, it might not happen.

Pop one's clogs

Take the expression **to pop one's clogs**. On the surface, it doesn't sound final at all. You could almost imagine it meaning to perform a dance or to clap your hands. It sounds rhythmical and light-hearted. But this belies its essential seriousness. 'To pop your clogs' means 'to die'. The verb **to pop** is a hardy English perennial, 700 years old at least, and its original meaning – borrowed from its sound – was to deliver smack or a blow to something. In fact, when you think of a paper bag (rather than a champagne cork) popping, it does seem to have a note of finality. In the eighteenth century 'to pop' on its own meant just that: to die.

So where did clogs come in? Well, they were once everyday footwear in the north of England, and perhaps the most likely item to pop (a slang expression for **pawn**) when people wanted to rustle up some cash. The combination of popping and clogs in the context of death is relatively recent, though, and spotted by no lesser personage than a *Balderdash* wordhunter in a 1970 copy of *Punch* magazine, by which time it could be said to be an analogous expression to **hanging up your boots** (or **hat**). So the phrase harks back from a non-clog era to a much older time.

Clogs were a common item of footwear not only in northern towns, but also in the Netherlands, so it seemed reasonable to ask if that fine country includes references to clogs in any of its euphemistic expressions for death. Luckily, *Balderdash*'s small but fast-growing band of Dutch wordhunters rose enthusiastically to the challenge, and the answer appears to be: absolutely none, though Hollandophiles will enjoy some equally colourful expressions, such as *Tussen zes planken de deur uitgaan* (Leave the door [i.e. house] inside six pieces of wood), and *Er groeit gras op zijn buik* (There's grass growing on his belly). But nothing about clogs.

Kick the bucket

There are plenty of other ways to die, of course. Some offer comfort to the religious – **to be in the arms of Jesus**, **to go to a better place**, **to be at rest** – while some adopt an almost insolent attitude to the brutal finality of extinction. One of these is the cryptic phrase **kick the bucket**. Why should death result

'I could cope with him passing on. It's the thought of him dying that's so awful.'

from a kick to a bucket? Is **bucket** perhaps a medieval expression for the Black Death? Did buckets collect recently guillotined heads during the French Revolution? Or did the kick lead to a fatal toe infection? None of the above, of course, since the great joy of such euphemisms is that if you stare straight back at them in search of logical explanation, you won't get anywhere. Nor is there any etymological help from Dr Samuel Johnson's *Dictionary of English* (1755), which defines buckets as 'the vessels in which water is carried, particularly to quench a fire'. The *OED* points to the Old French *buket*, which meant 'a washing tub or a milk-pail', so we still don't seem to be any the wiser.

You might have thought that of all the words in the English language, 'bucket' was one of the most stolid, reliable words: never the type to give us the slip. Well, you'd be wrong. There is another bucket, with a wholly separate life. In part of Norfolk, in fact, where certain ancient practices persist, they still use this other bucket pretty much for its original purpose, since it comes not from the Old French *buket*, but from another Old French word, *buquet*, which gave us the word **trebuchet**. A trebuchet was 'a large medieval siege engine' (*Collins*), as anyone who has sat through the film of *The Lord of the Rings* will already know. This bucket, then, has nothing to do with carrying water or milk: it's a balancing operation. The *OED* includes this comment: 'The beam on which a pig is suspended after he has been slaughtered is called in Norfolk, even in the present day, a "bucket".'

The theory goes that the condemned pig was suspended by its heels from the bucket, or the **bucket beam**. Perhaps, during its death spasms, the poor animal's trotters clanged against this bucket, giving rise to the phrase. That particular kicking of the bucket is noted by Captain Francis Grose in his *Dictionary of the Vulgar Tongue* (1785). It's a fine story, and it works well, but some people still have a lingering feeling for that other bucket, the one we know better. It suggests, in fact, another series of images – a poor soul standing on an upturned bucket with a noose around his neck, a foot then flying out to knock the bucket away, leaving the body swinging from the gibbet. Could 'kicking the bucket', then, be associated with hanging, either as execution or suicide? It seems possible, but no written evidence attests to this.

Death in combat

As a general rule, those bodies that have pursued war with the greatest zeal have been the most adept at using military euphemisms as camouflage, or sometimes sand-bags, to deaden the shock of their weapons. These days, the US Army is a key player in this theatre of war. Terms such as **collateral damage** have been around for so long – since the Vietnam War – that they even merit definition in the US Air Force's own *Intelligence Targeting Guide*, namely: 'unintentional damage or incidental damage affecting facilities, equipment or personnel, occurring as a result of military actions directed against targeted enemy forces or facilities'. The adjective 'friendly' had been in use since the First World War to describe a missile passing overhead that turns out not to be hostile since it was fired by your own side. The American journalist C.D.B. Bryan wrote *Friendly Fire*, a bestseller about the Vietnam War, in 1976. The phrase **friendly fire** caught on in the UK during the first Gulf War, in 1991, when more American troops were killed by their own firepower – or turned into basket cases (see page 28) – than by Iraqi weapons.

According to a November 2003 report on a Toronto-based website called *Common Dreams*, the new euphemism for death in the army keeps evolving. During the Vietnam conflict, in which 58,000 US soldiers died, the term **body bag** was in common currency to describe the article in which a corpse was wrapped for storage and transport. Perhaps the comparisons with the Vietnam era – when President Lyndon Johnson was accused of hiding the body bags – were regarded as unwelcome. At any rate, during the 1991 Gulf War, body bags were replaced by **human remains pouches**. Perhaps this was a bit close to the bone, for, according to *Common Dreams*, the preferred term among Pentagon briefers is now **transfer tubes**. You couldn't really have a phrase that better embalms the real effects of violent death.

BODILY FUNCTIONS

We can't all be love gods, and very few of us want to be proficient at dying, but if there's one thing we should all have mastered by an early age, it's **going to the toilet**. Yet the subject has always fascinated us, to the point where we are still thinking up new ways of referring to weeing or pooing – these are not medical terms but they'll do for now – with varying degrees of self-mockery. The acute embarrassment that many of us suffer when mentioning our need to use the **rest-room** makes for fertile ground for euphemism. Frankly, most of us would rather say anything than admit that we need to **have a dump**. You don't even have to make a huge attempt to connect the wish with the activity, which is perhaps why a phrase such as **going to see a man about a dog** (see page 86) has achieved its vague and uncertain popularity. The **privy** has for long been the room where one goes to **drain the spuds**, though 'privy' used to mean – at least in 1225 or so – a circle of intimate friends. It extended its use from people to a private place, a **latrine** in fact, in 1375. Now it's time to meet some more examples of **number ones** and **number twos** (urination and defecation, from 1902).

Toilet

The word **toilet** is, in fact, a euphemism par excellence. It's a diminutive from the French *toile*, which had various meanings according to a Cambridge scholar called Randle Cotgrave who was writing in 1611, including 'a bag to put night-clothes' and 'other stuffe to wrap any other clothes in'. During the seventeenth century, 'toilet' kept retiring to **powder its nose** (see page 177), returning each time with a new definition. Thus we have 'a cloth cover for a dressing-table' from 1682 vying with 'a towel or cloth thrown over the shoulders during hair-dressing' from 1684. To the great diarist John Evelyn (1620–1706), 'The greate looking-glasse and toilet of beaten and massive gold' was an item of furniture used when dressing, as he noted in 1662. By the time Alexander Pope (1688–1744) wrote his famous poem *The Rape of the Lock* (1712–14), his reference to 'The long labours of the Toilet' made it clear that 'toilet' didn't mean squatting over the privy after a curry, but hours spent in pampering and preparing oneself by washing and grooming.

During the eighteenth century, it was fashionable for a lady to entertain visitors as she approached the closing stages of her toilet. Sir Walter Scott (1771–1832), in his romantic novel *Kenilworth* (1821), was one of many nineteenth-century writers for whom 'toilet' referred to a way of dressing, or to the costume itself. But it was Lord Byron (1788–1824) who pipped everyone to the post for giving it the contemporary slant: 'There is the closet, there the toilet' begins stanza 153 of his mock-epic poem *Don Juan* (1819). And so 'toilet' came to mean 'the bowl', and **to go to the toilet** meant 'to empty one's bladder or bowels into a piece of enamel', rather than to fish among the contents of one's wardrobe.

Lavatory

No word for toilet can tell it like it is. What about **lavatory**? It's the place where one washes, from the French verb *laver* (to wash), but in 1375 or thereabouts it meant the jug containing the water that you used to wash your face or have a bath. The actual room called a lavatory, where hands and face were washed, appeared in print in 1656. It wasn't until Europe was on the brink of war, 1913, that this word was shortened in print to **lav**.

The Britain preference for 'toilet' over 'lavatory' marks a peak in the ongoing class struggle, but, characteristically, the war was conducted through language. Class warfare in other countries has seen such horrors as the invention and enthusiastic adoption of the guillotine in France, the purging of the entire royal family in revolutionary Russia, and Pol Pot's genocidal campaign against middle-class Cambodians. In pre-Second World War Britain it took the form of certain people flaring their nostrils on hearing the word 'toilet' as opposed to 'lavatory'.

Loo is a mystery too: is it from *l'eau*, the French for 'water'? The *OED* doesn't even hazard a guess, maybe since printed evidence for it comes, incredibly, not until the twentieth century was well established. James Joyce made a joke about Waterloo or **Watercloset** in his 1922 novel *Ulysses*, but the first incontrovertible evidence – 'In the night when you want to go to the loo' – comes in 1940, in a novel by Nancy Mitford called *Pigeon Pie*. How appropriate: she, of all people, would have known if loo was U (upper class) or non-U (not upper class): she pretty much invented the terms, after all.

At stool

The word **stool** was, and still is, a very simple chair. Around 1410 it came to mean the humble **privy** or room where you did your toilet activity. The *OED* includes the quotation 'Than go to your stole to make your egestyon' from 1582, at which the stool was the action of either weeing or pooing, though by 1533, the word 'stool' had become solidly – if you'll forgive me – associated with faecal matter. By 1597 it was 'a discharge of faecal matter of a specified colour'. Along the way the stool has had lots of other lives, including 'a stump from which sprouts shoot up' and 'a piece of wood to which a bird is fastened as a decoy' (both *Chambers*), and this is surely a welcome thing: it's good to vary your approach when you don't want to be associated with crapping.

Crap

No one could accuse **crap** of being a particularly delicate euphemism. 'To crap' meant 'to defecate' in 1846. In 1874 it was 'to ease oneself by evacuation', as John C. Hotten's *Dictionary of Modern Slang* informs us with delightful euphemism. As an aside, though, if you were a criminal in Victorian England, you'd probably have something else on your mind if you were over-heard talking about **the crap**: it was an underground term for 'the gallows' until around 1834. And yet, these days, crap, **having a crap** or **sitting on the crapper** are about as base and uneuphemistic as one can get – along with **shit, shitting** and **the shitter** – for the action of **opening one's bowels**. As for the origin of the word, the early Dutch noun *krappe* is closely related to the Dutch verb *krappen*, meaning 'to pluck off'. There's also the Old French noun *crape*, which means 'siftings', as in 'the grain trodden under feet in the barn, and mingled with the straw and dust', which is similar in meaning to the medieval Latin word *crappa*. All these meanings have the general sense of residue or dregs – *Residue Dregs*, great name for a film – and they're all pretty crappy.

Spending a penny

The origins of **spending a penny** are an object lesson in social history. The penny in question was the asking price for admission to public lavatories, which were introduced in this country at the Great Exhibition of 1851. Charging for admission was common from then on, it seems, wherever they were built, just as levying a toll for a newly constructed bridge was also widespread. The great advantage to saying you were spending a penny was its non-specificity. You didn't need to go into any detail about whether it was a **number one** or a **number two**: no further information was required, or, I'm sure, wanted. Even when prices rose, the expression remained and seemed set to continue in, albeit antiquated, use.

The decimalization of Britain's coinage in 1971 brought the beginning of the end for Britain's pay-as-you-go toilet system, but that was some time after the phrase 'spend a penny' had embedded itself in the nation's hearts, minds and bottoms. The first sighting of the phrase was not until 1945, though, in a book called *Strange Story* by H. Lewis: '"Us girls," she said, "are going to spend a penny!"' Were they really going to visit a **public convenience?** Surely not. And that's another marvellous euphemism for exactly the same item of street furniture, first noted in print by (Sir) Osbert Lancaster in 1938: 'The cathedral, the Dean's house ... and the public convenience ... are all "architecture",' wrote the great cartoonist, art critic and exotic character.

Call of nature

A need to defecate or urinate has long been known as **a call** or **a call of nature**, and people have been **paying a call** for some centuries now. First off the mark was Laurence Sterne, author of *Tristram Shandy* (1759–67), a novel that was one enormous shaggy dog story (see page 101), so no wonder there were a few exaggerations, such as 'A city ... who neither eat, or drank ... or hearkned [sic] to the calls either of religion or nature for seven and twenty days'. A helpful entry in the magazine *Tailor & Cutter* from 1852 advises that 'The calls of Nature are permitted and Clerical Staff may use the garden below the second gate'. The sequel to Jim Carrey's 1994 comedy film *Ace Ventura: Pet*

Detective was called *Ace Ventura: When Nature Calls*. A very funny title: funnier, said some who had seen it, than the script.

Caught short

The staff at the tailors above might have had to **relieve** themselves in a hurry, especially if they were **caught short**. The *OED* doesn't list this, but it has plenty to say on the subject of **to take short**. This means 'to take by surprise, at a disadvantage; to come suddenly upon', and is often to be found in a nautical context. As well as that, **to be taken short** means 'to have an urgent need to urinate or defecate'. For its first instance in English, we are indebted to *Funk's Standard Dictionary*, from 1890, which lists, 'To be taken short (colloquial), to be pressed with the need of evacuation of feces'. For its first use in literature we are directed to consult a poem by Ignatius Roy Dunnachie Campbell called 'The Wayzgoose' from 1928. This includes the line: ''Tis Nature's whim that dogs, when taken short,/ Still to the loftiest monument resort.' So it isn't just people who are taken short. 'To be caught short' is a good phrase, though, and useful in a joking context in cricket, such as 'Their big-hitting number three batsman went for a slog and was caught short by the boundary'. Ho ho.

Relieve oneself

Men and women have been relieving themselves since the dawn of time, but the precise phrasing **to relieve oneself** is no older than 1931 – 'I wanted to relieve myself' – and occurs in a book about the British murderer Alfred Rouse by Sydney Tremayne in 1931. (Rouse gave a lift to a hitch-hiker, whom he murdered by burning him alive inside his car. Nasty story.) The Revised

Standard Version of the Bible, published in 1952, renders a line in the first book of Samuel: 'And he came to the sheepfolds by the way, where there was a cave; and Saul went in to relieve himself'. The original Hebrew is **to cover his feet**, but this was evidently a euphemistic expression in itself, so one euphemism was being translated with another, which gives one a nice warm feeling. (Did they do it to keep warm?) The *Collins* definition of 'relieve oneself' is 'to urinate or defecate'. Presumably there was no ambiguity this time.

Vladimir Nabokov (1899–1977), one of the greatest text-teasers in the English language, wrote in his 1960 novel *Invitation to a Beheading* about 'The bliss of relieving oneself, which some hold to be on a par with the pleasure of love'. And if you're tempted to dismiss that as stuff and nonsense, just bear in mind that Nabokov was also a world-famous lepidopterist: his collection of male blue butterfly genitalia holds pride of place at the Harvard Museum of Natural History.

To powder one's nose

W. Somerset Maugham (1874–1965) was the first person we know about to put the words '**I must powder my nose**' into a woman's mouth, but there have been many since then. In a way it's the ultimate toilet euphemism because there is nothing in it that remotely refers to defecation or micturition, merely an acknowledgment that, outside the cubicle, a woman might take a few moments to retouch her make-up. Certainly if one were to suggest that she was going to **take a leak**, one would get a very dirty look indeed, perhaps because that phrase is even more recent. In fact it comes from a writer at the very opposite end of the scale of gentility from Maugham: Henry Miller (1891–1980), and his novel *Tropic of Cancer*, which was published in Paris in 1934. The novel was eventually published in the United States in 1961, prompting a furore similar to that generated by *Lady Chatterley's Lover* in the UK. If only Miller had shown more interest in euphemisms, there wouldn't have been any such fuss. In fact, 'I stood there taking a leak' is one of the most respectable lines in the whole book. Such an activity, of course, like many such instances of toilet euphemism, is more likely to apply to a lady than to a gentleman. It's a bit like the old adage that 'horses and soldiers sweat, men perspire; women merely glow'. So bulls shit, men obey calls of nature … and women powder their nose.

DRUNKENNESS

Every generation remembers its first drink, and likes to record the moment with a series of memorable phrases that always tell us much about a particular society and a particular age. So, for example, variations of the phrase **in one's cups** have, since Thomas Hoccleve used it in 1406, referred to the drinking of intoxicating liquor or drunkenness. A 1611 translation of the Book of Esdras, one of the Bible's apocryphal works, contains the line 'And when they are in their cups, they forget their love both to friends and brethren'. Around the same time, the word **legless** meant 'having no legs'. Flip forward three centuries, and it means 'drunk'. The first reference is from the pop song 'Wide-eyed and Legless' by Andy Fairweather Low, which rose to number six in the Christmas charts back in 1975.

A 1946 study of current English records that 'Synonyms for **drunk** now current in England … [include] **tiddley**, **oiled** or **well oiled**, **sloshed**'. The origin of 'tiddley' (or 'tiddly') – meaning mildly intoxicated – is mysterious, especially since, from the

1920s onwards, 'tiddly' was used in the services to mean 'smartly dressed or well-presented' (perhaps from tidy), which is quite the opposite of **pissed as a fart**.

It's interesting to compare these genteel expressions – like tiddly and so on – with today's barrage of more explosive terms for the same state, such as the not yet *OED*-listed **bladdered**, **twatted** and – heaven help us – **wankered**. Whereas the old-school euphemisms are designed to draw a discreet veil over what can be fairly anti-social behaviour, adjectives such as **arseholed** (1982) and **rat-arsed** (1984) are, if anything, more like dysphemisms – i.e. the deliberate crudities of an age that delights for satirical purposes in putting an ugly gloss on stuff and calling a spade a bloody great mechanical digger.

Three sheets

The joy of being drunk, unless you're doing it every day before breakfast, is that you can pretend not to be. Hence the barrage of phrases that unite to persuade the drinker that he or she can, variously, dance, sing or in some other way entertain someone who is clearly not very interested.

Think of the word **sheet** and you'll think … bed? That's from the Old English word *scíete*. Now change your location so that you're on board a clipper, snaking its way over the sea to Java in search of spices and exotica. 'Sheet' also meant 'the sail of a ship', so if your mainsheet, your jib sheet and your spinnaker sheet all become detached, your ship is **three sheets to the wind**, and unable to control itself or be controlled. Spinning around like a **piss-head**, in other words. Some of our most imaginative and colourful expressions denoting the intake of excess alcohol have come out of the army and navy, which for centuries have housed and trained many of our most successful and enthusiastic drinkers.

The expression **three sheets in the wind** was first recorded by Pierce Egan (1772–1849), a chronicler of London life who had his ear very close to the (under)ground on account of the many slang expressions he noted. 'Old Wax and Bristles is about three sheets in the wind' comes from his book *Real Life* (1821). Sixty years later, Robert Louis Stevenson (1850–94) noted, 'Maybe you think we were all a **sheet in the wind's eye**'.

The navy also gave us the archaic and much less well-known phrase **half-seas-over**, or simply **half-seas**. When originally transcribed, in the mid-sixteenth century, it meant literally 'half-way across the sea'. Then, in the seventeenth century, it meant 'caught in two minds' and was used by such distinguished writers as the playwright Sir John Vanbrugh (1664–1726) and the poet Lord Byron. In between times *A New Dictionary of the Terms Ancient and Modern of the Canting Crew* (1700) explained 'half-seas-over' – perhaps connected to seasickness, though I can't state it with confidence – as 'almost drunk'. This has not survived into the twentieth century.

Cut

Another phrase whose meaning is not immediately apparent is **half-cut**, but one of the meanings of the word **cut**, when used as a participle, is 'lessened or reduced'. In 1624 this could refer to something being diluted or even castrated; then, in 1673, we find 'He is flaw'd, fluster'd, Cup shot, cut in the leg or back', which appeared in a marvellous slang dictionary called *The Canting Academy* by Richard Head, a seventeenth-century rogue who probably knew from first-hand experience every euphemism for drunkenness he collected. A popular book of the time, *Chrysal,*

or the Adventures of a Guinea by the Irish lawyer Charles
Johnstone (?1719–1800), contains the wonderfully forgiving line:
'Your excellency was a little cut, but you broke up much the
strongest of the company.'

'Three sheets' and 'half-cut' are among our best expressions
for drunkenness, but there is no shortage of other ways of saying
pissed. (That term, by the way, evolved from meaning 'splashed
with urine'. It appears first in Ben Jonson's 1616 play *The
Alchemist* and is an occupational hazard for the inebriated.) And
how appropriate that it was first spotted in a volume called *The
Tyneside Songster* in 1889: 'Sit still, you pist fool'.

Tired and ...

One of the most successful twentieth-century phrases for
drunkenness was born in 1967, care of the satirical magazine
Private Eye. It owes its creation to the antics of first deputy
leader of the Labour party, George Alfred Brown (1914–85).
Brown, or Lord George-Brown as he became better, if mockingly,
known upon being elected to the peerage by Harold Wilson
in 1970, was an effective politician and campaigner, and an
inveterate drinker. Unfortunately, when he'd been **at the bottle**
(Scotland's most famous poet Robert Burns seems to have hit
upon this phrase first, in 1789) his behaviour became unpredict-
able and often unacceptable. This habit increased when he was
under pressure, which was so frequent in the 1960s that his
colleague Anthony Crosland referred to the 1963 leadership
election campaign as 'a choice between a crook and a drunk'
(respectively, Harold Wilson and George Brown).

Of course, as Patrick Marnham recounts in his book *The
Private Eye Story* (1982), it was 'quite impossible in those days

for the press to say that a cabinet minister was drunk'. Instead, *Private Eye* produced a spoof report of a memo from the Foreign Office (FO): 'Following the appointment of Mr George Brown as Foreign Secretary, I am reliably informed that a special memo has been dispatched by the F.O. to embassies and consulates abroad.' The memo, it went on, 'is intended as a guide to ambassadors and embassy spokesmen when dealing with the Foreign Press.' There followed a list of English words that were obviously intended to be helpful when dealing with Brown: 'Tired, Overwrought, Expansive, Overworked, Colourful, Emotional'. Translations were provided in French, Italian, German and Russian. Thus the phrase **tired and emotional** tottered into the language. By the time Peter Paterson came to write the biography of Lord George-Brown in 1993, the phrase was so well established that it was used as the book's title. How very different from our own dear politicians of today.

Chapter Eight

X-rated

Kinky Marital aids Jerk Pole-dancing Wank To wap Porn Dogging Fluffer Kinky Marital a Pole-dancing W orn Doggi inky Mar aid J ing Wanki Porn Dogging Fluffer Kinky Marital aids Je Pole-dancing Wanking To wap Porn Doggi

*T*he usual definition of **X-rated** implies that the material described thus is suitable only for adults. In practice, adults are some of the last people who should be exposed to such material. It's not as if we don't think about sex too much anyway. Feeding X-rated material to an audience that's perpetually hungry for more may not be such a great idea.

Society is still struggling with its attitude to **adult** matters. Indeed, the word 'adult' is something of a euphemism itself, having evolved from meaning 'a mature person', most often a man (1531), to 'a grown-up attitude' (as late as 1929). From there, according to the *OED*, it came to be 'applied euphemistically to premises or productions ostensibly restricted to adult access, such as **adult cinema**, entertainment, movie, etc.; pornographic, sexually explicit'. That usage originated in the fleshpots of North America, naturally, but it has travelled to places as far apart as Kent and Burnham-on-Sea, as we shall soon find out.

The joy of dictionaries lies in witnessing the utter demo-cratization of language. There are no priorities in this system of headwords: each word gets the attention it deserves, and just that. Thus, the etymological roots of 'sublime', 'beautiful' and 'culture' (none of which you will find in this book) are investi-gated just as passionately and scrupulously as the stories that lie behind **wank**, **jerk** and **dogging** (all of which you *will* find – and in this very chapter).

The democratic nature of lexicography is evident in the dating process that lies behind every word, for without that information, no word is properly 'dressed'. Britons may grumble that their society is obsessed with bureaucracy and form-filling these days, but it was the Victorians who really set the ball rolling with their learned disquisitions on every – well, nearly every – English word that had ever been.

And yet, for all the *OED*'s unparalleled, unrivalled, unapologetic and unshakable intellectual excellence, anecdotal evidence suggests that it's not just the common people – the hoi polloi – who enjoy luxuriating in the detail of rude words. You might think that all those highfalutin types in their libraries would have eyes only for posh words, but you'd be wrong. Whisper it not in the reading rooms of the British Library and the Bodleian, but there is evidence that the *OED Online*'s wordsearch tool receives a disproportionate number of enquiries for its X-rated words. Surprising? Perhaps not. Maybe it's because the dictionary is just the place from which to examine some of the language's most dangerous elements. Seeing these words on the screen, you can inspect them at your leisure. Downloading child porn is, of course, illegal, and rightly so – even if you're writing a book about it. But examining **pornography**, the word, is not a crime, and rightly so.

Seeing how different centuries have dealt with X-rated issues – mostly, in some form, to do with sex – is as important a part of our shared social history as any other. Did Victorians wrap up difficult words in Latin just as they encased 'naked' piano legs in satin? Was Geoffrey Chaucer's readiness to use a word such as **cunt** an act of daring, or merely frankness?

Our aim is not to tiptoe around the long shadow cast by some of our most shocking words, so be warned: this chapter starts with **kinky** and ends with **fluffer**. In other words, it goes from bad to worse.

Kinky

The *OED* tells us that the word **kink** is probably from the Dutch word *kink*, meaning a 'twist or a twirl'. (German, Danish and

Swedish all have the same word.) The *OED* speculates that it comes from a root *kink-* (which seems logical) or *kik-*, meaning 'to bend or twist'. That's hypothesis, but we are fortunate to have physical evidence from contemporary Icelandic, which uses the verb *kikna*, meaning 'to bend at the knees', or *keikr*, meaning 'bent back'. The word 'kink', when first used in English in 1678, meant 'a short twist or curl in a rope, thread, hair, wire, or the like, at which it is bent upon itself'.

Kinky was first attached exclusively to hair. More specifically, and since 1844, it was used to describe Afro-style curls. In fact, it seems to have been a traveller's term because references to **kinky-headed** and **kinky-haired** Africans were most often used by nineteenth-century voyagers. But in that same century it also began to acquire a more figurative sense. This is clear from John Russell Bartlett's *Dictionary of Americanisms* (1860) in which he defined kinky as 'queer, eccentric, crotchety'. In his 1907 novel *The Longest Journey* E.M. Forster (1879–1970) described a jaundiced young philosopher as having a 'kinky view of life'.

'Kinky' became kinkier as the twentieth century progressed, and varied according to where on the planet you were standing. In the USA, until the First World War, 'kinky' could mean 'lively or energetic': 'You seem to be feeling pretty kinky to-day' comes from a US publication called *Dialect Notes*, dated 1914. The next twist in the story of kinky comes in 1927, when it appeared in *Collier's Weekly*, a magazine that published a mixture of fiction and investigative journalism in a distinctive narrative style. This has to be fiction: 'Why, you can't tell me that you didn't know those five big cars were kinky.' 'Kinky?' … 'Those cars were bent.' This suggests that the word was popular with the criminal fraternity and could also mean 'dodgy' (see page 109). This sense continued, certainly until 1954, as the *OED* includes the citation 'kinky gambling paraphernalia' from that year. But kinky could also be used in its original sense of 'curled': for example, the offspring of an artificially irradiated mouse in 1956 had tails that were 'kinky'.

From criminality, kinky then became associated with **perverted** behaviour, as it was then called. It first broke through in that touchstone novel of postwar London *Absolute Beginners* (1959) by Colin MacInnes. The unnamed nineteen-year-old narrator has a girlfriend called Crepe Suzette. 'Suze … meets lots of kinky characters … and acts as agent for me, getting orders from them for my pornographic photos.' Thus 'kinky' became associated with the seamier side of sex. A **kinky advert**, reported the *Daily Telegraph* in 1963, implied 'irregular sexual practices', but there is evidence from a variety of novels, films, journals and other memoirs of the time that people were capable of feeling kinky towards teapots (1960), sweetbreads (1964) or Black Russian cigarettes (1967). They probably thought that these objects were – to use a popular word from the time – exceptionally 'groovy'. These uses of 'kinky' seem to have pretty much flushed out any earlier ideas about innocent fun or simple liveliness.

'Kinky' could also connote **gay sex**, though it more often meant – and still does – what is nowadays called **fetishism**. This is illustrated in an extract from the *Daily Telegraph* (again) in 1971: 'In a moment of excessively kinky passion a husband strangles his mistress'. We're not told, of course, whether a husband's urge to strangle his mistress with his bare hands would be called deranged or perverted. Perhaps he (or she) was wearing **kinky boots** at the time: made of leather, these were first spotted in 1964.

The last part of kinky's journey has been from 1960s' **creepiness** to late 1990s' **funkiness**. Where the word was once a synonym for 'perverted' or **deviant** behaviour, these days couples of all types are being urged to inject a little **kinkiness** into their lives. Esther Freud wrote a bestselling novel called *Hideous Kinky* in 1992. Cinema audiences also enjoyed a British comedy called *Kinky Boots* in 2005. And, of course, there's also the detective writer Kinky Friedman, still ploughing his lonely but entertaining furrow as the world's only Jewish cowboy. Being kinky is now seen as pleasantly eccentric, and is certainly inclusive. Kinkiness no longer means skulking around the edge of society in a pair of rubber trousers. In fact, we seem to have got to the point where being kinky has fused with being **sexually adventurous** and can now be worn as a badge of pride to show that the 'romance' or 'fun' hasn't gone out of your love life. These days there's a global design agency called Kinky, a Ghent-based record label called Kinky Star, and over in San Francisco the Kinky Salon is building 'a community dedicated to sex-positive self-expression'. Wherever you look the world seems to be pointing in an ever-kinkier direction.

Marital aids

On the surface, **marital aids** sound vague and respectable enough. Like 'athletic support' or 'passing wind', they get away with masking their actual function, but the *OED* tells us that a marital aid is 'any device for the production or enhancement of sexual stimulation'. The first printed reference to the term – 'We sell a wide range of marital aid appliances ... Send for our ... catalogue – it'll help you put more life into loving' – is from the *Burnham-on-Sea Gazette*, dated April 1976. That definition strains the link between 'marital' and 'marriage' to bursting point, but maybe that's the intention. If it's 'marital', goes the thinking in Burnham-on-Sea, it must be all right. No doubt that rather windy area of Somerset in 1976 was not the sort of place whose newsagents' windows were full of adverts for ticklers, dildoes, leather straps and butt plugs, but the successful mass marketing of marital aids is attributable to the fact that the words contain a wink and a discreet nod. The term sounds wholesome, but we sense that there is something else going on too. It's post-Philip Larkin, who claimed that sexual intercourse began in 1963,[1] but *before* the anything-goes era of today. It's a prime example of a euphemism (see page 156).

To understand the attraction of certain words, you need first to read the manual. Take the **Wartenberg wheel**, for example. This device, designed by Dr Robert Wartenberg (1886–1956), is made of stainless steel and has a rotating head studded with evenly spaced pins. It can still be found in most medical catalogues. In the field of neurology it is rolled across the skin to test nerve reactions, but it is also popular within the **BDSM community**.

BDSM? The letters refer to **B&D** (Bondage and Discipline), **D&S** (Domination and Submission) and **S&M** (Sadism and/or Masochism). The Wartenberg wheel enhances sexual pleasure for a consenting community with a distinctive approach to pain and sensitivity. The wheel, along with the use of a **vaginal speculum**, are employed to heighten pleasure. In the online world the Wartenberg wheel is listed more prominently as a sex or marital aid than as part of orthodox medical practice.

---

1 From 'Annus Mirabilis' in the collection *High Windows* (Faber & Faber, 1974).

The fact that certain groups are finding sexual gratification from items more usually found in a medical context reflects a blurring of social divisions, and crossover at its most inventive. In fact, electrical **vibrators** were invented in the 1880s as a means of treating 'hysteria' in women. In her book *The Technology of Orgasm* (1999), Rachel P. Maines begins with her own shock at finding an advertisement for such vibrators within 1906 copies of *Modern Priscilla, Needlecraft* and *Woman's Home Companion* – all respectable women's magazines. These days, however, women are not being prescribed genital massage by their physician: they are shopping online and buying the necessary equipment for themselves, batteries not included.

The rise to near-respectability of what has long been called the marital aid is either a miracle of marketing or an acceptance that a quick shag (see page 202) is not the only means of relaxation after a hard day's work. Unusually, the *OED* seems rather coy about defining **dildo**: 'a word of obscure origin, used in the refrains of ballads'. Now you don't need to be making a living from writing about words to know that *that* is not a definition – it's more a historical note. It's only in the small print, written underneath, that we learn it is 'also a name of the penis or phallus, or a figure thereof; *spec.* an artificial penis used for female gratification'. As well as Dr Wartenberg and his wheel, the dildo has been pleasuring women – and men too, whatever the *OED* might say – for centuries, and was originally made of stone, wood or other materials.

The commercial success of the 'Jack Rabbit Vibrator', along with a plethora of other **ticklers** and **teasers**, is evidence of the **sex toy** as a form of home entertainment, though the topic of 'marital aids' is still some way from becoming chatter around the dinner party table. The main difference these days is that this

category of marital aid is made from rubber or latex rather than wood or stone.

Nowadays you don't have to be married to enjoy the improvements that a marital aid can bring to your sex life. The term was once a kind of code encompassing **butterfly strap-ons**, **vibrating panties**, **love eggs** and suchlike, but it's now 'out there' in common parlance. Where Burnham-on-Sea led the way, the rest of the country has followed. It's almost as if women are claiming that they can do perfectly well on their own, thank you very much, or with just a little help from their battery-operated friends.

Jerk

While Philip Larkin's tongue was firmly in his cheek when he wrote his now-famous lines about sexual intercourse beginning in 1963, there had long been another type of sexual act that, if it came to a contest, would have triumphed, one-handed, over intercourse. It was masturbation. We know for sure that people were **jerking off** in the nineteenth century because they have told us. The extracts in the *OED*, listed under the word 'off', introduce us to the verb **to jerk off** – the jerking in this case being to the point of orgasm. One is from a rare 1865 work called *Love Feast* by a writer who took the pen-name Philocomus: 'I'll jerk off, thinking of thee'. That's the earliest, but a pantomime called *Harlequin Prince Cherrytop* was performed in 1879 and this contained the line 'To the privy I would repair, And **toss it off** in the basin there'. The *OED*, admirably thorough as ever, also suggests we look up **bring, jack, pull, suck, toss, wank** and **whack**. By adding the word 'off', all these verbs can be extended to the point of orgasm, though not on the same evening.

The noun/verb 'jerk', along with its Scots cousin **yerk** (1509–1871, but not much since), is assumed to have arisen in imitation of the sound of a whip or rod. 'Jerking' has implied masturbation since the Victorian era, according to Barrère and Leland's 1889 *Dictionary of Slang*, but, like adolescence in its later stages, the word seems to have shed its obsession with self-abuse and can be applied to the wider world. The implication is never kind, of course, but **a jerk-off** could mean 'a simpleton' in 1968 or 'a fool' according to a 1970 edition of *Playboy*. These days, **a jerk** or a jerk-off is more likely to be a time-waster, especially in the States, than someone engaged in what used to be called **self-pollution**.

'Jerk', like many of our X-rated words, lost its impact after a while and began popping up in less threatening environments. Who knows: perhaps it's time for 'jerk' to return to the meaning it had 300 years ago – 'to lash with satire or ridicule'. There is no shortage of institutions that richly deserve the sting of its lash.

Meanwhile, 'jerk' should not be confused with the cured meat known as **jerky**, since this latter word comes from the Spanish-American verb *charquear*, which means either 'to dry' (of meat) or 'to carve up' (of a person). Hmm... There is also the Peruvian dialect word *charqui*, which means 'dried flesh, unsalted, in long strips'. It's hard to see how any confusion could arise between jerking off and laying out long slivers of tender meat, isn't it?

Pole-dancing

In 1992 the *Chicago Tribune* reported on 'girls soliciting, performing naked **pole dances** and erotic carnival tricks in the bars that blanket the area'. And yet, in October 2006, the *Guardian* newspaper reported that 'The country's biggest supermarket chain [Tesco] has upset parents by selling a pole-dancing kit in its toys section'. The BBC would evidently have approved, judging by this comment, made two years earlier: 'In recent years, pole dancing has been attracting a steady stream of women keen to improve their fitness, flexibility and have fun at the same time'.

Just a bit of fun? Fun and fertility, more like. Dancing around the **maypole**, as it was originally known, was originally a Germanic custom and has long inspired ambivalence among northern Europeans about what that pole represents. It combines springtime fun and a much older, darker, pagan-influenced adoration of the male member. Put it this way: if, instead of a maypole, there were a giant carved wooden phallus plonked down on the centre of village greens, would the churches, the girl guides and the morris dancers be so keen to endorse it?

Of course, there are theorists – or spoilsports – who deny the pagan or penis/pole connection, and insist that sometimes a pole is simply a pole, or a tree, but not a penis.[2] Whatever form the ceremony takes, though, it has long been a central feature of May Day celebrations, but evidence suggests that even some Victorians were growing weary of it, as this quotation from *Appletons' Journal* – a magazine devoted to literature, science and art – reveals: 'When next a **May-pole dance**, that long since worn-out and always wearisome affair, is introduced in a drama, the exasperated audience will rise *en masse* … and exterminate the May-pole.'

Our earliest reference to the May Day maypole is from 1529. Eighty years later, the royalist journalist John Crouch had already carved out a more ribald idea of it in his 1655 'newsbook' *Mercurius Fumigosus*: 'Wee'l Increase and Multiply, and may with any man. You may, indeed good Sir, you May, your May-pole stiff and strong.' That doesn't leave much doubt about how he viewed the pole.

Pole-dancing can be done with varying degrees of sensuality, and either fully clothed or butt-naked, but that isn't the key to the commercial success of, for example, the telescopic X-pole (with its own carrying case and nylon strap). For the fact is, to pole-dance your way to success, you need the sort of upper thigh muscles that would not look out of place on a bucking bronco rider, and the fitness industry has not been slow to spot the potential health benefits from the activity.

That's what pole-dancing has in common with its maypole ancestor. Raunchier aspects have been deliberately played down

---

2 If they're so confident, I dare them to tell a group of twelve-year-olds that the Latin for 'pine tree' is *pinus*.

in favour of something more wholesome. It used to be about crowning the Queen of the May, the embodiment of the Earth's energy. These days, no doubt helped by movie stars such as Angelina Jolie having their own poles installed at home, it's more about having well-toned bums and tums.

Wanking

Etymologically, **wanking** is a huge anti-climax. It gives the impression of having impeccable baggage from northern Europe, and we turn to the dictionary, expecting to find references to similar words such as *wenken*, Icelandic for 'to squeeze', or *wengen*, very Old German for 'to tug', or possibly the Old Norwegian *wanka*, meaning 'to stand up'. Alas, no such history exists. The word **wank** seems to have embedded itself in the (largely British) lexicon of self-abuse as recently as 1948, and is the bastard offspring of a Mr and Mrs Slang, according to Eric Partridge.

The *OED* doesn't support this comparison in any way, but we couldn't help our eyes wandering over to the noun **whang**, a 1536 variant of **thwang**, meaning 'thong' (see page 57). *Chambers English Dictionary* defines whang as 'a leather thong; a thick slick; a penis'. The *OED*'s last reference to it in this form is from Robert Louis Stevenson's *Travels with a Donkey in the Cévennes* (1879): 'With a glass, a whang of bread, and an iron fork, the table is completely laid'.

The next thing we know is that 'whang' has indeed morphed from a hunk of cheese into a penis. It sounds like an early feminist joke in reverse. 'Leave them horses alone or I'll cut your whang off' is a line from *Honey in the Horn* (1963), a novel of pioneer life in eastern Oregon by Harold Lenoir Davis, which drew a lot of praise at the time. In sightings since then, 'whang' has been used, mostly by admiring male writers, about well-endowed men.

Again, though, 'wanking' and its associates have turned a sort of corner. Granted, it's unlikely to turn into a euphemism for a bouquet of roses – although you never know with the English language – but it has developed a further array of meanings in recent years, beginning in 1970, when Peter Laurie's book *Scotland Yard: A Study of the Metropolitan Police* contained the unedifying comment that 'Fred's counsel is a fat wank'. The use of 'wank' as a synonym for 'rubbish' continues to this day, as do more recent coinages, such as 'Oh, do stop **wanking on**' – which is merely a request for someone to talk less. At this point it seems entirely appropriate to move on, though not before we pause to pay tribute to some of the proliferation of entries on the urbandictionary.com site for 'masturbation'. These include: **buffing the banana**, **holding your sausage hostage**, **jackin' the beanstalk**, **rounding up the tadpoles**, **spanking the frank** and on and on and on …

To wap

Amid the profusion of words for the sexual act these days, and despite marvelling at every college kid's eagerness to include his own well-rehearsed – physically and verbally – neologism on the latest list, it's also fascinating to wander back into the past to see which words have come into and then fallen out of fashion. One such is the verb **to wap**, evident around the year 1400, and with a meaning similar to throw or pull. Between 1567 and 1725 it was a slang term for **copulation**. We owe its first reference in this context to the irrepressible Mr Thomas Harman, a Kentish gentleman active during the sixteenth century. His one book was called *A Caveat or Warning for Common Cursitors, Vulgarly Called Vagabonds.* It was first published in 1566, and – from later copies – we know that Harman was a dab hand at chatting to many of the ne'er-do-wells and itinerants (frequently failing to distinguish between the two) who passed his door. Harman writes of a man who 'tooke his Iockam in his famble, and a wapping he went', which means something like, 'He took his penis in his hand and went away copulating (or jerking off)'. **Iockam**, incidentally, lingers on in the members-only area of the jockstrap.

The activity of **wapping** is not to be confused with Wapping, the part of London named after a Saxon called Wæppa, even though, given the area's dodgy reputation, it probably saw a fair amount of wapping over the years. Now, of course, since Rupert Murdoch moved his newspaper operation there, the area enjoys unrivalled respectability, especially the lorries driving bundles of the *Sun* and *News of the World* with headlines screaming 'What a **whopper**!' This word, marked 'colloquial or vulgar' by the *OED*, is defined in *Chambers Dictionary* as 'one who whops; anything very large, especially a monstrous lie'. It began its career in print in 1785, thanks to Captain Grose and the *Dictionary of the Vulgar Tongue*, when it meant 'a large man or woman'. To study it further, etymologists direct us towards the verb **to whop**, a variant of 'to wap'.

More recently, 'wap' went all upper case, in which style it stands for Wireless Application Protocol, an international standard for applications that allow you to connect to the Internet from your mobile phone or PDA (Personal Digital Assistant). WAP technology dates from 1997, though in some circles it is regarded, for various reasons, as a failure, leading to its rebranding as

Worthless Application Protocol. It would be nice to think that some wag had 'wap' in mind when WAP was conceived, or that if WAP achieves universal admiration, 'wap' will also return to fashion. Maybe that's too much to hope for. After all, it's not as if we have don't have enough words for having sex.

Porn

In between **porn** and **porny**, the *OED* stops at twenty-one other headwords along the way, like a British tourist taking a wide-eyed stroll on his first night in Amsterdam's red-light district. These entries include freakish one-offs from serial neologists such as James Joyce: he invented **pornosophical** in 1922 – it didn't catch on. Nor did Arnold Toynbee's **pornographico-devotional**, which means 'both pornographic and devotional'. ('Rare', comments the *OED*. Unique, you might wish to add.) Along the way, we are exposed to all the various shapes into which the word **pornographic** has been squeezed, the very earliest of which appears to be the noun **pornography**. This seems to have entered English from an 1800 French (who else?) treatise on *la pornographie*, though it took until 1842 to make the transition. How would we define it? The depiction of sexual subjects or activities 'in a manner intended to stimulate erotic rather than aesthetic feelings', says the *OED*. And then, of course, there's the **hard** or **soft porn** split, depending on how explicit the material is.

Sir William Smith's *Dictionary of Greek and Roman Antiquities* (1842) distinguishes between 'rhyparography, pornography, and all the lower classes of art'. **Rhyparography**: there's a word to conjure with. It's Greek in origin, as is 'porn', in fact. The Greek word *rhuparos* means 'filthy'. Add the verb

grapho (to write) and you have someone who writes about filthy things. Of course the Greeks didn't just write about sex: they drew it, painted it, sculpted it and – sometimes telling us more often than we need to know – had it. Turn it into English and you have 'a painter of mean or sordid subjects'. Rhyparography is a lovely-looking old word, first spotted in 1656, which did not survive into the twentieth century.

As for 'porn', it's from the Greek work *porne*, meaning 'prostitute' – simple as that. A *pornuboskos* was 'a brothel-keeper', and someone described as *pornophiles* was 'fond of prostitutes'. In English, 'porn', as the shortened form of 'porno-graphy', dates from 1962 (mentioned in the 10 May issue of *John o' London's Weekly*, where a character called the Captain, a seedy but not at all unsympathetic individual, is described as making a precarious living by writing 'porn'). It took 120 years for us to drop the -ography bit, but it is interesting that we are habituated enough with porn now to settle for the simple word. Here's hoping one day soon we'll all be into 'lexico', rather than having to spell out our passion for lexicography.

It's striking how many of these early references to pornography are taken from the world of classical Greece and Rome. It seems that Victorian scholars had quite enough on their hands weighing up what to do with the recently discovered treasures of Pompeii, and doubtless preferred to immerse themselves in that world, rather than pass comment on contemporary porno mores. Given the subsequent history of porn, from soft to hard – from rumpled knickers to aggrieved-looking mongrels – and given that distinction between material stimulating erotic rather than aesthetic feelings, it's interesting to see how pornography has turned something of a corner in recent years. Onlookers can see a hint of it in non-sexual writing, such as Kathryn Flett's description of the BBC's remake of *Dracula* – 'more **property porn** than an entire series of *Grand Designs*' – in the *Observer* newspaper in December 2006.

If you love reading cookery magazines, but prefer gazing at beautiful images of food to making it yourself, you are participating in **food porn**. If you like reading about exotic places rather than actually visiting them, you're indulging in **travel porn**. All tastes are catered for: **gastro porn**, **disaster porn**, **war porn**, even **weather porn**. The *OED* has been on to this trend since 1973, when an article in the *Journal of Pop Culture* mentioned **horror porn**. In fact, almost any activity that seduces its audience with glamorous images – emphasizing 'the sensuous or sensational aspects of a non-sexual subject' as the *OED* says – can now be said to have its own style of porn, and this may be where the word is going. Alongside this is the still depressingly rapid spread of **Internet pornography**.

Dogging

The verb **to dog**, as language buffs never tire of telling us, reveals a sizeable linguistic shift, made possible because English verbs had begun to shed themselves of their grammatical constraints from the time of Geoffrey Chaucer and onwards. In 1519 'to dog' (see page 92) meant what it still means: 'to follow closely and not a little menacingly'. These days the verb **to stalk** has partially supplanted it, though that has – or had – more obviously sexual undercurrents.

If you were a spy (or espie) in the seventeenth century, as a snippet from Randle Cotgrave's *Dictionarie of the French and English Tongues* (1611) shows, you would have indulged in 'ambushes, waylayings … treacherous dogging, of people'. The term was also applied to the sport of grouse-shooting, where dogs, rather than human drivers or beaters, were used to stir up the birds. (You can imagine the Royal Family and half the toffs in the country going to that kind of dogging.) A good **dogging moor**, in the first seventy or eighty years of the twentieth century, was a moor fit for this activity. What happened next?

What happened next has not yet been documented by the *OED*,[3] though if its lexicographers could get their hands on the network of closed-circuit TV cameras that is slowly tightening its grip on all aspects of life in Britain, they might begin to see how many people are engaging in semi-public sexual activities. This new form of alfresco sex is known as **dogging**. The BBC reported on it in September 2003: 'Dogging is an extension of "swinging" parties – and involves exhibitionist sex in semi-secluded locations such as car parks or country parks'.

----

3 The revised entry was being prepared as this book went to press.

It is indeed a strange mixture of back-door sexual exhibitionism, voyeurism and yet another excuse for forming a queue – an old English habit that takes going to the dogs in quite a different direction. Like a cross between a cockfight and an orgy, it involves groups of people watching two others having sex. The Internet is used as a message-board, alerting people, very often at the last minute, about locations. An NHS team in Kent noticed a rise in hepatitis cases towards the end of 2002, and they put it down to dogging. It's interesting to note where the locations for illicit sex have moved to. It used to be a sea-front hotel – or its rustic and more romantic alternative, the shady copse. These days it's supermarket car parks and motorway lay-bys. *O tempora!* as the Roman orator Cicero observed in 63 BC, *O mores!*

While the health risks are worrying hospitals, the etymology is causing concern to wordsmiths. Is it called 'dogging' because dogs have no objection to **shagging**[4] in public? Or is it playing with the idea of the innocent and morally unobjectionable practice of taking the dog for a walk? Maybe it's linked to the sense of tracking, which dogs have been doing since at least the sixteenth century. After all, aren't contemporary **doggers** meant to follow a trail that ends with them watching couples making out in a car or on the ground?

Wherever 'dogging' comes from, it will be interesting to see where it goes now that the cat – so to speak – is out of the bag. The activity received an intense blast of publicity in March 2004, when the former England international footballer Stan Collymore was pursued – dogged, in fact – by reporters from the *Sun* until he is said to have admitted: 'I've been to dogging sites maybe a

---

4 The first recorded 'shag' dates from 1788. Even if you weren't aware of its origins, this reeks of the farmyard: you can really imagine two shaggy-haired dogs getting down and having a good rut.

dozen to fifteen times and, yes, I have taken part and had sex'.
Whether it was preferable to being a Five Live match comment-
ator – since he was sacked from that post forthwith – poor
Mr Collymore hasn't so far revealed in public.

It seems likely that the publicity generated for dogging
will lead to its gaining greater acceptance, since it was always
destined to take place on the threshold of society. An explosion
of cold sores and hepatitis infections will tell its own story, but
the questions that bother *Balderdash* wordhunters – would
'word-doggers' have made a greater impact? – is whether outdoor
sex enthusiasts felt more inclined to indulge in this activity once
it had a name, and whether the welter of references in the media
has legitimized or even encouraged the practice. 'There's nothing
wrong with dogging: it's in the dictionary.' Is that really how
social licence works?

Fluffer

The word **fluff** is surely one of the skimpiest words in the
language. It feels like a gentle breeze could simply knock it over.
Just the thing, in other words, to describe 'downy particles that
separate from dressed wool', or 'the fluff of a peach' as Captain
Francis Grose wrote in his 1790 *Provincial Glossary*. Given its
wispy nature, it is perhaps not surprising to see the term **a bit
of fluff** used to describe a young girl in a little-known novel
called *Fluff-hunters*, written in 1903 under the pseudonym
'Marjoribanks'.

And there, as blameless as the skin of a peach, matters would
have rested, had not the world of filmed pornography ruptured
the purity of this innocent tableau. The *OED*, in a draft entry
dated September 2004, defines **fluffer** thus: 'In the pornographic

'Sorry, I think I fluffed my entrance.'

film industry: a person employed to stimulate a male actor to ensure that he has an erection when required. Hence: a person employed to prepare or warm up an audience for another act.' The first quotation to back this up is from a 1979 issue of the magazine *Screw*: 'One of the black guys was nearly demanding a warm-up, some contrivance to stiffen his johnson before the main event … "No fluffers," screamed someone.'

It is rather extraordinary, isn't it, that this sordid term is sharing the same pages – well, online pages – with some of the noblest and most uplifting sentiments ever translated into words, from Shakespeare to the King James Bible and onwards? It illustrates the *OED*'s absolutely rapacious appetite for all words. One might almost say they're promiscuous for words, but they're not: they're simply wholly and non-judgementally democratic. There is no censorship or discrimination, no matter how unsavoury.

Fluffers were also the people employed by London Underground to clean the railway system at night. They were 'the char-ladies of the Underground' as a Pathé film from the 1950s referred to them, flossing the railways lines with knives and brushes. Perhaps they got their name because of the huge amount of fluff and dust – and human hair – that was sucked into the tunnels every day.

The verb **to fluff** was by no means lacking in experience before. It has been around, one way or another, since 1790, but it had never known times like these. It could mean 'to pant' or 'to knock the breath out of someone', as if literally to wind them. To these nineteenth-century meanings could be added a rare sense that ran similar to 'flash in the pan': a **fluff in the pan** (1825) was what you did to gunpowder to cause it to ignite. So there at least the word had a bit more backbone.

To fluff someone in the nineteenth century also referred to the practice – evidently quite common among railway clerks – of giving passengers the wrong change, presumably in those scrambled moments when the train was pulling into the station and people were thinking more about racing to catch it than whether they had been given the right change. (I might suggest a link with 'to fleece', but I'd be alone.)

If you mis-speak your words on stage or on air you have **fluffed your lines** – a meaning extant since 1936. 'Fluff', at its most fly-away, came to mean something utterly insubstantial, as in this 1906 letter from the Bloomsbury Group art critic Roger Fry: 'Having to see reporters … and being careful to give them a lot of fluff with nothing inside it.'

You could also, of course, **fluff your hair**, which may have influenced – ironically of course – the porn usage, since the porn world's fluffer is, albeit contemptibly, something of a make-up artist.

And all the actions involved in these centuries of cleaning, scrubbing, primping, rejuvenating and lifting somehow coalesce on the set of a **blue**[5] movie, converging and dancing upon the tip of a man's penis in a series of pampering manoeuvres carried out by someone who, one at least hopes, might find themselves referring rather vaguely to a certain period on their CV in years to come.

It's notable how, perhaps because of its somewhat arcane job specifications, the fluffer of the porn industry has not pushed the other types of fluffing out of the way. Fluff, for all its apparent flimsiness, is not as insubstantial as you might think.

---

5 'Blueness', as first described by the writer Thomas Carlyle in 1840, can refer to indelicacy or indecency, perhaps because of its connection to blood or the equally sensual colour purple. 'Blue-blooded' dates from 1853: 'The old blue-blooded inhabitants of Cranford', in the novel *Cranford* by Mrs Gaskell. Blue can go either way, it seems, from classy and upmarket to seamy and downmarket.

Endword

The First *Balderdash & Piffle* Wordhunt

In June 2005 *The Oxford English Dictionary* and the BBC jointly launched a national Wordhunt, asking the public to seek out ante-datings and information about the origins of fifty words and phrases. Although this was a twenty-first-century campaign, conducted largely online, it was very much in the traditions of the *OED*'s original 'Appeal to the English-speaking and English-reading Public' back in April 1879.

More than 1500 emails and letters arrived in response to the BBC/*OED* Wordhunt. Many of the correspondents were utterly convinced they knew an earlier use of a word, or offered attractive, exotic and sometimes downright implausible theories as to its origins. All fascinating stuff, but not always of much help in rewriting the dictionary. However, among these tall tales and adamant correspondents were hundreds of offerings giving clear evidence of the sought-after words in books, newspaper articles, sheet music, records, TV programmes and handwritten diaries. These were used to make the six programmes of the BBC2 series *Balderdash & Piffle*, first broadcast in January 2006. Each programme focused on a different letter of the alphabet – P, M, N, C, S and B being the favoured ones.

A tribunal of senior editors from the *OED* (associate editor Peter Gilliver, etymologist Tania Styles and chief editor John Simpson) sat in judgement on the submissions of wordhunters. And over the course of the series, they agreed to revise a whopping twenty-one entries in the dictionary – all thanks to the new evidence.

While the series was broadcast (to an average audience of 2.7 million viewers), 4500 more emails came flooding in. The quality of the evidence supplied by this ever-growing band of keen wordhunters was such that the BBC sprang into action and commissioned a one-off follow-up programme, *Balderdash & Piffle – The Results Show,* to demand further action by the judges. Yet more rewrites followed – twenty-two of them to be exact – fourteen of which were for words and phrases that had stumped the original wordhunters.

Perhaps the most distinctive feature of the first *Balderdash* Wordhunt was the nature of much of the evidence we were sent. While the *OED*'s editorial teams and reading programme members have ready access to mainstream books and newspapers, that doesn't always help them. Many modern words and phrases are first recorded in sitcoms, football fanzines, local newspapers and classified advertisements, and, increasingly, online. Our wordhunters could lay their hands on this type of material where professional lexicographers could not. They also offered handwritten evidence, which presented a challenge to the dictionary's bibliographers. How reliably was it dated? How could future scholars consult it? Ultimately, thanks to *Balderdash* wordhunters (now honoured on the 'Wordhunt Wall of Fame' on the *OED*'s website), thirty-five of the *OED*'s 300,000 or so entries have had a makeover. And here they are.

Balti

Thanks to *Balderdash & Piffle*, there is now a corner of the *OED* that is forever Balsall Heath in Birmingham. Journalist Tazeen Ahmad found a perfectly preserved copy of a magazine called *The Balsall Heathan*, dated July 1982, which contained an otherwise unremarkable advertisement for a restaurant boasting

'Specialists in Kebab, Tikah, Balti Meats, Tandoori Chicken and all kinds of curry'.

That was a two-year ante-dating of **balti** for the *OED*, and as crucial as garam masala is to a curry chef. What it didn't settle, however, was the question of where the balti was born. Word-hunter Harry Bell watched the programme and also came forward with evidence from 1982, of 'Balti mince' on a special menu for a sci-fi fans convention – held not in Birmingham, which has long claimed paternity of the balti, but Newcastle! In any event, it seems that one place the balti definitely didn't originate in is the Indian subcontinent.

Beeb

Apart from **Auntie**, the most common nickname for the BBC is the **Beeb**. The *OED* calls it a 'colloquial contraction', but evidence of its use in print hadn't come any earlier than the 1970s. Now surely someone must have been using it earlier than that? In fact, Jeff Walden of Caversham came across an interview with the colourful and eccentric disc jockey Kenny Everett. Here, surely, was a man who wouldn't hesitate to use the affectionate colloquial contraction. And his hunch was right. Everett obliged in an *Evening News* interview from September 1968. The journalist writes, 'He gives the impression he doesn't worry about anything: least of all "Beeb", as he calls the BBC.' Those inverted commas suggest that the nickname was pretty new back then.

Boffin

The boffins at the *OED* – splendid chaps that they are – had two senses of **boffin** in the dictionary, dated just a few years apart. The first sense, from 1941, is 'an "elderly" naval officer'. The second sense is 'a person engaged in "back-room" scientific or technical research', first encountered in *The Times* in 1945 with reference to the early pioneers of radar. But surely, historian and uber-boffin Felipe Fernandez-Armesto asked in *Balderdash & Piffle,* the word has now moved on, being the denigration of choice to describe people who are frightfully clever but can scarcely tie their shoelaces. The *OED* judges were persuaded, and have unveiled a whole new sense for 'boffin': '3. *Brit. colloq.* In weakened use: an intellectual, an academic, a clever person; an expert in a particular field; *esp.* such a person perceived as lacking practical or social skills. Cf. EGG-HEAD *n.*'

Bog-standard

Mark Edwards from Coventry may have had to put up with years of mickey-taking (see page 79) for not disposing of his large pile of *Personal Computer World* magazines, but in the end the clutter proved its worth. The *OED*'s first use of the term **bog-standard** was dated 1983: *Balderdash & Piffle* just knew there had to be something earlier, and, more importantly, so did Mark Edwards. He rifled through his pile and dug out a copy from 1978 that had the very phrase we were looking for.

However, Gerald Dawson in Bristol could go not one, but five years better. His example, culled from a review of an Escort racing car in *Hot Car* magazine, is dated to October 1968, so we've pulled the bar back a whole fifteen years. What a Triumph! (Or an Escort.)

Bomber jacket

If the US-style **bomber jacket** was based on American flying jackets from the Second World War, why was there no textual evidence earlier than 1973? Is it possible that, as the *OED* suspected, the term was applied retrospectively, and only after they became a fashion item?

In a classic case of 'The Yanks are coming', Bill Mullins in the USA came to our rescue. He found an advertisement from the *Los Angeles Times* for December 1940 – 'This three-piece outfit for junior consists of a bomber jacket, drape trousers, and squadron cap' – which ante-dates the original front-runner by thirty-three years! Bill: Britain salutes you.

Bonk

The *OED* couldn't find anyone who had been **bonking**, sexually speaking, prior to the year 1975. Despite much frantic activity, *Balderdash* wordhunters could find no earlier reference to it either. But it was more than a consolation prize when Gerald Donovan from Bristol found us an ante-dating for the noun **bonk**, as in the sound of being hit on the head (see page 24). He uncovered this in a risqué little number from 1934 called *Cannibal Quest* by Gordon Sinclair, subtitled 'The Racy Record of a Cannibal Quest from Sydney to Afghanistan'.

Chattering classes

The originator of the term **chattering classes** was thought to be the journalist and quintessential chatterer Clive James. But we were sure that a certain section of the middle classes had been described in that way before 1985. In fact, it fell to a former editor of the *Spectator*, Frank Johnson, to offer one of his own cuttings from James Goldsmith's short-lived *Now!* magazine, dated March 1980. Sadly, Frank Johnson died in December 2006. He will be remembered as one of the wittiest journalists of his day, and could have few better memorials than to be quoted in *The Oxford English Dictionary*.

Cocktail

The model Jerry Hall went searching for the origin of **cocktail** in New Orleans, just days before Hurricane Katrina hit. Despite her efforts to find the answer at the bottom of a martini glass, she couldn't push the date back. After the broadcast, news came in from wordhunter David Barnhart of a sighting of 'cocktail' that predated the *OED*'s first 1806 reference. As a result, we now have evidence from a New Hampshire newspaper called *The Farmer's Cabinet*, dated April 1803: 'Drank a glass of cocktail – excellent for the head … Call'd at the Doct's … drank another glass of cocktail …' Not such good news for the bicentenary celebrations of the cocktail, which were held in 2006, but we hope the world of mixology will forgive us.

Codswallop

It feels like it's been around for as long as other silly-sounding words, such as 'nincompoop' or 'popinjay'. In fact, **codswallop** is a twentieth-century newcomer. The *OED*'s first recorded use of it was from a 1963 correspondent who wrote to the *Radio Times* to complain that some programmes were rubbish. (No doubt they'd revise their opinions if they experienced today's output.)

Thanks to Joe Cunningham, a resident of Canada, we have an earlier citation from those kings of radio and TV comedy – who never wrote a word of codswallop in their lives – Ray Galton and Alan Simpson. The extract is from a 1959 script for *Hancock's Half Hour*. Sid James is, as usual, upbraiding Hancock: 'Don't give me that old codswallop. You were counting your money.'

There is no proof, says the *OED*, for the attractive but sketchy story that the name came from a real person, a British soft drinks manufacturer called Hiram Codd (1838–87), who produced several designs for mineral water bottles in the 1870s, and that it became a derogatory term used by beer drinkers to refer to soft drink. No, says the *OED* severely: no evidence for that.

Cool

Jazz saxophonist Courtney Pine went hunting for the roots of **cool**, as a term of approval or sophistication, certain that it must pre-date 1948. Sure enough, thanks to a tip-off from wordhunter Kate Carter from Putney, he found a reference to that kind of 'cool' in a short story of 1933 by Zora Neale Hurston, a writer who recorded dialect terms from the exclusively African-American Florida town she grew up in.

But that was just the start. Alan Dobson of Sheffield put his hand on the lyrics to a travelling minstrel show performed by white people in black-up with the very of-its-time title *Evah Darkey Is a King*. That was from 1902, and included the line 'de way we dress is cooler'. And then the phrase 'Dat's cool!' was found as an interjection from as far back as 1884. Dat is indeed cool – a sixty-six year ante-dating for such a ubiquitous and magnificent word.

Full monty

This has to be one of the most mythologized phrases ever used. Did it arise from Field Marshal Montgomery or Montague Burton the tailors? The most recent citation was 1985: *Balderdash* word-hunters resolved to do better. The *OED* had – and still has – a slight preference for the term as a shortening of Burton, the tailor: the Montgomery theory is described as 'popular but unsubstantiated'. The *OED*'s damning verdict on the latter was that 'the sheer variety of often vague, purely anecdotal, and mutually contradictory explanations for the connection – ranging

from his wartime briefing style to his breakfasting habits –
renders this less credible'.

Balderdash may not have settled the argument, but wordhunters did send in several references to fish and chip shops
called The Full Monty from before 1985, which made it into the
OED's revised etymology, albeit with a pinch of salt (and a dash
of vinegar). Could the 1982 edition of the Yellow Pages: Manchester
North (where these shops were listed) be the most boring cited
work in the entire *OED*? And that's saying something, since there
are 2,436,600 quotations.

Mackem

The word **mackem** has long been a nickname for a fan of
Sunderland Football Club, or more generally for someone who
lives in Sunderland or the Wearside. It recalls the days when ships
were made there and taken back for repairs (hence 'We mack
'em and we tack 'em'). Local radio DJ Mike Elliott was outraged
that the *OED* had no record of this word in between **mackelerage**
and **Mackenzie bean**, so he set out on a quest for the grail of
printed evidence. Answers came in thick and fast, and 'mackem'ly
as far back as 1980–1.

In fact, it was Jerome Borkwood of London who supplied the
earliest printed evidence of the word 'mackem'. It comes from –
what an irony! – *The Magpie*, a Newcastle United Supporters
Club fanzine. Now that Sunderland fans claim 'mackem' as their
word, it might be better for them to remain in denial that it was
probably coined by their arch-enemies.

Made-up

The term **made-up** is a regional expression for being happy,
originally from Ireland, and now distinctive of Liverpool. The

wordhunt for it led, via a dose of Beatlemania, to a first for the *OED*. Professor Stephen Fletcher of Loughborough University remembered 'made-up' from the mid-1960s, and tracked down its use to the wedding day of Ringo Starr to Maureen Cox on 11 February 1965. In an *ITV News* interview, Starr said, 'John and George were at the wedding, and they were made up, you know. They're happy.' Tania Styles of the *OED* enjoyed that: 'He's even glossing it,' she said excitedly.

This was the first time in the *OED*'s history that it had cited a TV interview, as opposed to something scripted. And it's Ringo's eighth appearance in the *OED*: he'll be made-up about that too.

Management-speak

It seemed to fall naturally to Ian Hislop, the editor of *Private Eye*, to investigate **management-speak**, which (curiously) hadn't yet made it into the *OED*. The *Sunday Times* dates the phrase back to 1986, and *Balderdash* submitted its own definition to the dictionary's top team: 'a load of balderdash and piffle, spouted by self-important morons in an attempt to feign intelligence and authority, has the effect of rendering the most simple concepts completely unintelligible; the bastard son of *newspeak*, coined by George Orwell for the lies of corrupt politicians'.

The *OED* team seemed reluctant to buy that wholesale, so they had a bit of a think and came up with: 'a form of language considered typical of business managers or consultants, esp. in being obfuscatory, needlessly complex, or empty of useful meaning'. Well, that's their job, after all.

Mark/Gas mark

These unlikely candidates actually provoked the greatest number of entries to the first Wordhunt. It seems that cookery books are the one type of publication that people never throw away. We were seeking uses prior to 1963, and entries for both **Mark** (noun 1, sense 34) and **Gas mark** – both used in relation to ovens – came in by the ladleful. For 'Gas mark' the first prize was won by *The Berkshire Cookery Book*, published by the Berkshire Federation Women's Institute, and the date was pushed back to 1958. We trust that their 2007 jam output will be of a particularly high quality. For 'Mark', the alarmingly titled *Radiation Cookery Book* from 1929 took the honours.

Minger

As the *Balderdash* Wordhunt heated up, the *OED* judges were put to the test on the type of material they would accept, especially in the case of **minger**. This rather rude word for 'an ugly or unattractive person, especially a woman' had been dated at 1995, but that was before *Balderdash* was inundated with poetry from teenage Goths.

The trump card came in from Clare Washbrook of Derbyshire, who'd dug up her own teenage poetry-filled note-books. One, entitled 'They Ming Therefore They Are', contained the lines, 'They bandy around the tag of minger/Slap it on teacher, pupil, parent, singer.'

The *OED* team wrestled long and hard over this one. Did this handwritten poem, albeit date-marked 1992, count as evidence? John Simpson, reigning chief of the *OED*, finally delivered his verdict: yes. Rejoice! (Note to Goths: that means 'be happy'. Try it some time.)

Moony

The moon has been a synonym for the buttocks since 1756, but **mooning**, or **doing a moony**, is of more recent vintage. Will

Weaver of Eastbourne overcame his natural embarrassment and showed us a comic that he and his childhood friend Ben, then aged ten, had created in 1990, replete with references to buttocks, **moonies** and other pre-teenage thrills. Respect also to the editors of the Leicester University student magazine *Ripple* for re-creating an attack by 'The Moonie Squad', in which a lecture-hall is invaded by a gaggle of students who run in, expose their buttocks and run out. This activity was first glimpsed in print in 1987. Some students are still in therapy.

Mullered

The trouble with words for drinking is that they don't tend to come up in a situation where one is armed with pen and sober enough to use it, so written evidence is often thin on the ground. One such is **mullered**, a word for 'drunk' that the *OED* sought before 1995.

Our wordhunters must have been too busy getting mullered to better this, but then Paul Davies found a reference to another sense of the word, meaning 'to destroy or comprehensively beat another team on the sports field'. This came from *All Played Out* written by Pete Davies just after the 1990 World Cup, and beating (mullering?) the *OED*'s first entry by three years. As Davies wrote, 'It had been a dreadful game. Macca asked Gazza, had he heard? – they were getting "mullered" back home…'

Gazza is, sadly, now more familiar with both senses than he was in 1990.

Mushy peas

As most people know, **mushy peas** are a northern delicacy. Not to everyone's taste, perhaps, but whatever you think of their nutritional value, we were sure wordhunters had encountered them before 1975. In fact, we might have known that Roy Clarke, writer of *Last of the Summer Wine* and identifier of so many northern traits, would have bettered that, or indeed battered that, as he did in 1973, with a serving of fish and chips.

One group of hopefuls felt that it could do better – but, failing to find any evidence, decided to make it up. These scoundrels, who shall remain anonymous, produced a *Guide to Tenby* (Pembrokeshire) from 1950. On closer inspection, the cover turned out to have been Photoshopped (yes, that's in the *OED*) to include not only the fake date, but also the term 'mushy peas' itself. Nice try, chaps, but we weren't fooled! It just shows the lengths people are prepared to go to in order to gain *OED* immortality.

Ninety-nine/'99'

We asked Daniela Nardini, whose family have connections with the catering business, to try to find out why a '99' ice cream is so called. If we'd known the controversy that it would unleash, we might never have gone there. Ante-dating it from 1977 to 1935, thanks to a price list in Cadbury's archives, was the easy bit. It was exploring pre-war ice-cream history that turned things ugly. The Arcari family, purveyors of fine ice cream from 99 Portobello High Street in Edinburgh since the 1920s, said they invented it. But so did the Dunkerleys from 99 Wellington Street in Gorton, and Marino Bianco from Barrow-in-Furness. Not to mention two other ice-cream dynasties.

To complicate matters, what exactly was a ninety-nine originally? This is an important matter for a historical dictionary like the *OED*. The definition as 'an ice-cream cone made with soft ice cream with a stick of flaky chocolate inserted into it' would no longer suffice. Thanks to *Balderdash*, there was now also evidence of '99' meaning a short Cadbury's flake (on its own, without ice cream or cone); a sandwich of ice cream and wafers with flake in the middle (but no cone); and, most challenging of all, a cone (manufactured by Askeys from 1937) called the '99', despite the absence of either ice cream or flake! All of these needed to be encompassed in the new post-*Balderdash OED* definition.

As to why it's called a ninety-nine, the arguments continue. The *OED* judges were persuaded to distance themselves from suggestions that they had previously quoted uncritically – 'that something really special or first class was known as "99" in allusion to an elite guard of ninety-nine soldiers in the service of the King of Italy'. But they were unpersuaded by several *Balderdash* wordhunters' ingenious suggestion that the letters IC stand not only for ice cream, but also – and here's the clever bit – that they make the number ninety-nine in roman numerals. Nice theory, said the *OED* top brass, licking their lips. But it wasn't good enough to think of the answer first and then work your way back.

Nip and tuck

The September 2003 *OED* entry for **nip and tuck** reads: 'minor cosmetic surgery, especially for the tightening of loose skin' and comes from 1980. US-based wordhunter Katherine Flynn thought this was showing its age a bit, though, so she got out her scalpel and took it back to 1977. Result: it looks years older, which is just how ante-dating ought to look.

Nit comb

Where would the nit nurse be without a fine **nit comb**? In the process of tracking down the former, we also improved the *OED*'s entry for the latter. Fiona Bourne from the Royal College of Nursing in Edinburgh came up with a citation from 1917, in the *British Journal of Nursing*, beating the previous reference by twenty-six years. Job well done, we thought. But proving that nits have been irking us for a very long time, the *OED* has subsequently rooted out a 1662 quote – from Giovanni Torriano's *Proverbial Phrases*. 'To enter into the Nit-comb, *viz.* to sift and examine strictly and impartially, sparing none'. This reads as if it's lifted from the *OED*'s own mission statement. We were proud of our ante-dating, but a further 255 years really is astonishing.

Nit nurse

A **nit nurse** is a colloquial British term for 'a school nurse who periodically checks children's hair for lice'.

The first recorded use of 'nit nurse' in the *OED* was from the *Guardian* in January 1985. But since this said, 'Whatever happened to the nit nurse?', it seemed manifestly to miss the itchy spot by several decades. Anton Dil of Milton Keynes scratched his head and found a reference to 'nit nurse' from a 1942 copy of *The Lancet*. But once you find one, you have to deal with the whole damn lot ...

Nutmeg

There may not be a lot of footballers who know this, but a **nutmeg** is actually 'the hard, oval, aromatic kernel of the seed of the evergreen tree *Myristica fragrans*'.

The usage known to most Premiership players (not, it would be fair to say, usually avid *OED* readers) is of a football manoeuvre in which the ball is cheekily played between an opposing player's legs (see also 'flip-flop', page 52). Author Giles Milton went on a surreal journey, aided by the hallucinogenic properties of nutmeg, to try to better the *OED*'s first reference.

It was Michael Parkinson who came to the rescue. Delroy Gayle of London spotted a reference in his biography of George Best – a player who certainly drifted past a few opponents in his time – from 1975. Best, ever obliging, even glosses the phrase himself: 'I love taking the piss out of players too. Like "**nutmegging**" them. That's sticking it between their legs and running round them.'

Pass the parcel

This game must have been doing the rounds at children's parties for donkey's years, but whereas people have been pinning the tail on the donkey since 1887, paper evidence for **pass the parcel** as the name of a game wasn't unwrapped earlier than 1967. In the rush to clean the room afterwards, it all seemed to have been swept away. *Balderdash* got it back to 1953, but the *OED* was worried about that citation because all the people playing seemed to be grown-ups.

Step forward Vivian Clear (née Smith), who was sure she'd written a story about the game in 1955 when she was all of seven and a half. She consulted her carefully preserved exercise book and there it was – 'Then the party began. Molly, who always had good ideas said to everyone "Should we have pass the parcel?" "That's what we're going to play," said Mr. Brown.' Vivian can now lay claim to being the youngest contributor to the *OED*. The dictionary now says 'V. Smith *Bk. about Browns* (MS story) (O.E.D. Archive) xxi. 46.' If you didn't know otherwise, you'd think it was a reference to some classic of English literature.

Phwoar

Most of us probably know what **phwoar** implies, but how many of us could define it? It's a word that positively begs for an exclamation mark afterwards, as the *OED* acknowledges: 'an enthusiastic expression of desire, approval, or excitement, especially in regard to sexual attractiveness: "cor!" "wow!"' But who first wrote it down? Naturally, *Carry On …* aficionado Graeme Johnston went to the spiritual home of the word, *Carry On Doctor* (1967), but the *OED* team was not convinced whether a wiggling Barbara Windsor had elicited the comment 'Phwoar!' or, as typed in the script, 'Cor!' from the man under the car.

More satisfying, though, was the ante-dating of the word from 1980 (an entry in *Viz* comic) to *c*.1976. Why only *circa* and not exactly 1976? Because the citation came from the autograph book of Michele Grange, formerly of Scunthorpe, and the remark was made about a very shapely pair of legs belonging to her school gym teacher: 'We *love* Mr Blackburn's legs. Phwor! Cor! Wow!!! Phew! Get Em Off!' This entry caused considerable discussion within the *OED* trinity: could they really accept a teenager's autograph book? An affidavit from Michele finally swung it, and her autograph book has now gained lexicographical immortality, referred to in the *OED* as '*MS Inscription* in *Autograph Bk.*' But given the unusual circumstances, the *OED* felt it safer to make the date *c*.1976.

Ploughman's lunch

The delightfully specific definition of **ploughman's lunch** is: 'cold snack, usually including bread, cheese, and pickle, and frequently served in a public house at lunch-time'. But the *OED* had found no evidence for it before 1970. There is a citation from 1837 regarding a **ploughman's luncheon**, but this wasn't eaten in pubs, and hardly ever included pickled onions, so it was ring-fenced with square brackets in the *OED*.

One wordhunter found a reference to a **ploughboy's lunch** from a 1958 copy of *The Times*, which was close – but not quite close enough to cut the mustard (or pickle). It fell to *Balderdash*'s own crack research team to uncover some minutes at the National Archives from a meeting of the English Country Cheese Council in 1960, referring to 'Ploughman's Lunch Showcard[s]' and proving that, far from being traditional fayre, the ploughman's lunch was the clever invention of cheese marketers. The big cheeses at the *OED* were duly impressed.

Pop one's clogs

There are many ways of referring to the act of dying (see page 166), of which to **pop one's clogs** is among the most colourful. It was David Johnson of Wembley who produced a copy of *Punch* from 1970 that couldn't have been plainer. 'He was forced to retire in 1933 after a disastrous Catholic/Protestant punch-up among the bugs,' reads the entry in that lightly witty style *Punch* was so renowned for throughout the 1970s and before. 'He's just popped his clogs.' This was a whole six-year improvement on what had come before.

Pull, on the

The phrase **on the pull** is defined in the *OED* as 'intending or hoping to attract a partner, especially for sex'. Until wordhunters got busy, the earliest evidence the *OED* had was from a 1988 copy of *Jackie* magazine: 'Poor Dave, on the pull, as usual'. But thanks to David Parkins and Geoffrey Cunnington, we were able to back-date it to a Dick Clement and Ian La Frenais 1975 screen-play. Their film, released as *The Likely Lads*, included this line from one of Rodney Bewes's exhausted girlfriends: 'The answer to all your problems – look up the lads and go on the pull – isn't that the expression?' That's a massive thirteen-year ante-dating. Whoever said being a lexicographer didn't have pulling power?

Ska

The term **ska** had music-lovers reaching for their old 45s, which is fine because that's what most music-lovers love doing anyway. Poet Benjamin Zephaniah's explorations took him – where else? – to Jamaica, where he eventually tracked down the word in a copy of the *Gleaner* newspaper from 1964, ante-dating the *OED*'s previous first citation of 'ska' by a precious six months.

London-based record collector Dave Edwards went one better, digging out an Island Records recording from 1963 by saxophonist Tommy McCook with the title on the label 'Ska-ba'. Thanks to this, the *OED* was able to issue an improved etymology, suggesting that ska was 'probably imitative of the distinctive guitar sound typical of this music'.

Smart casual

The challenge for wordhunters here was to find a reference to **smart casual** earlier than the *New York Times* in 1945. They responded, and lo and behold, 'smart casual' has been traced even further back in the annals of fashionable acceptability, to a 1936 advertisement from the *Toronto Daily Star*. In fact, an even earlier use – from the *Davenport* (Iowa) *Democrat & Leader* in 1924 – was found, but the *OED* remained sceptical that it was exactly the right sense, and put it in square brackets – the lexicographical equivalent of purgatory.

Snazzy

A bit passé these days, but **snazzy** was *the* word to describe something stylish and attractive throughout the 1950s and 1960s. The first reference in the *OED* was from 1932; could word-hunters do any better? The *OED* defines it as 'excellent, attractive; classy, stylish, flashy', but, apart from saying it comes from the United States, gives its origin as 'unknown'. We pulled it back by one year, to the *Los Angeles Times* of 1931. This was spotted by eagle-eyed Bill Mullins (he of earlier 'bomber jacket' fame). Only one year, but every day counts. Snazzy work, Bill.

Something for the weekend

Certain phrases slip through the net, especially when they refer to our foibles and sexual antics. We were in no doubt that **something for the weekend** predated 1990, but finding documentary evidence proved unusually difficult. *Balderdash* word-hunters Michael Glass, Timothy Freeman, James Barrett and Mrs E. Blatherwick provided helpful evidence that the *OED* drew on in composing the first-ever entry for this word. The earliest reference came, funnily enough, from a 1972 Monty Python record, which referred to 'a herd of zebras visiting the same chemist to ask for something for the weekend'. But of course.

Square one, back to

This was one of those phrases where we were berated by numerous wordhunters for our apparent ignorance – many were utterly convinced that its origins lay in BBC radio commentary of the 1930s, with its numbered grid system for following football and rugby matches. However, it was **back to square one** with them, for none was able to furnish us with any evidence of this.

Nor, in fact, could anyone find a board game – a more likely origin of the phrase – where you really did go back to square one. In the end, American wordhunters Darren Hick and William C. Waterhouse trumped the *OED* by finding the phrase in a 1952 issue of the *Economic Journal*, so they definitely get another turn on the board.

Could do better ...

You might be able to trump any of the findings described in this section. You might also be able to make some progress with those words and phrases that, despite the best efforts of *Balderdash* wordhunters, still managed to get away. The search goes on. Can you trace any of them back to an earlier date? For those marked with an asterisk, the *OED* is also somewhat mystified about the word or phrase's origins.

Bouncy castle (1986)	**Naff*** (1966)
Crimble (1963)	**Nerd*** (1951)
Cyberspace (1982)	**Pear-shaped*** (1983)
Cyborg (1960)	**Pick and mix** (1959)
Minted (1995)	**Porky** (1985)
Mullet* (1994)	**Posh*** (1915)

Find out more about the series and join the Wordhunt at www.bbc.co.uk/balderdash

Visit *The Oxford English Dictionary* online at www.oed.com and explore the *OED*'s own *Balderdash & Piffle* section at www.oed.com/bbcwordhunt/

Further reading

SOME OF THE BIG HITTERS IN THE FIELDS OF LEXICOGRAPHY AND ETYMOLOGY

Brewer's Dictionary of Phrase and Fable (1923)
Chambers English Dictionary (1988)
Collins Concise Dictionary (2nd edition 1988)
J.A. Cuddon, *The Penguin Dictionary of Literary Terms and Literary Theory* (1977, 3rd edition 1992)
Fowler's Modern English Usage, revised by Sir Ernest Gowers (1965)
Funk's Standard Dictionary (1890 and subsequent editions)
Jonathon Green, *Slang Down the Ages* (1993)
Iona and Peter Opie, *The Lore and Language of Schoolchildren* (1959)
The Oxford English Dictionary (1st edition 1928, 2nd edition 1989, 3rd edition 2004)
Eric Partridge, *A Dictionary of Slang and Unconventional English* (1949)
Eric Partridge (ed.), *A Classical Dictionary of the Vulgar Tongue* by Captain Francis Grose (1931, original edition 1785)
Eric Partridge, *A Dictionary of Forces Slang* (1948)
Michael Quinion, *POSH* (2004)
Hugh Rawson, *A Dictionary of Invective* (1989)
Nigel Rees, *A Man About a Dog* (2006)
Nigel Rees, *A Word in Your Shell-like* (2006)
Tony Thorne, *Shoot the Puppy* (2006)
Sir Henry Yule, *Hobson-Jobson: Being a Glossary of Colloquial Anglo-Indian Colloquial Words and Phrases and of Kindred Terms* (1886)

OTHER WORKS CITED

Chapter One – *One sandwich short*
Joseph Alexander Baron in *From the City, from the Plough* (1948)
Albert Barrère and Charles Leland, *A Dictionary of Slang, Jargon and Cant* (1889)
W.H. Downing, *Digger Dialects* (1919)
W. Granville, *A Dictionary of Sailors' Slang* (1962)
Adam Hart-Davis, *Taking the Piss: The Potted History of Pee* (2005)
T.E. Lawrence, *Mint* (1935)
James A. Michener, *Tales of the South Pacific* (1946)
Harold Pinter, *The Birthday Party* (1959)

Chapter two – *Fashionistas*
Edward Fraser and John Gibbons, *Soldier and Sailor Words and Phrases* (1925)
John Galt, *The Provost* (1822)
James Joyce, *Ulysses* (1922)
David Lodge, *Ginger You're Barmy* (1962)
Sir Thomas Lodge, *A Fig for Momus* (1595)
Richard Lowe and William Shaw, *Travellers: Voices of the New-Age Nomads* (1993)

Chapter three – *Who were they?*
Joyce Cary, *Mister Johnson* (1939)
Geoffrey Chaucer, *The Canterbury Tales* (1386, 2003)
W.H. Downing, *Digger Dialects* (1919)
Stephen Fried, *Thing of Beauty: The Tragedy of Supermodel Gia* (1993)
Guinness Book of Records (1992)
Joseph Scott and Donald Bain, *The World's Best Bartender's Guide* (1998)
Sir Walter Scott, *Rob Roy* (1818)
Tony Thorne (ed.), *A Dictionary of Contemporary Slang* (1988)
Mark Twain, *Letters from Hawaii* (1866)

Chapter four – *Man's best friend*
C.L. Anthony, *Touch Wood* (1934)
William Bullein, *A Dialogue against the fever pestilence* (1564)
Thomas Carlyle, *Frederick the Great* (1864)
Thomas Cooper, *Thesaurus linguae Romanae & Britannicae* (1565-73)

J.S. Curtis, *The Gilt Kid* (1936)

Sir Arthur Conan Doyle, *The Hound of the Baskervilles* (1902)

William Horman, *Vulgaria* (1519)

Washington Irving, *A History of New-York from the Beginning of the World to the End of the Dutch Dynasty* (1809)

Charles Kingsley, *The Water Babies* (1863)

Peter Laurie, *Scotland Yard: A Personal Inquiry* (1970)

Maurice Levinson, *Taxi!* (1963)

Colin MacInnes, *To the Victors the Spoils* (1950)

Hippo Neville, *Sneak Thief on the Road* (1935)

George Puttenham, *The Arte of English Poesie* (1589)

Edward Topsell, *The History of Four-footed Beasts* (1607)

Edward Topsell, *The History of Serpents* (1608)

Dean Stiff, *The Milk and Honey Route: A Handbook for Hobos* (1931)

John Wainwright, *The Last Buccaneer* (1971)

William Wycherley, *The Plain-Dealer* (1676)

Chapter five – *Dodgy dealings*
Albert Barrère and Charles Leland, *Dictionary of Slang, Jargon, and Cant* (1889)

Alison Cross, *A Death in the Faculty* (1981)

W.S. Gilbert, *The Hooligan* (1910)

William Gillette, *The Astounding Crime on Torrington Road* (1928)

Louis E. Jackson and C.R. Hellyer, *A Vocabulary of Criminal Slang* (1914)

Lehmann Hisey, *Sea Grist: A Personal Narrative of Five Months in the Merchant Marine, a Rousing Sea Tale* (1921)

Thomas Keneally, *Schindler's Ark* (1982)

Lord William Pitt Lennox, *Fifty Years' Biographical Reminiscences* (1860)

Paul Tempest, *Lag's Lexicon: A Comprehensive Dictionary and Encyclopaedia of the English Prison To-day* (1950)

Andrew Wynter, *Our Social Bees: Or Pictures of Town and Country Life* (1860)

Chapter six – *Put-downs and insults*
Joan Aiken, *Black Hearts in Battersea* (1965)

Melvyn Bragg, *Without a City Wall* (1968)

Noel Coward, *Play Parade* (1939)

Joey Deacon, *Tongue Tied* (1974)

Thomas D'Urfey, *Wit & Mirth* (1719)

John Florio, *Worlde of Wordes* (1598)

Martin Handford, *Where's Wally?* (1987)

Thomas Hoccleve, *Letter to Cupid* (1402)

Gwyn Jones and Islwyn Ffowc Elis (eds) *Twenty-Five Welsh Short Stories* (1971)

Ben Jonson, *Poetaster* (1602)

John Lyly, *Maides Metamorphosis* (1600)

G.F. Newman, *Sir, You Bastard* (1970)

Roger Scruton, *Fortnight's Anger* (1981)

Roger Scruton, *A Short History of Modern Philosophy* (1984)

Peter Wildblood, *The Main Chance* (1957)

Henry Williamson, *The Patriot's Progress* (1930)

P.G. Wodehouse, *Right Ho, Jeeves* (1934)

P.G. Wodehouse, *Tales of St Austin's* (1904)

Joseph Wright, *The English Dialect Dictionary* (1898)

Chapter seven – *Spend a penny*
C.D.B. Bryan, *Friendly Fire* (1976)

Pierce Egan, *Real Life* (1821)

Germaine Greer, *The Female Eunuch* (1970)

Richard Head, *The Canting Academy* (1673)

Joseph T.J. Hewlett, *Parsons & Widows* (1844)

John C. Hotten, *A Dictionary of Modern Slang* (1874)

Aldous Huxley, *Time Must Have a Stop* (1945)

Samuel Johnson, *Dictionary of English* (1755)

Charles Johnstone, *Chrysal, or the Adventures of a Guinea* (1821)

Ben Jonson, *The Alchemist* (1616)

D.H. Lawrence, *Lady Chatterley's Lover* (1932)

H. Lewis, *Strange Story* (1945)

E. Lighter, *Historical Dictionary of American Slang* (1997)

Patrick Marnham, *The Private Eye Story* (1982)

George Melly, *Owning-Up* (1965)

Henry Miller, *Tropic of Cancer* (1934)

Nancy Mitford, *Pigeon Pie* (1940)

Vladimir Nabokov, *Invitation to a Beheading* (1960)

A *New Dictionary of the Terms Ancient and Modern of the Canting Crew* (1699)
Peter Paterson, *Tired and Emotional: The Life of Lord George-Brown* (1993)
Alexander Pope, *The Rape of the Lock* (1712–14)
Daniel Richler, *Kicking Tomorrow* (1993)
Sir Walter Scott, *Kenilworth* (1821)
George Bernard Shaw, *Geneva* (1938)
Albert R. Smith, *The Struggles and Adventures of Christopher Tadpole* (1847)
Laurence Sterne, *Tristram Shandy* (1759–67)
Sydney Tremayne (ed.), *The Trial of Alfred Arthur Rouse* (1931)

Chapter eight – X-rated
John Russell Bartlett, *Dictionary of Americanisms* (1860)
Randle Cotgrave, *Dictionarie of the French and English Tongues* (1611)
John Crouch, *Mercurius Fumigosus* (1655)
H.L. Davis, *Honey in the Horn* (1963)
E.M. Forster, *The Longest Journey* (1907)
Esther Freud, *Hideous Kinky* (1992)
Captain Francis Grose, *A Provincial Glossary* (1790)
Thomas Harman, *A Caveat or Warning for Common Cursitors, Vulgarly Called Vagabonds* (1566)
Peter Laurie, *Scotland Yard: A Study of the Metropolitan Police* (1970)
Rachel P. Maines, *The Technology of Orgasm* (1999)
'Marjoribanks', *Fluff-hunters* (1903)
Colin MacInnes, *Absolute Beginners* (1959)
Sir William Smith, *Dictionary of Greek and Roman Antiquities* (1842)
Robert Louis Stevenson, *Travels with a Donkey in the Cévennes* (1879)

Endword
Pete Davies, *All Played Out* (1990)
Elizabeth Gaskell, *Cranford* (1853)
Gordon Sinclair, *Cannibal Quest* (1934)
Giovanni Torriano, *Proverbial Phrases* (1662)

We have done our best to acknowledge all the authors of works cited and apologize for any omissions.

Index

Ace Ventura: Pet Detective 175–6
Ace Ventura: When Nature Calls 176
Adams, Fanny 72–3
Adams, George 72
Adams, Harriet 72
Adams, Lizzie 72
Addison, Joseph 79
Ade, George *Artie* 26, 27
adult 184
adult cinema 184
Aesop 94
African-American 15, 213
Agnew, Jonathan 157
Agnew, Spiro 115
Ahmad, Tazeen 208
Aiken, Joan *Black Hearts in*

Battersea 140
Alfred, King 161
all is bob 76
Allen, Woody 166
American Saturday Review 28
American Speech 28
Americanisms 28, 48, 124, 225
Anglo-French 18
Anglo-Indian Words and Phrases 129–30
Anglo-Norman 144
Anglo-Saxon 152
Anne, Queen 90
Annie Hall 166
anorak 37–9
anoraks 39

Anthony, C.L. *Touch Wood* 100
Appletons' Journal 194
Arabic 45
Arcari 218
Archbold: Criminal Pleading, Evidence and Practice 108
Aristophanes *The Birds* 31
arse 152–3
arsehole 134, 152–4
arseholed 179
Artful Dodger 110
Aryan 160
as happy as Larry 62
as mad as a gum tree full of galahs 29
as quickly as Jack

Robinson 62
Ascham, Roger 112
Askeys 219
asshole 152
at stool 173
at the bottle 181
Atlantic Monthly 15
Attenborough, David 96
Auden, W.H. 144
Austen, Jane *Emma* 164-5
Australian National
    Dictionary Centre 29
Australianisms 29, 44, 45,
    65, 79

B&D 189
bad dog 87
Bain, Donald *The World's
    Best Bartender's Guide*
    69
Baker, Frederick 73, 77
balaclava 35-6
Balderdash & Piffle 7, 9
    OED 207-8
Balfour, Arthur 76
ballocks 104
balm 20
balmy 20
Balsall Heathan 208-9
balti 208-9
Bangs, Lester *Psychotic
    Reactions* 102
barm 19
barmy 19-21, 145
barmy army 21
Barnhart, David 212
Baron, Joseph Alexander
    *From the city, from the
    Plough* 80
Barrère, Albert *Dictionary
    of Slang, Jargon and
    Cant* 73, 121-2, 192
Barrett, James 225
Bartlett, John Russell 186
basket case 28
bats 145
batty 145
BDSM community 189
Beano 64
Beaumont, Francis 30
bed 160-1
Bedlam 12
Bee Gees 152

bee's knees 104
Beeb 209
Bell, Harry 209
Belloc, Hilaire 93
Benchley, Robert 17
Bennett, Gordon 64, 66
Bennett, Henry Gordon 66
Bennett, James Gordon
    64-5
bent 109
berks 143
Berkshire Cookery Book
    216
Best, George 221
Bewes, Rodney 224
Bible 14, 59, 160, 177, 178,
    204
bird-brained 31
bit dodgy 109
bit of fluff 203
blackmail 116-18
Blackwell's magazine 36
bladdered 179
Blair, Tony 52-3, 110
Blatherwick, E. 225
blogmail 118
Bloody Mary 67-9
blue 206
Blue Peter 146-7
bob's your uncle 67, 74-7
bobbies 75-6
bobby's job 75
bodily functions 170
body bag 170
boffin 209-10
bog-standard 210
bollocks 104
bomber jacket 210-11
bonce 24
Boney M 152
bonk 24, 211
bonkers 24
bonking 211
Borden, Lizzie 63
Borkwood, Jerome 214
Boston Herald 124
Botham, Ian 157
bounce 24
bouncy castle 226
Bourne, Fiona 219-20
Boyz N the Hood 40
Bragg, Melvyn 154
    Without a City Wall 150

Breval, John Durant *The
    Play Is the Plot* 54
*Brewer's Dictionary of
    Phrase and Fable* 98
bring 192
British Journal of Nursing
    220
British Medical Journal 22
Broadus, Calvin Cordozar Jr
    103
Brockett, Linus B. 15
Brown, George 181-2
Brudenell, James 43
Bryan, C.D.B. *Friendly Fire*
    170
Bryson, Bill 98
bucket 168
bucket beam 169
Buckingham, Lord 90
buffing the banana 196
bulldog spirit 87
Bullein, William *A Dialogue
    against the fever
    pestilence* 94
bung 118-20
bunged 118
bung-hole 119
Burnham-on-Sea Gazette
    188
Burns, Robert 181
Burton, Montague 213
bust some booty 159
butt plugs 189
butterfly strap-ons 191
Byron, Lord 180
    Don Juan 172

Cadbury 218
call 175
call of nature 175-6
camel toe 45
Cameron, David 39, 52-3,
    126, 142
Campbell, Ignatius Roy
    Dunnachie 176
cant 113
Canting Academy 180
Carangi, Gia 34
cardigan 43
care-in-the-community
    25
Carlyle, Thomas 131, 206
    Frederick the Great 96

Carrey, Jim 175
Carry on Doctor 222
Carter, Kate 213
Cary, Joyce *Mister Johnson*
104
Casanova 159
cat's pyjamas 104
cat's whiskers 104
caught short 176
Caxton, William 115
Chambers Dictionary
47, 56, 94, 135, 150, 151,
197
Chappell, Greg 112
Chappell, Trevor 112
chattering classes 211
Chaucer, Geoffrey 94, 135,
185, 201
Canterbury Tales 136-7
Chicago Tribune 193
Cicero 202
Cincinnati Commercial
120
Clarke, Roy 218
Clash 26
*Classical Dictionary of the
Vulgar Tongue* 53, 76,
110, 114, 169, 197
Clear, Vivian 221
Clement, Dick 223
cockfighting 48
cocktail 212
Codd, Hiram 212-13
codswallop 212-13
Coleridge, Samuel Taylor 83
'Kubla Khan' 36
collateral damage 169-70
Collier's Weekly 186
Collins Concise Dictionary
42, 56, 94, 116, 126, 135,
151, 169
Collymore, Stan 202
combat fatigue 23
coming from behind
103
Common Dreams 170
Concise Oxford Dictionary
51
cool 213
Cooper, Thomas *Thesaurus*
97, 98
copulate 160, 164
copulation 196

Cotgrave, Randle 171, 201
could do better... 226
Coward, Noel *Play Parade*
150
Cowper, William 96
Cox, Maureen 215
crackers 145
crackpot 145
crap 174
creepiness 188
cretin 14, 15-17
crimble 226
Crippen, Dr 123
Crosland, Anthony 1812
Cross, Alison *A Death in the
Faculty* 116
Crouch, John *Mercurius
Fumigosus* 194
cuckold 31
cuckoo 30-1
Cunningham, Joe 212
Cunnington, Geoffrey 223
cunt 185
Curtis, J.S. *The Gilt Kid* 100
cut 180-1
Cuthbert, St 136
cyberspace 226
cyborg 226

D&S 189
D'Urfey, Thomas *Wit &
Mirth* 138
daffy 145
daft 145
Daily Chronicle 119
Daily Graphic 122, 123
Daily Mirror 24, 151
Daily News (UK) 20, 47
Daily News (US) 122
Daily Telegraph 25, 39, 187
Danish 19, 88, 138, 185
*Davenport Democrat &
Leader* 224
Davidson, David 39
Davies, Paul 217
Davies, Pete *All Played Out*
217
Davis, Harold Lenoir *Honey
in the Horn* 195
Dawson, Gerald 210
Deacon 147
Deacon, Joey *Tongue Tied*
146-7

deal or no deal 78
death 166
death in combat 169-70
dementia 12
derr 32
deviant 188
Dialect Notes 186
Dickens, Charles *Pickwick
Papers* 110
*Dictionarie of French and
English* 201
*Dictionary of
Americanisms* 186
*Dictionary of
Contemporary Slang*
38-9
Dictionary of English 18,
168
Dictionary of Forces Slang
24
*Dictionary of Greek and
Roman Antiquities* 198
*Dictionary of Modern
Slang* 174
Dictionary of Sailors' Slang
73-4
*Dictionary of Slang and
Unconventional English*
69, 74, 100, 103, 195
*Dictionary of Slang,
Jargon and Cant* 73,
121-2, 192
died 156
Digger Dialects 72
Dil, Anton 220
dildo 189, 190
dippy 145
disaster porn 200
dithering 145
Dixon, William 92
Dobson, Alan 213
dodginess 110
dodgy 108-11
dodgy back 111
dodgy dossier 110-11
dodgy geezer 110
dodgy motor 109
dog 86, 87-90
dog don't eat dog 98
dog does not eat dog 98
**dog does not eat a dog's
flesh** 98
dog-eared 95

dog-earing 96
dog eat dog 98–9
dog-end 95
dog-fight 88
dog-Greek 94
dog in the manger 94
dog knot 105
dog-Latin 94
dog leg 106
dog oogie 106
dog people 106
dog perch 106
dog poo sandwich 106
dog-rimes 94
dog roza 106
dog skidder 106
dog tubbing 105–6
dog's bollocks 87, 103–5
dog's breakfast 100–1
dog's chance 87
dog's dinner 86, 100–1
dog's prick 103
dogged 92–4
dogged determination 93
dogged harte 92
doggedness 94
doggerel 94–6
doggers 202
dogging 92, 106, 184, 201–3
dogging moor 201
doggish 102
doggone it 106
doggy business 105–6
doggy paddle 101–2
doggy (doggie) style 101–3
doghouse 87
dogs of war 89
dogsbody 106
doing a moony 216
Donovan, Gerald 211
doolally 21–2
doolally tap 21
doss 111
doss-house 111
dossier 111
Downing, W.H. 72
Doyle, Roddy 39
Doyle, Sir Arthur Conan
    Hound of the
    Baskervilles 90–1
Dracula 200

drain the spuds 171
dropped a bollock 104
drunk 178
drunkenness 178–9
duh 32
Dunkerley 218
durr-brain 31–2
Dutch 41, 88, 119, 167, 174

Economic Journal 226
Edmonds, Noel 78
Edwards, Dave 224
Edwards, Mark 210
Egan, Pierce Real Life 180
Elgin, Lord 27
Elliott, Mike 214
Elyot, Sir Thomas 112
Empire 149
Encyclopaedia Britannica 55
English Dialect Dictionary 151
Eskimo 37–8
Evah Darky Is a King 213
Evelyn, John 171
Evening News 209
Everett, Kenny 209
every dog has its day 87
extracting the michael 80

fall in love 164
Farmer's Cabinet 212
fashion-conscious 35
fashion industry 35
fashion journals 35
fashion-monging 34
fashionable 34
fashional 34
fashionate 34
fashionative 34
fashionist 34
fashionista 34–5
fashionly 34
Fellows, Graham 18
fetishism 187
51st State 104
Fisher, Samuel 78
Flemish 115
Fletcher, John 30
Fletcher, Professor Stephen 215
Flett, Kathryn 200

flip-flap 53
flip-flopping 53
flip-flops 52–3
Florio, John 94
    World of Wordes 138
fluff 203
fluff in the pan 205
fluff your hair 205
fluffed your lines 205
fluffer 185, 203–6
Flynn, Katherine 219
Foley, Larry
food porn 200
Foot, Michael 21
football bung 119
Forster, E.M. The Longest Journey 186
FourFourTwo 139
Fraser, Edward Soldier and Sailor Words and Phrases 22
Freeman, Timothy 225
French 17, 27, 46, 50–1, 53, 55, 56, 83, 171, 172
Freud, Esther Hideous Kinky 188
Fried, Stephen Thing of Beauty 34
Friedman, Kinky 188
friendly fire 170
Frisian 115, 119, 152
Fry, Roger 205
full monty 213–14
Funk, Charles Earle 121
    Funk's Standard Dictionary 127, 176
funkiness 188

G-spot 57
G-string 57–8
Galt, John The Provost 19
Galton, Ray 212
gas mark 215–16
Gaskell, Elizabeth Cranford 206
gastro porn 200
Gawd Almighty 64
gay sex 187
Gayle, Delroy 221
Gentleman's Magazine 83
German 8, 19, 88, 90, 93, 113, 121, 185
get it on 164

getting a bollocking 104
getting your leg over 157
Gibbons, John *Soldier and Sailor Words and Phrases* 22
Gilbert, W.S. *The Hooligan* 123
Gillette, William *Astounding Crime* 127
Gilliver, Peter 207
gipsy 126-7
Gladstone, William 76
Glass, Michael 225
Gleaner 224
Goddard, Henry 17
going belly up 159
going to bed with 157
going to the dogs 97-8
going to the toilet 171
Goldsmith, James 211
gone to the dogs 97-8
good dog 87
Gorblimey 64
Gordon Bennett 63-6
Gothic 15, 91
Gräfenberg, Ernst 57-8
Grange, Michele 222
Granville, W. *Dictionary of Sailors' Slang* 73-4
Gray, Charles 98
Greek 12, 14, 17, 56, 88, 90, 153, 156, 198, 199
Green, Jonathon 159
Greer, Germaine *The Female Eunuch* 162
Grimaldi, Joseph 147
Grimm brothers 93
Grose, Captain Francis 114 *Classical Dictionary of the Vulgar Tongue* 53, 76, 110, 169, 197 *Provincial Glossary* 203
Guardian 57, 193, 220
Guide to Tenby 218
Guinness Book of Records 65, 73
gyp 126-7

hair of the dog 106
half-seas 180
half-cut 180
half-seas-over 180
Hall, Jerry 212

Hancock's Half Hour 212
Hand & Heart 140
Handford, Martin *Where's Wally?* 151
hanging gardens of Babylon 45
hanging up your boots 167
hanky panky 159, 162-3
hard or soft porn 198
Harlequin Prince Cherrytop 192
Harman, Thomas *A Caveat for … Vagabonds* 196-7
Harper's Magazine 54, 113, 114
Harris, Robert 97-8
Hart-Davis, Adam *Taking the Piss* 81
have a dump 171
have it away 162
have it off 162
have sex 160
having it off 161-2
Head, Richard *The Canting Academy* 180
heeled 47
Hellyer, C.R. *Vocabulary of Criminal Slang* 126
Hemingway, Ernest 68
Henry VIII, King 67, 143
Heywood, John 96
Hick, Darren 226
hide the salam 166
hiding the salami 159
Hindley, Myra 63
Hisey, Lehmann *Sea Grist…Five Months in the Merchant Marine* 123
Hislop, Ian 215
Historical Dictionary of American Slang 166
hit skins 159
Hobart, G.V. 28
Hobson's choice 77-9
Hobson, Thomas 77-8
Hobson-Jobson: Anglo-Indian Words and Phrases 130
Hoccleve, Thomas 136, 178 *Letter to Cupid* 135
holding your sausage

hostage 196
hood 40, 122
hoodie 39-41
hoodlum 40, 120-2
hooley 123
Hooley's gang 122
hooligan 122-3
hooligan navy 123
hooliganesque 123
hooliganic 123
hooliganism 122
Horizon 147
Horman, William *Vulgaria* 92
hornswoggle 124
horror porn 200
Hot Car magazine 210
Hotten, John C. 174
hound 86, 87, 88, 89, 90-1
Hound of the Baskervilles 90-1
Houndsditch 91
how's your father 164
hug a hoodie 39
human remains pouches 170
hump 165
Humphries, Barry 29
Hurston, Zora Neale 213
hustler 115
Huxley, Aldous *Time Must Have a Stop* 161

I must powder my nose 177
I'm all right Jack 71
Icelandic 186, 195
idiot 14
imbecile 14, 18
in bed 161
in fashion 34
in heaven 159
in one's cups 178
insanity 12
insult 134
International Herald Tribune 65
Internet pornography 200
iockam 197
Irving, Washington *A History of New York* 98
Italian 46, 49, 88

jack 192
Jack in the water 70
Jack Muck 71
Jack Sheppard 70
Jack Shilloo 71
jack tars 73
Jack the lad 69-71
Jack Weight 70
Jack's the lad 70
Jackie 223
jackin' the beanstalk 196
Jackson, Louis E.
  *Vocabulary of Criminal
  Slang* 126
Jade 63
James, Clive 211
James, Sid 212
Jefferson, Thomas 46
jerk 184, 191-3
jerk-off 192
jerking off 191
jerky 193
Jessel, George 67, 69
jew 113-14
Jew 114
Jew's Rolls-Royce 114
Joey 146-7
John o'London's Weekly
  199
John of Trevisa 89
Johnson, David 223
Johnson, Dr Samuel 18, 92,
  93
  Dictionary of English
  18, 168
Johnson, Frank 211
Johnson, Lyndon 170
Johnston, Brian 157
Johnston, Graeme 222
Johnstone, Charles *Chrysal,
  or the Adventures of a
  Guinea* 180-1
Jolie, Angelina 195
Jonson, Ben 154
  Poetaster 153
  The Alchemist 181
*Journal of Political
  Economy* 147
Journal of Pop Culture 200
*Journal of Psycho-
  asthenics* 17
Joviall Crew 149
Joyce, James 15, 141, 198

Ulysses 57, 173
jump 41
jumper 41-2

Kael, Pauline 145, 146
Kama Sutra 103
Kath & Kim 44
Keneally, Thomas
  Schindler's Ark 125
Kerry, John 53
kick the bucket 167-9
Kingsley, Charles *Water
  Babies* 93
kink 185-6
kinkiness 188
kinky 185-8
kinky advert 187
kinky boots 187
Kinky Boots 188
kinky-haired 186
kinky-headed 186
Kinnock, Neil 21
knitting 41
knotting 41
Krumpelmann, Dr John T.
  120

La Frenais, Ian 223
Lady Chatterley's Lover
  178, 189
Lancaster, Sir Osbert 175
Lancet 220
Lane, Lord 124
Larkin, Philip 189, 191
larrikin 62
Likely Lads, The 224
Last of the Summer Wine
  218
Latin 12, 17, 18, 45, 54, 76-7,
  89, 90, 134, 138, 154, 160,
  174
latrine 171
Laurie, Peter *Scotland Yard:
  A Personal Inquiry* 104,
  196
lav 172
lavatory 172-3
Lawrence, D.H. 160
Lawrence, T.E. *Mint* 80
legless 178
Leland, Charles *Dictionary
  of Slang, Jargon and
  Cant* 73, 121-2, 192

Lennox, Lord William Pitt
  *Fifty Years'
  Reminiscences* 125
let sleeping dogs lie 96
Levinson, Maurice *Taxi!* 99
Lewis, H. *Strange Story* 175
Lighter, J.E. 166
like a dog 87
like a dog with two tails
  105
Lincoln Chronicle 42
Lindisfarne Gospels 59
Lindsay, Sir David 138
Lithuanian 88
Livingstone, David 64
Lodge, David *Ginger You're
  Barmy* 19
Lodge, Sir Thomas 13
  A Fig for Momus 20
long-heeled 48
loo 173
loon 13
Looney Tunes 13
loons 13
loony 13
Lord of the Rings 169
*Lore and Language of
  Schoolchildren* 145
Los Angeles Times 225
lose your marbles 27-8
love eggs 191
Lovelace, Earl 153
Low, Andy Fairweather 178
Low, David 101
Lowe, Richard *Travellers:
  Voices of the New-Age
  Nomads* 29
lunacy 12
lunatic 12-13
lying doggo 106
Lyly, John *Maides
  Metamorphosis* 143

Macelhome, Harry 68
MacInnes, Colin
  Absolute Beginners 187
  To the Victors the Spoils
  104
MacKay 62
Mackay, Charles 130, 131
mackelerage 214
mackem 214
Mackenzie bean 214

mad 13
made-up 214–15
Magpie 214
mail 117
Maines, Rachel P. *The Technology of Orgasm* 190
making love 164–5
mammet 143–4
management-speak 215
Manchester Guardian Weekly 115
mania 12
man's best friend 86
Marashi, Ibrahim al- 110
Marino Bianco 218
marital aids 188–91
Marjoribanks *Fluff-hunters* 203
mark 215–16
Marnham, Patrick *The Private Eye Story* 181
Mary I, Queen 67, 69
masturbation 192
Maugham, W. Somerset 177, 178
mawmets 143
May, Caroline 65
Mayhew, Henry 20
Mayo, Simon 57
maypole 193–4
McCook, Tommy 224
McCoy, Bill 62
McCoy, Elijah 62
McKechnie, Brian 112
Melly, George *Owning Up* 162
Melody Maker 115
Mencken, H.L. 153–4
Michener, James A. *Tales of the South Pacific* 69
Middle East Review of International Affairs 110
Middle English 13, 149
Miller, Henry *Tropic of Cancer* 177–8
Milligan, Spike 23
Milton, Giles 220–1
Milton, John 20, 78
minger 216
minted 226
Mitford, Nancy *Pigeon Pie* 173

Modern Priscilla 190
Monroe, Marilyn 50
Montgomery, Field Marshal 213
Monty Python 225
moonies 217
mooning 216
moony 216–17
moose knuckle 45
More, Sir Thomas 143
Morison, Sir Richard 93
moron 14, 17–19
Mowlam, Mo 139–40
moyles 51
muffin top 44–5
muffins 45
mules 50–1
mullered 217
mullet 226
Mullins, Bill 211, 225
Murdoch, Rupert 197
mushy peas 217–18
my arse 153

Nabokov, Vladimir *Invitation to a Beheading* 177
naff 226
naked-heel 48
Nardini, Daniela 218
Needlecraft 190
negligee 53–5
neighbourhood 40, 122
Nenets 36–7
nerd 226
Neville, Hippo S*neak Thief on the Road* 95
New Dictionary of … the Canting Crew 180
New English Dictionary 56
New Society 114
New Statesman 50
New Testament 14
New York Herald 64
New York Herald Tribune 67
New York Times Magazine 101, 224
New Yorker 68, 145
News of the World 120, 197
Nganasan 36
ninety-nine/'99' 218–19
nip and tuck 219

nit comb 219–20
nit nurse 220
Norwegian 140
not the sharpest knife 31
Now! 211
number ones 171, 175
number twos 171, 175
nutmeg 220–1
nutmegging 221
nuts 30
nuts on (upon) 30
nutty 30
nutty as a fruitcake 30

Observer 38, 111, 200
OED 7
    arsehole 154
    back to square one 226
    blackmail 117, 118
    bob 75, 76
    boffin 209–10
    bonkers 24
    bucket 168, 169
    bulldog 87
    Charlie 151
    codswallop 212–13
    cuckold 31
    dildo 190
    dog 88,
    dog someone 92
    dog's bollocks 104
    dogged 93
    doggerel 95
    doggie style 102
    duh 32
    euphemism 159, 184
    full monty 213–14
    hiding the salami 166
    Hobson's choice 78
    hoodlum 120
    hooligan 122
    hornswoggle 124
    in bed 161
    Jack's the lad 70
    jerk off 191–2
    Jew 113
    kink 186, 187
    losing your marbles 28
    made-up 215
    making love 164
    mammet 143
    management-speak 215
    marital aids 188

minger 216
negligee 54–5
ninety-nine (99) 218–19
nip and tuck 219
nits 220
nutmeg 220–1
OED Online 67, 185
on the pull 223
pass the parcel 221
phwoar 222
plonker 148
ploughman's lunch 222–3
porn 198, 200, 203–4
prat 149, 150
relieve oneself 177
rip 115
ska 224
sleeping dogs 96
smart casual 224
snazzy 225
something for the weekend 225
special needs 147
stool 173
style 49–50
swindle 113
take the mickey 79
Thug 130
to take short 176
tosser 140
Turk 125–6
wally 151
well heeled 48
welsher 125
whang 195
whopper 197
off the straight and narrow 109
off your trolley 24–7
Official Lawn Tennis Bulletin 83
oiled 178
Old English 13, 41, 58, 88, 90, 119, 134, 149, 161, 179
Old French 26, 169, 173, 174
Old German 195
Old Norse 13
Old Norwegian 90, 195
Old Saxon 90
Old Turks 126

on trend 34
one sandwich short… 28–9
Only Fools and Horses 149
opening one's bowels 174
Opie, Iona and Peter 145
    Lore and Language of Schoolchildren 145
Orwell, George 215
Osborn, Hon. Sarah 96
out of fashion 34
out to lunch 29–30
Oxford English Dictionary see OED

pantaloons 56
panties 56
panting 56
pantomime 56
pants 55–7
paragraphers 67
parka 36–7
Parkins, David 223
Parkinson, Michael 221
Partridge, Eric 53, 71, 75, 114, 124, 151, 162
    Dictionary of Forces Slang 24
    Dictionary of Slang and Unconventional English 69, 74, 100, 103, 195
pass the parcel 221
passed away 156
Patrick Hooligan 123
pawn 167
paying a call 175
pear-shaped 226
Pearl 141
Peel, Sir Robert 75
pelicocks hill 138
Penguin Dictionary of Literary Terms 101
Penguin New Writing 71–2, 80, 100
penis 79, 149, 193–4
Penn, William 92
Pepys, Samuel 137
Peronistas 35
Persian 22, 45
Personal Computer World 210

perverted 109, 187
Pétiot, Fernand 68–9
Phillips, Caryl 153
Philocomus *Love Feast* 192
phlid 146
phwoar 22
pick and mix 226
pile of pants 57
pilkoc 138
pill 138
pillicock 138
pilloch 139
pillock 137–40
Pine, Courtney 213
Pinter, Harold *The Birthday Party* 80
piss-head 179
pissed 181
pissed as a fart 179
Playboy 192
plink 147, 148
plonk 147, 148
plonker 147–9
ploughboy's lunch 223
ploughman's lunch(eon) 222–3
plug ugly 63
plunk 147–8
podex 154
pointing percy at the porcelain 158
pole dances 193
pole-dancing 193–5
pomp 52
pop one's clogs 166–7, 223
Pope, Alexander *The Rape of the Lock* 172
porky 226
porn 198–200
pornographic 198
pornographico-devotional 198
pornography 185, 198
pornosophical 198
porny 198
posh 226
post-traumatic stress disorder 23
prat 149–50
pratfall 150
prats 149
Prescott, John 142

prick 149
Private Eye 181, 182, 215
privy 171, 173
Proclus 140
property porn 200
Proverbial Phrases 220
Provincial Glossary 203
Prudentius 89
psychosis 12
public convenience 158, 175
pull 192
pull, on the 223–4
pull over 42
pull-over 42
pullover 42
pull the pud 166
pump 52
pumps 52
Punch 20, 162, 167, 223
Purchas, Samuel 36
put down 134
put someone down 134–5
put someone's name down 134
put your foot down 134
Puttenham, George *Arte of English Poesie* 95

Queen 36
Queen of the May 195
Quinion, Michael 48
Quote ... Unquote 27

racketeer 115
Radiation Cookery Book 216
Radio Times 212
raining cats and dogs 87
Rambler 92
rat-arsed 179
real McCoy 62
real thing 62
Rees, Nigel *A Word in Your Shell-like* 27, 28
relieve oneself 176–7
rest-room 171
retard 146
rhyparography 198–9
Richler, Daniel *Kicking Tomorrow* 166
riding to hounds 90

rip 114–15
rip-off 114–16
Ripple 217
Rivelino, Roberto 52
Roberts, Ernie 146
robin 83
Robin Hood 41
Robinson, Jack 62
Rooney, George 63
Rooney-ugly 63
Rooney, Wayne 63
round robin 814
round robin tournament 83–4
round the bend 27
rounding up the tadpoles 196
Rouse, Alfred 176–7
rumpy-pumpy 159
rym doggerel 94

S&M 189
salam 166
salami 165–6
Salisbury, Lord 76
Samoyed 37
Sandinistas 35
sandwich short of a picnic 29
Sanskrit 88
Schindler's List 125
Science Digest 30
Scott, Joseph *The World's Best Bartender's Guide* 69
Scott, Sir Walter *Rob Roy* 93
Kenilworth 172
Screw 204
Scruton, Roger 154
see a man about a dog 86, 171
self-pollution 192
Sellers, Peter 71
Senderistas 35
sequin 46
sequins 45–7
set of heels 48
sex 159–60
sex act 160
Sex Pistols 17
sex toy 190
sexed up 111

sexually adventurous 188
shagging 202
shaggy dog story 101
Shakespeare, William 12, 20, 160, 164, 204
As You Like It 97
Julius Caesar 90
King Lear 138
Richard III 161–2
Romeo and Juliet 144
Twelfth Night 128
Sharapova, Maria 84
Shaw, George Bernard *Geneva* 163
Shaw, William *Travellers: Voices of the New-Age Nomads* 29
sheet 179
sheet in the wind's eye 180
shell shock 22–4
shifty 109
sicca rupee 46
Simpson, Alan 212
Simpson, John 207, 216
Simpson, O.J. 63
Sinclair, Gordon *Cannibal Quest* 211
siphoning the python 158
ska 224
slap and tickle 165
slap the salami 166
slattern 135
sleep 161
sleeping dogs 96–7
sloshed 178
slut 135–7
slut bagel 137
slut's wool 136
sluttish 136–7
smart casual 224
Smith, Albert R. *Christopher Tadpole* 163
Smith, Sir William 198
snazzy 225
Snoop Doggy Dogg 103
snuffed it 156
snuffed out 156
Soldier and Sailor Words and Phrases 22
something for the

weekend 225
South Bank Show 150
South Pacific 69
spacker 145
spacko 145
Spanish 46
spanking the frank 196
spanner 145
spastic 145
spastic paralysis 145
spaz 145-6
spear the bearded clam 159
special needs 32, 147
Spectator 78-9, 211
Speight, Johnny 139
spending a penny 158, 174-5
square one, back to 225-6
Stanley, Henry 64
Starr, Ringo 215
Steele, Sir Richard 79
Steptoe & Son 65
Sterne, Laurence *Tristram Shandy* 175
Stevens, Lord 120
Stevenson, Robert Louis 180
  Travels with a Donkey in the Cévennes 195
Stiff, Dean *The Milk and Honey Route* 99
stiletto 49-50
stiletto heel 50
stool 173
Stopes, Marie 160
Strand, The 91
strictly for the birds 31
stubbie short of a sixpack 29
Stuyvesant, Peter 98
style 49
Styles, Tania 207, 215
suck 192
Sullivan, John 149
Sun 197, 202
supermarket trolleys 26
Sutcliffe, Peter 63
Swedish 19, 88, 137, 140, 185
sweet FA 71-4
swindler 113-14

Sydney Morning Herald 44, 45

Tailor & Cutter 175
take a leak 177
take it or leave it 78
take the mickey 79-81
taken short 176
taking a mickey bliss 79
taking the Michael 80
taking the mick 81
taking the mickey 79-80
taking the piss 81
Taking the Piss: The Potted History of Pee 81
Tate, Harry 164
Taylor, John 95
Taylor, Thomas 140
teasers 190
Test Match Special 157
Thévenot, Jean de 129
thick 32
Thing of Beauty: The Tragedy of Supermodel Gia 34
third degree 127-9
third-degree burns 128
Thomas, Dylan 154
Thomas, Lesley 39
thong 57-9
thongs 52
Thorne, Tony *Dictionary of Contemporary Slang* 38-9
three sheets 179-80
three sheets in the wind 180
three sheets to the wind 179
Thug 129-30
thug 129-31
thuggery 131
thuggish 131
thwang 58, 195
ticklers 189, 190
tiddley 178
Till Death Us Do Part 139
Times 26, 100-1, 151-2, 210, 223
Times Literary Supplement 158
tired and... 181-2
tired and emotional 182

to be at rest 167
to be brought into love's dance 164
to be caught with one's pants down 57
to be cuckoo 31
to be dogged 93-4
to be in the arms of Jesus 167
to be nuts 30
to be taken short 176
to be third-degreed 127
to bed 161
to bung 119-20
to cover his feet 177
to dog 92, 200-1
to dog nose 105
to dog someone 92
to drain the spuds 171
to fluff 205
to gee up 127
to get the third degree 127
to go, send or throw to the dogs 97
to go to a better place 167
to go to bed 161
to go to the toilet 172
to have 161
to have kangaroos in the top paddock 29
to hide the sausage or weenie 166
to hooligan/ize 123
to jerk off 192
to jew 113
to know someone 160
to make love 164
to pop 166
to powder one's nose 171, 177-8
to pull someone's plonker 148-9
to rip off 115
to sleep with 161
to spend a penny 158, 174-5
to stalk 201
to take short 176
to take the mike out of 80
to throw a spanner in

the works 145
to toss 140, 192
to wap 196-8
to whop 197
toilet 171-2
took the micturate 80
took the piss 80
top dog 87
Topsell, Edward 96
   History of Four-footed
    Beasts 96
   History of Serpents 96
Toronto Daily Star 224
Torriano, Giovanni
   Proverbial Phrases 220
toss 192
toss a drink back 141
toss a pancake 140
toss it off 192
toss off 141
toss off a book 141
tosser 134, 140-3
tosser-up of omelets 140
tossers-off of beer 140
tossing 140
tossing the caber 140
Toynbee, Arnold 198
transfer tubes 170
travel porn 200
Travellers: Voices of the
   New-Age Nomads 29
Travolta, John 159
trebuchet 169
Tremayne, Sydney 176
troll 26
trolley 26
trolley-car (tram) 27
Trollope, Anthony
   Claverings 27
tuppence short of a
   shilling 25
Turk 125-6
Twain, Mark *Letters from*
   Hawaii 48
twatted 179
Twenty-Five Welsh Short
   Stories 144
twinge 58
Tyneside Songster 181

underhand 111-12
underhand cricket 112
urbandictionary.com 39, 84,

104, 105-6, 137, 196
US Air Force *Intelligence*
   Targeting Guide 170
vaginal speculum 189
Vanbrugh, Sir John 180
Vanity Fair 17
Varro, Marcus Terentius 98,
   99
vibrating panties 191
vibrators 190
visible panty line 45
Viz 103, 222
Vocabulary of Criminal
   Slang 126
Vogue 35, 38
Vulgaria 92

Wainwright, John *The Last*
   Buccaneer 100
wake a sleeping dog 96
Walden, Jeff 209
Walliams, Wally 151
Wallies of Wessex 151-2
wally 151-2
wally acts 152
wallydrag 151
wallydraigle 151
Walter 151
wank 184, 192, 195
wankered 179
wankers 142
wanking 195-6
wanking on 196
WAP 197-8
wapping 197
war neurosis 23
war porn 200
Ward, Thomas 79
Warner, Minnie 72
Wartenberg wheel 189
Wartenberg, Dr Robert 189
Washbrook, Clare 216
watercloset 173
Waterhouse, William C.
   226
weather porn 200
Weaver, Will 217
Wedderburn, E.A.M. 38
Weekly Journal 82
well heeled 47-8
well oiled 178
welsher 125
welshing 124-5

Westminster Gazette 21,
   122
whack 192
whang 195-6
whopper 197
Wildblood, Peter *The Main*
   Chance 151
Williamson, Henry *The*
   Patriot's Progress 148
Wilson, Harold 181
Windsor, Barbara 222
Wintour, Anna 35
Wodehouse, P.G.
   Right Ho, Jeeves 146
   Tales of St Austin's 148
Woman's Home
   Companion 190
Woods, Tiger 146
World's Best Bartender's
   Guide 69
Worth, Mary 68
wriggle navels 159
Wycherley, William *The*
   Plain-Dealer 92
Wyclif, William 160
Wynter, Andrew *Our Social*
   Bees 110

X-rated 184

Yank 28
Yellow Pages: Manchester
   North 214
yerk 192
Young Turks 126

Zephaniah, Benjamin 224
Zigzag 142

Acknowledgements

This is the no-but-seriously moment. It is, again, a tremendous privilege to be able to call on the resources of *The Oxford English Dictionary* online, the greatest linguistic research tool in the English-speaking world.

A very warm thank you to my Dutch researcher Jon van Hodes, and to two Latin teachers: Richard Loe of Trevor Roberts School and Peter Dennis-Jones of Monmouth School. Classics teachers have, in my experience, always been a supportive and humane community, but special thanks go to these two for their help.

Essential and well-deserved agent-thanking: to Antony Topping, at Greene & Heaton at this end, and to Julian Alexander at LAW at the other end. Thanks also to Martin Redfern of Random House and to Trish Burgess, a reassuringly unflappable editor.

Thanks to Andy Davey for his very funny cartoons, which more than capture the spirit of the book. And to the marvellous people at Takeaway: thanks to Jayne Rowe (and Muffin) for her unchequered assistance, and to Kim Lomax and her team for some very timely factual back-up. Above all, I owe an enormous debt to Archie Baron and to Kate Carter for their painstaking and thoughtful reading of my text. If this book still contains any errors after their supreme efforts, I have no hesitation in saying that it's entirely their fault, and not mine.

Thank you to my parents for setting the ball rolling in the first place – they are more than welcome to skip the slightly racier passages. Last and most importantly, thanks to Esther, Fergus and Edie, who, to misquote Lerner and Loewe, really make the day begin.

BIRDS OF THE WORLD
WATERFOWL

JOHN P.S. MACKENZIE

NorthWord
PRESS, INC

Originally published in Canada by Key Porter Books, Toronto

Published in the United States by:
NorthWord Press Inc.
Box 1360
Minocqua, Wisconsin
54548

ISBN: 0-942802-94-2

Library of Congress Catalogue Card Number: 88-061092

For a free catalog describing NorthWord's books call 1-800-336-5666

Design: First Image
Composition: First Image
Printed and bound in Italy

90 01 02 6 5 4 3

Photograph page 2: Canada Goose (*Branta canadensis*)   The distinctive chin strap, black stocking neck, and white front identify the Canada Goose, probably the most widely recognized goose in the world.

Photograph pages 4-5: Trumpeter Swan (*Olor buccinator*)   The small population of these swans south of Canada lives in the Red Rocks Lake area where Montana and Idaho meet. They winter in the neighborhood where thermal springs and streams keep the available water from freezing.

CONTENTS

Introduction   9

Swans   17

Geese   35

Ducks   67

Grebes and
Cormorants   131

Photograph Credits   143

Index to Photographs   144

Greater Scaup (*Aythya marila*)   The Greater Scaup nests from the Arctic
Ocean south to about 60 degrees north latitude. In winter it moves to salt
water where it dives for food. Rafts of thousands of birds are common.

INTRODUCTION

Mallard (*Anas platyrhynchos*) This is a male Mallard in full nuptial plumage. It is the most widely distributed and common of all the ducks, its range covering the Eastern and Western hemispheres, and extending as far as northern Australia.

The term "waterfowl" is normally understood to include only swans, geese and ducks. For this volume we have added grebes and cormorants which often share the same habitat.

Waterfowl have a number of features in common. All feed to some extent in water. Some, such as the dabbling ducks, geese and swans, feed from the surface. They up-end, with their tails in the air, and stretch their necks to reach food under the surface. The diving ducks submerge completely, and swim under water for their food, sometimes to a considerable depth. Their diet tends to consist of animal matter in the form of fish, molluscs, crustacea and insects.

Six years ago, when we were exploring the arid plains west of the Murray River in Victoria, Australia, we were guided to a shallow lake which was crowded with ducks and swans. After hours of heat and dust, the water and green margins were a restful and relaxing change. There were several dozen Black Swans, indigenous to Australia and New Zealand, Chestnut-breasted Shelduck, Chestnut and Grey Teal, the striking Southern Shoveler and Blue-billed Duck. Altogether, there were over a thousand birds. This lake, the only standing water for several miles, acted as a magnet for waterfowl and the wading birds that dotted the shore. Our visit was during the dry season. When the rains came, the birds would range widely to nest, for the area was too small to support such a population for a long time.

The waterfowl that we saw in Australia migrate only within the country in search of lakes, rivers and marshlands in which to feed and nest. In the Northern Hemisphere, most waterfowl are migratory. In the spring, they leave the ice-free areas where they have wintered in ponds, lakes, swamps, estuaries, and on the edges of the oceans, to move northward. Some wood duck, teal and mergansers do not go very far, but settle in suitable watered areas. Others, including the Tundra Swan, spread out across the tundra of North America and northern Europe, and throughout the vast taiga of Siberia. Still others, including the King Eider and the Oldsquaw, whose ranges extend as far north as there is land on which to nest, press farther, to the limits of the Arctic islands.

Geese, swans and ducks that nest in the Far North are often faced with conditions critical to successful nesting, and to their own survival. Although migrating waterfowl build up reserves of fat prior to their long journeys, they arrive on their breeding grounds in a weakened condition. This is especially true of swans, for example, which make long, non-stop flights, or stop to rest and feed only briefly. Snow geese, in contrast, make long intermediate stops — sometimes as long as a month. If the migrants arrive at the nesting grounds before the snow has gone, or before the ice has left the shores, they may starve. They can, however, survive for two or three weeks, and nest before arctic vegetation has started to grow. The period between thaw and freeze-up may be as short as eight weeks. Since incubation takes from three to five weeks, depending upon the species, and since the young must be fledged before freeze-up, they must grow very quickly.

Waterfowl born in the Far North grow more quickly than those in the south, due to the abundant food supply and continuous daylight. Canada Geese, for example, which nest over most of North America, gain about one pound a week, and may be fully grown in eight weeks in the south. The same process in the Arctic may take six weeks. For this species, it takes approximately 100 days to nest, incubate and raise the young to the flying stage.

The marshes at the margins of rivers, lakes and the oceans which attract waterfowl on their autumn migration are exciting locations for avid birders during the half hour or so before sunrise. Then, at first light, they can hear the marvelous chorus of marsh sound. First, there is the splashing as birds rise from their resting positions and flap their wings. The croaks and cackles of grebes and coots follow. Both species indulge in nervous splashing and grunting in the reeds. There is the occasional feeding quack of a Mallard, and then the rustle of wings as ducks start to move about the marsh. Most species can be identified at a considerable distance by the experienced observer: flight patterns differ, shapes are slightly different, wings beat at varying speeds. Pintails, for instance, have pointed wings and long tails; scaup have a rapid wingbeat and fly close to the water; teal are small and dart about erratically. When it is full light, the drama subsides.

The chicks of waterfowl are "precocial." This means that they are born with protective down and their eyes open. They are also "nidifugous," meaning that they have well-developed legs and are capable of leaving the nest as soon as their down is dry. In fact, they head almost immediately for the nearest water, sometimes a long way off, where they can swim, dive and feed themselves within a few hours of emerging from the egg.

Another feature common to waterfowl is the leathery web which joins the three front toes. The single rear toe is vestigial, usually no more than a tiny spur emerging slightly above the foot on the tarsus. Grebes' feet are exceptional in that they are not webbed, but the toes have lobes which bend sideways when they are swimming, providing added propulsion.

Most waterfowl have short legs and tails, narrow wings and longish necks. Most also have long, flat bills, with varyingly serrated edges, which they use to strain water while retaining food. All members of this group have a complicated system of feathers of which the outer layer is virtually impervious to water. By preening regularly, arranging the barbs on the feathers, and by the application of oil from a gland near the tail, the feathers are kept lubricated.

Ducks, geese and swans are designed primarily for swimming and flying. Their legs emerge relatively far back on the body. This varies among species, as does the ability to walk on land. The dabbling ducks, with legs at the center of the body, waddle quite well, as do geese and swans. The diving ducks, with legs near the rear, are clumsy on land.

Many species of waterfowl, particularly the dabbling ducks, geese and swans, vary their feeding habits between land and water. Geese and swans graze on grasses, seeds and the various clovers. In agricultural areas they eat wheat and other grains in huge quantities. During the autumn migration, large flocks descend on uncut fields and strip the grain from the stalks. The damage can be so great that the fields are not worth harvesting. In the spring, migrating waterfowl may do comparable damage to the young shoots of grain crops. In North America some prairie regions are particularly hard hit; the worst offenders are usually Mallards.

Waterfowl nesting in the Northern Hemisphere tend to migrate much farther than those south of the equator where, for the most part, migration may be limited to the search for suitable habitat. This is usually due to seasonal precipitation rather than freezing. In much of Africa, Asia, Australia and South America, it is necessary for waterfowl to follow the rains, more often east-west than north-south. Several species, including the Black Swan, the Plumed Whistling Duck, the Freckled Duck and the Chestnut Teal, occur only in Australia and New Zealand. Some, such as the Yellow-billed Duck, the Cape Wigeon and the Hottentot Teal, are seen only in Africa. And a few are found only in fairly restricted areas in South America. In some remote islands, such as New Guinea, Madagascar, the Falklands, the Crozet Islands, the Andamans and New Zealand, there are isolated species that occur nowhere else.

During the first half of the twentieth century, counting methods were primitive and the records are suspect. Since about 1950, most wildfowl counts have been conducted from light aircraft with fair accuracy. It has been determined that the North American population averages 40 million birds at the beginning of the breeding season, and 80 million at its end. It does not appear to be declining seriously. The game laws that were first introduced in the United States in 1918 limited the daily bag to 25 ducks. Now the limit has been generally reduced to more modest numbers.

In the early years of the present century, both in North America and Europe, it was not unusual for a single hunter to kill hundreds of birds in a day. North American species still face uncontrolled slaughter when they reach Mexico, which does not enforce the Migratory Bird Treaty. Some years ago in Merida, in the Yucatan Peninsula, I met two North Americans who boasted that on that day they had killed 500 duck.

Natural hazards remain a constant threat to waterfowl populations. Disease caused by blood parasites, botulism and fowl cholera, is probably the largest destroyer. Fowl cholera strikes large bird populations feeding in stagnant ponds, in areas where there is not enough suitable habitat. Periods of drought have a serious impact on the capacity of waterfowl to nest and raise young. Prolonged winters and violent storms kill many young birds. Predators, both avian and animal, threaten eggs and young birds.

Unnatural hazards are increasing, despite solid efforts to control them. Regular shooting by hunters has carpeted the bottom of many marshes with lead pellets. These pellets, ingested by feeding birds, lodge in their gastrointestinal tracts. Some birds can tolerate a few pellets, but when the number of pellets exceeds their tolerance, the birds are poisoned. It is estimated that two to three percent of the fall and winter populations of waterfowl die from lead poisoning. (In many areas, hunters are now required to use steel rather than lead shot.)

Oil spills, in both fresh and salt water, not only poison waterfowl as they try to clean their feathers, but also kill them by destroying their waterproofing.

The nesting habits of waterfowl are generally consistent, in that they lay their eggs as close to the water as they can, although late arrivals and less aggressive individual birds lose out on the best territories. Some ducks are exceptional, in that they nest in uplands away from the water. Most species nest on the ground, or on an elevation in a marsh. Nests vary from a scrape lined with down, to substantial piles for some of the geese.

Pair relationships differ considerably among waterfowl and between species of the same family. Swans and geese pair and tend to remain together for long periods, often for life. Among ducks, pair bonding is strong while it lasts, but is often of short duration. Bonding may take place in the autumn and continue through the winter and migration. With some species, the male attends the female during nest building and during egg laying, but departs when incubation begins. Among other species, the male will remain until incubation is well advanced. Once hatched, the young are capable of feeding themselves, and need brooding only at night and during harsh weather.

Longevity varies considerably. Trumpeter Swans have lived in captivity for 29 years. Ducks' longevity is much shorter. The life expectancy — as opposed to longevity — is another matter. It has been estimated that the average life expectancy of a Mallard in Europe is six months. In North America, the annual mortality rate from all causes, for those species subject to shooting, is about 60 to 70 percent, so the chance of reaching old age is slight. About one half of the mortality is due to shooting; the rest to other causes. Since waterfowl are prolific breeders if habitat is available, they can tolerate relatively high mortality. Swans average five eggs per clutch; geese slightly more. Most duck species average about nine eggs per clutch. Nesting success varies enormously depending upon human interference, predation, and weather, but, on average, less than half the eggs laid produce flying birds.

Throughout most temperate regions, a fast-growing human population has, for centuries, demanded increasing areas of land for agricultural production. Much of this land has been claimed from natural wetlands. With the invention of powered machinery in the nineteenth century, the process was accelerated. In the United States, for instance, there were originally about 127 million acres of natural wetlands. By 1968, this had been reduced to 75 million acres. Much more has been lost since then. In Canada, where vast areas of northern forest and tundra account for some 2.24 billion acres, the losses have not been so great in relative terms, but much of the best of the pothole country and estuaries is being drained. From a human point of view, food production is, of course, essential, but so is the maintenance of wetlands for water storage and natural drainage. Drained land does not hold spring rain or melting snow, and consequently leads to drought conditions in a dry summer. From the point of view of maintaining waterfowl populations, the loss of habitat is disastrous. Recently, it has been recognized that human interference and loss of habitat to agriculture have put pressure on waterfowl populations that may become intolerable. In North America, particularly, an enormous effort in terms of money and research has resulted in the retention and creation of wetlands. This has to some extent halted the decline in the vast populations that once existed.

Whooper Swan (*Olor cygnus*) The trumpeting call of the Whooper gives it
its name. It nests in Iceland, across northern Europe and Asia and moves
south as far as North Africa in winter.

SWANS

Coscoroba Swan (*Coscoroba coscoroba*) The short neck, white body, red bill, and relatively small size identify this bird. It lives entirely south of the equator from southern Brazil to Argentina and Chile.

Many people tend to think of swans as ornamental birds, because they are usually seen floating majestically on ponds in zoos and botanical gardens. The bird most commonly seen is the Mute Swan, an enormous, all-white bird, with a pinkish bill surmounted by a black knob. This swan has been semi-domesticated in Europe for centuries, and is recognized as a symbol of elegance and grace in myth and legend. Tchaikovsky immortalized it in his ballet, *Swan Lake*. In the British Isles, where the swans nominally belong to the monarch, the wild population is probably descended from semi-domesticated birds of the medieval period. Mute Swans were imported into North America in the nineteenth century for ornamental purposes, and escapees have established themselves in the wild.

Populations of Mute Swans that have become established in some parts of North America, for example on Chesapeake Bay in New England, have caused some disruption to the local environment. They tend to drive other waterfowl out of the nesting territory. They pull up a lot of the aquatic vegetation. And generally, they may be at least partially responsible for a local decline in habitat suitability for other waterfowl.

There are — arguably — seven swan species: Whooper, Trumpeter, Tundra (or Bewick's), Mute, Black-necked, Black and Coscoroba. Some years ago the Whistling Swan of North America was re-named the Tundra Swan. More recently, it was agreed among ornithologists that the Bewick's Swan of Europe and the Tundra Swan of North America were, in fact, the same species. To further complicate matters, some authorities now consider the Trumpeter Swan of North America to be conspecific with the Whooper of Eurasia, although this has not been recognized in official circles. The Tundra-Bewick's and the Whooper both nest across northern North America, in the Arctic islands and in northern Russia. They visit the British Isles in winter to feed in ponds, rivers and protected estuaries. Both are straight-necked birds. The necks of Mute Swans, in contrast, form a distinct S. Finally, ornithologists now maintain that the Coscoroba and Black Swan are members of the duck tribe. I include them here because swans are what they are called and what they look like.

The Black-necked, Coscoroba and Black Swan live only in the Southern Hemisphere. The first two are found from Brazil southward, and the Black in Australia and New Zealand.

In Europe and North America swans, with the exception of the Mute Swan, nest in remote regions and require large territories to themselves. (The Mute Swan of Europe nests quite happily in parks and farmland.) Swans usually choose wetlands in the tundra, or land surrounded by water. Here they build a bulky nest on a mound they have made themselves or, quite frequently, by scooping out the top of a muskrat mound. The Tundra Swan claims and maintains a territory of at least one square mile. It will tolerate duck and other small birds, but drives off most geese and other swans. It is because the Trumpeter Swan requires a similarly large territory that it was driven, by the expansion of agriculture on the Great Plains, to the brink of extinction.

Swans are gregarious outside the nesting season, and some species nest in loose colonies. On a visit to the evaporating ponds of the salt works of Imperial Chemical Industries in Adelaide, Australia, we saw one flock of Black Swans estimated to be more than 1,000 birds. When our host put them to flight, they presented a magnificent roaring display of brown-black bodies and red bills. Migrating swans in the Northern Hemisphere tend to settle for feeding stops of a week or so, as they follow the spring north. Near Chatham, in Ontario, several thousand Tundra Swans litter the fields in March, feeding mostly on last year's corn and some early shoots.

The species particular to the northern part of the Western Hemisphere are the Trumpeter and Tundra swans. The Trumpeter is rare south of Canada, outside the Red Rocks Lakes area near where Wyoming, Montana and Idaho meet. Due to heavy shooting and restricted habitat, the Trumpeter population declined to a low of 69 birds in the U.S. and south of Canada in 1932. Concentrated and intelligent work by federal, state and private agencies has led to an increase in the group to about 700 birds, at which level it remains more-or-less stable. Further expansion is limited by restricted nesting habitat. Another and separate population of Trumpeters, numbering about 3,500 birds, lives in southern Alaska and northern British Columbia. This bird once nested widely and was common throughout the central and northern part of North America, but it could not withstand encroachment and the draining of its habitat for farming.

The Tundra Swan remains abundant in North America and, as its name suggests, nests from the Aleutians, across northern Alaska and the Northwest Territories. Once, when flying westward to Prudhoe Bay in Alaska, we were able to see the nesting birds clearly against the dun-colored tundra. Although swans usually fly in flocks with their own kind, sometimes on migration young swans fly with Canada Geese, usually in the lead.

Swans establish strong bonds and pairs mate for life. They remain together throughout the year, keeping the surviving cygnets, or young, with them until they nest again. If one of a pair dies, the survivor usually takes a new mate, but when they are together their mutual affection (if birds can be said to feel affection) is apparent. Swans and geese carry out mutual displays prior to mating. Aggression displays to intruders involve a lowering of the neck, hissing, and forward rushes. Success in sending off an intruder is heralded by a display of triumph. At the nest it appears that the female does most, if not all, of the incubating of the eggs. The clutch averages about five eggs, but may be as many as 10. Incubation for most swan species is about 30 days. The survival rate of the young is reasonably high during the next 60 to 75 days that it takes them to develop to the flying stage. For those species nesting in the Far North, about half the young birds perish on migration to the south, for they must leave the Arctic before they have grown strong.

Swans of the Northern Hemisphere migrate to their wintering area in flocks of about 20 to 40 birds. In winter they are gregarious, feeding together in very large groups.

Tundra Swan (*Olor columbianus*)   Formerly known as the Whistling Swan, this is a Holarctic species which nests in northern North America and in Siberia.

Left: Trumpeter Swan (*Olor buccinator*)   Swans of this species were once widespread, from James Bay to the Mackenzie River in the north, to Nebraska and Missouri in the south. They once wintered as far south as the Gulf of Mexico.

Mute Swan (*Cygnus olor*)   This is the swan most often seen in zoos and ornamental gardens. It was introduced into North America in the nineteenth century and breeds in the wild.

Mute Swan (*Cygnus olor*)   This large swan takes off from land or water
ponderously, with a heavy flapping of wings, and with its feet pattering
along the surface. In bogs it may even be grounded.

Whooper Swan (*Olor cygnus*)   The Whooper nests on firm spots in the
Arctic tundra as well as on islets in lakes and bogs. It winters on sea coasts,
lakes and large rivers around the British Isles, northern Europe and at the
head of the Adriatic.

Left: Tundra Swan (*Olor columbianus*)   Migrating from the Chesapeake Bay area where it winters, to the shores of the Arctic Ocean, the Tundra Swan takes a month-long intermediate rest part way, and then flies non-stop to the Northwest Territories, Baffin Island and Siberia.

Mute Swan (*Cygnus olor*)   Note the long, curving S-shaped neck and the orange, nobbed bill. The yellow stain on the neck is the result of constant feeding with the head below the surface. The raised wings are typical.

27

Trumpeter Swan (*Olor buccinator*)   Once widely distributed through the plains of North America, only about 700 birds remain south of the Canadian border. A separate population of about 3,000 birds lives in British Columbia and Alaska.

Mute Swan (*Cygnus olor*) Although gregarious in winter, often gathering in groups of a hundred or more birds, in the breeding season Mute Swan pairs are apt to be isolated.

Black-necked Swan (*Cygnus melancoryphus*)   The striking black neck and face, and the brilliant red nob on the bill contrast markedly with the white body. The Black-necked Swan lives only in South America, from southern Brazil to Argentina.

Black Swan (*Cygnus atratus*) A native of Australia and New Zealand, this swan congregates in large numbers when not nesting. It is abundant in both fresh and salt water.

Left: Black Swan (*Cygnus atratus*)   The black-brown color and straight neck are typical of this swan. They lay an average of five eggs, with both the male and the female incubating.

Black Swan (*Cygnus atratus*)   The Black Swan is often found in a pond or small lake many miles from standing water. The white tip on the red bill can be seen for some distance.

Tundra Swan (*Olor columbianus*)   The Tundra Swan chooses nesting sites anywhere from the water's edge to low hilltops as much as half a mile from water.

GEESE

Barheaded Goose (*Anser indica*)   This attractive goose nests, usually at high altitudes, in central Asia and Tibet, laying three or four eggs. It winters in northern, and occasionally central India. It feeds mostly at night and congregates in flocks to rest during the day.

Ornithologists differ in their classifications of waterfowl, but there appear to be about 37 Anserinae species around the world, of which nine fall into the whistling duck category, and 28 are called geese and swans. As an example of the problem of classification, there are five species of sheldgeese in South America that, in evolutionary terms, are more closely related to ducks than to geese. Both sheldgeese and shelducks, however, may be classified as geese.

Geese are intermediate in size between swans and ducks, and tend to have longer and heavier necks than ducks. They are agile on land, where most species do much of their feeding. Their legs are relatively longer than those of swans, and emerge close to the center of the body. They also feed in shallow water, where they up-end in order to reach aquatic vegetation with their bills. Most geese are almost entirely herbivorous in their feeding habits, although some feed partially on insects and shellfish. Geese will adapt to changing circumstances, however. For example, before the European settlement of North America, geese fed exclusively on wild food, probably obtained mostly in the water. With the expansion of grain farming, geese, particularly the Canada Goose, became upland feeders. Some species, such as Brant and Snow, used to feed almost entirely on eel grass, bullrush roots, and sea lettuce. Some 50 years ago, as agriculture expanded, they moved into farming areas for grain.

Goose habitat varies considerably between species. The Nene Goose, which lives only in the mountains of Hawaii, would probably be extinct by now had not Sir Peter Scott obtained a few birds many years ago, and bred them at Slimbridge in England. The experiment was so successful that a regular program of returning birds to the wild has led to a modest recovery. The Blue-winged Goose lives only in the Ethiopian highlands. The Upland Goose lives at high elevations in South America and in the Falkland Islands.

The Canada Goose is certainly the best-known of its family in North America and, perhaps, in the world. Its long black-stocking neck and white chinstrap are familiar to people who might not recognize any other species of goose. In and near cities, these birds have become accustomed to protection. Here they feed and nest in parks, and tolerate the close proximity of people. Geese generally are attracted to urban parks where food is plentiful on the fertilized grassy areas. Indeed, so many have settled in some cities that their droppings foul the lawns. Even in rural areas the Canada Goose now nests close to farms, usually at the edge of ponds and streams, choosing, where possible, firm ground surrounded by water. During the past 30 years or so, the North American population of the Canada Goose has been exploding, both in terms of numbers of birds and of habitat. This has been due, in large part, to thoughtful wildlife management, which includes restoration of wet areas, reduction of bag limits, and the provision of artificial nesting sites in settled areas.

The Canada Goose has developed in the course of its evolution into at least 12 sub-species, ranging in size from the Cackling Goose, which weighs about three pounds, to the Giant Canada Goose which, while averaging 10 to 14 pounds, may sometimes exceed 20 pounds. Geese breeding in the Far North grow progressively smaller. The various sub-species of Canada Goose become darker from east to west.

The Snow Goose comes in two forms: the Greater, which is pure white with black wing tips, and the Lesser, which may be white or blue-grey. These two forms were previously considered to be separate species, but are now recognized as one. The Lesser Snow Goose nests from eastern Siberia, across northern Canada, and migrates through central and western North America. The Greater nests in the extreme northern islands of the Arctic, and migrates through Labrador and the east.

On migration, and in their winter feeding areas, these birds travel and feed in great flocks. One of the most thrilling experiences available to birders is to crouch on the tidal flats on an island in the lower St. Lawrence River when, during their evening flight, thousands of these birds come to land.

With the exception of the Magpie or Pied Goose of Australasia, geese molt their flight feathers after nesting, and cannot fly for about a month. Then they seek open, shallow water for protection and food. The Magpie Goose is unusual in that its long toes are only slightly webbed. It has long, heron-like legs and a long, thin, black neck, rather like a swan's. Its body is black with large, irregular patches of white on the flanks and belly, and it has a yellow face.

The most strongly marked of the geese is the Red-breasted Goose. It ranges across northern Europe, where it nests on the coastal tundra, and wanders in winter as far as Britain, France and Hungary. It is covered with patches of white and red on a black upper body and wings. The most distinctive marking is a large red patch behind the eye, surrounded by a white line. The Emperor Goose of Siberia and Alaska has a lovely ocher-colored head, with a contrasting black throat, pink bill and speckled body.

African Shelduck (*Tadorna cana*)   Living only in South Africa, this
bird has a chestnut-colored body with a white head surmounted by a black
crown. There are, or were, seven species of shelduck, but the Crested
Shelduck of Japan is probably now extinct.

Ruddy Shelduck (*Tadorna ferruginea*)   An attractive chestnut-orange bird, this shelduck ranges from the eastern Mediterranean to eastern Asia. It nests in holes in banks, walls and trees. It is more terrestial than most ducks and can sometimes be found in the arid steppes.

Magellan or Upland Goose (*Chloephaga picta*)   The Magellan Goose lives in
the semi-arid plains of the interior of southern Argentina and Chile. In
winter it migrates north as far as Buenos Aires. It is also found in the
Falkland Islands.

Barnacle Goose (*Branta leucopsis*) In its breeding areas of the high Arctic of Greenland, Spitzbergen and northern Russia, this goose nests in colonies on rocky ledges and hillsides. In winter it can be seen around the British Isles and the Baltic where it feeds mostly on salt flats.

Brant Goose (*Branta bernicla*)   Like the Canada Goose, the Brant has a black-stocking neck, but its white ring is on the neck below the head. It nests on the arctic coasts of North America, Europe, and Asia, and feeds in salt water farther south in winter.

Cape Barren Goose (*Cereopsis novaehollandiae*) As the scientific name implies, this goose is native to Australia which was originally known as "New Holland." The handsome blue-gray mantle is dotted with dark spots, and the base of the bill is yellow.

Canada Goose (*Branta canadensis*)   The family of a Canada Goose may consist of up to ten chicks. They may grow at the prodigious rate of almost one pound per week to reach a weight of six or seven pounds in two months.

Right: Canada Goose (*Branta canadensis*)   There are some ten sub-species of the Canada Goose, ranging in size from the three-pound Cackling Goose to the Giant which is known to have reached 24 pounds.

Snow Goose (*Chen caerulescens*)   The Snow Goose winters in the southern
United States and nests in the eastern Arctic. In spring and fall it stops in
the St. Lawrence River east of Quebec City for about a month.

Egyptian Goose (*Alopochen aegyptiaca*)   This relatively small goose is common in ponds and rivers in Africa and Asia Minor. During the rains it extends its range from permanent waters to newly-formed ponds in the plains.

47

Cape Barren Goose (*Cereopsis novaehollandiae*)   While the Cape Barren Goose lives in both Australia and New Zealand, it is uncommon in both. This is a grazing goose, and although a strong swimmer, it seldom enters the water.

Snow Goose (*Chen caerulescens*)   The Snow Goose feeds principally on eel grass, but in winter it may devour grain in cut fields.

White-fronted Goose (*Anser albifrons*)   A circumpolar nester almost
everywhere except in eastern North America, it moves south in winter as
far as Mexico, India, North Africa and Asia. Nesting is often gregarious in
the tundra, deltas and valleys, always close to water.

Greylag Goose (*Anser anser*) There are two forms of the Greylag, the western (found in Britain and western Europe) with an orange bill, and the eastern (found in eastern Europe and Asia) with a pink bill. Some individual birds migrate only locally, while those nesting in Iceland move south.

Magellan or Upland Goose (*Chloephaga picta*) The Magellan Goose may attain a 28-inch wingspan. Its white head and neck, white rump and black barred back are striking.

Emperor Goose (*Philacte canagica*)   The Emperor Goose breeds mostly on the coast of northeastern Siberia and in northwestern Alaska. Some birds straggle south in winter along the coast of western Canada. The pink bill, black throat and white head and neck, set off the strongly-barred body.

Magpie Goose (*Anseranas semipalmata*) The Magpie Goose is unusual in that it does not molt or lose its ability to fly for a period each year. The toes are only partially webbed, the legs very long. It regularly perches in trees. It lives only in Australia and New Guinea.

Orinoco Goose (*Neochen jubata*) A native of Columbia, Venezuela and the Guianas, this attractive long-legged goose nests principally on the forested banks of the Orinoco River and its tributaries.

Pacific White-fronted Goose (*Anser erythropus*)   This is the Asian form of the White-fronted Goose. It is much browner and somewhat smaller than its eastern counterpart.

Nene Goose (*Branta sandvicensis*)   This beautiful bird, which nests in the highlands of Hawaii, was close to extinction some 40 years ago. Sir Peter Scott brought a few birds to England where he has built up a breeding flock, returning birds gradually to the wild.

Pink-footed Goose (*Anser brachyrhynchus*) Their nesting area in Iceland was discovered by Sir Peter Scott. He trekked to the center of the island to band them during the flightless period of the molt. They winter around the British Isles and on the European coasts of the North Sea.

Barnacle Goose (*Branta leucopsis*)   Flocks of Barnacle Geese tend not to
associate with other geese. They can be quarrelsome amongst themselves
and are often noisy. Their call is similar to the yelp of a dog.

Red-breasted Goose (*Bernicla ruficollis*) This is the most spectacularly marked of all the geese. The heavy body is large in relation to the small head and neck. It is Palearctic and is seen in Asia.

Left: Ross's Goose (*Chen rossii*)   Rather like a diminutive Snow Goose, the Ross's is white with black wingtips (not shown in this photograph). It nests in the low Arctic on the tundra, near fresh-water lakes. It winters principally in central California, and occasionally in Louisiana and Texas.

Snow Goose (*Chen caerulescens*)   The markings of the Snow Goose are shown clearly here: the pure white body, extensive black wingtips and the deep pink on the bill of the male.

White-fronted Goose (*Anser albifrons*)   On its circumpolar breeding grounds
the White-fronted Goose often nests in loose colonies. The four to six eggs
are laid in a down-filled nest on the ground. The female incubates while the
male stands guard during the four weeks that they take to hatch.

Shelduck (*Tadorna tadorna*)   From a distance the Shelduck appears to be black-and-white, despite the strong coloring that can be seen at close quarters. It is widespread on the coasts of Britain, Europe, North Africa and Asia. It often nests in rabbit warrens and bushes near the shores.

Snow Goose (*Chen caerulescens*)   The Snow Goose comes in two phases, blue
and white. Western birds are mixed blue and white, while the eastern birds
are white only. This appears to be a first-year bird in the blue phase. As
they age the bill turns pink.

Swan Goose (*Anser cygnoides*)   The breeding range of the Swan Goose is central Siberia, east to the Kamchatka and Commander islands, and south into Mongolia. It is almost always seen close to water, whether in mountain rivers or on the sea.

Magellan or Upland Goose (*Chloephaga picta*)   On pages 40 and 51 there are
pictures of the Magellan Goose which show a distinct break between the
white head and black neck and breast. The birds seen here are not in
breeding plumage and vary considerably.

DUCKS

Australian Wood Duck (*Chenonetta jubata*)   In Australia this bird is also known as the Maned Goose because of its long neck and legs. The brown head and strong markings of the male on the right contrast with the more sober female.

There are about 127 species of ducks in the world. They appear almost everywhere, with the exception of Antarctica, the Sahara, central Greenland and central Australia. Some, like the Wood Duck, the Harlequin and the Baikal Teal are brilliantly colored, while others, including the Black Duck of North America and the Grey Teal of Australasia, are mottled and rather drab. In weight, they range from the tiny teal at well under a pound, to the Common Eider at over five pounds. The wings are short and pointed, with the high ratio of weight-to-wing area making it necessary for them to pump their wings continuously and fast to remain airborne. Even at a considerable distance, it is possible to tell a duck from a goose in flight, but it requires considerable experience to tell one duck from another.

Ornithologists divide families of birds (in this case the Anatidae, being all the swans, geese and ducks) into sub-families and the sub-families into tribes, of which there are 11. These 11 tribes are further subdivided into 43 *genera*. Some of these *genera* have only one or two members, while others have many. The dabbling ducks, for instance, are of the genus Anas, of which there are 46 species. (Dabbling ducks are those that up-end and feed with only their heads and necks below the surface of the water). Examples of dabbling duck are the Mallard, Pintail, teal and wigeon. The diving ducks, or those that take their food while swimming under the surface, mostly in fresh water, are called Aythyini, and include the North American Canvasback and pochards or scaup. There are, in addition, some 20 species of sea ducks, or Mergini, which feed mostly in the oceans. They include the mergansers, eiders, and scoters. Next there are eight species of stifftail, Oxyurini, including the Black-headed Duck of South America, the Ruddy Duck of North America, and the Blue-billed Duck of Australia. Other tribes of duck are the Freckled Duck (one species), steamer ducks (three species), and perching ducks (13 species). The various species of each *genus* will have more characteristics in common than those at the base of the family tree.

Ducks generally have shorter necks than geese or swans. They molt, usually twice each year, lose their ability to fly while molting, have webbed feet, and in most cases have wide, flat bills. Most are more mobile on the water than on land. Within the range of these generalizations, the habits and appearance of the species differ widely. The most fundamental difference in habit is the method of feeding. One group takes all or most of its food while swimming under water, and the other group feeds either on land, or by up-ending and feeding just below the surface of the water.

Among the first group we find the sea ducks and bay ducks such as the eiders, Harlequin, Oldsquaw, scoter, Bufflehead, merganser, scaup, pochard and steamer ducks. In the more land-oriented group, are the whistling ducks, and dabblers. There is a further tendency for those ducks that feed under water to take a higher ratio of animal matter in the form of molluscs, crustacea and fish, than of vegetable matter. On the other hand, many adult dabblers are almost entirely vegetarian, although the young feed on insects when they are growing.

Diving ducks are divided into three tribes, and further subdivided into 12 *genera* worldwide. They have evolved with special skills for diving and remaining submerged for fairly long periods. The legs are set near the rear of the body, which facilitates swimming under the surface. A few species, including mergansers, also use their wings to swim. On land they are clumsy, at best able to shuffle along, often pushing themselves on their breasts. As a consequence, most diving and bay ducks nest as close as possible to water, although some, such as Common Mergansers, Hooded Mergansers and Goldeneyes, nest in cavities in trees many feet above the ground. When the young of cavity-nesting ducks hatch, they scramble in turn to the entrance, and tumble to the ground. The female then leads them to water. The young develop quickly, but still require nearly two months before they are capable of flying.

Diving ducks are well adapted to their environment. The location of the legs and webbed feet, near the rear of the body, give them strong propulsion under the surface; their lungs and metabolism are such that they can remain submerged for several minutes. The sea ducks, in particular, can reach their prey below the surface. Most, including the scaup, scoters and eiders have wide, flat bills.

The mergansers, however, have sharp, pointed bills. The sides of the bills are strongly serrated, enabling them to hold struggling fish. They are carnivorous, feeding mostly on fish, but also on eels, frogs and insects. Mergansers are unpopular on fishing rivers and lakes, although sometimes without cause. If coarse fish and game fish are both present, mergansers will concentrate on the more sluggish fish that compete for food with game fish. If only game fish are present, as is often the case in Atlantic salmon rivers, mergansers may do considerable damage to the stock of young.

Dabbling ducks, and other species that feed in shallow water and on land, are considerably more agile out of the water. They are capable of diving, but do so only when alarmed or when escaping from danger. For example, Bald Eagles and Peregrine Falcons often harass ducks, forcing them to dive time after time until they are exhausted, and can be picked up on the surface.

It is the dabbling ducks that take the greatest pressure from shooting, for their flesh is more palatable than others. Ducks that feed largely on fish and other animal matter tend to have a strong flavor.

The Mallard is probably the most abundant and widespread of the Anas group, for it lives from the Arctic areas of Europe, Asia and North America, to the sub-tropics. It is also the most heavily shot. It has been calculated that about 70 percent of young Mallards in North America die in their first year, about half from shooting, and half from other causes. When one considers that less than half of the nesting pairs are successful in producing young, one might wonder how the species can survive, but it does. Continued survival of all duck species relies on their capacity to lay large numbers of eggs (average 9 or 10 for most species) and their usual habit of nesting a second time if the first nest fails. Habitat loss in settled areas through drainage and drought is a more compelling pressure than shooting, although, as already mentioned, this situation has stabilized to some extent during the past quarter century.

In North America, governments, and private agencies like Ducks Unlimited, have done much to bring back marginal agricultural land into wetland. Significant areas have been set aside and protected, water has been impounded and controlled, and suitable plants introduced.

The vast majority of ducks, particularly those in the Northern Hemisphere, migrate. In areas like Australia and Africa, where there are seasonal periods of drought, ducks may only move far enough to find water. In a country such as New Zealand, where water is relatively plentiful, migration is quite limited. In the Northern Hemisphere, it would appear that the strongest urge to travel the huge distances to the Arctic and back comes from a little-understood need for light, as well as suitable food.

Most species of waterfowl breeding in the Northern Hemisphere nest in a wide band, from the high Arctic, to southern North America and Europe. It is not known why some Mallards in North America, for example, choose the northern limits of Alaska, and others choose Texas. It is known, however, that this bird with a North American breeding population fluctuating between 6 million and more than 13 million, centers its breeding activity in the Canadian prairies. The Oldsquaw, a long-tailed diving duck, nests only in the Arctic.

Most ducks travel principally over land and can, if they choose, rest and feed along the way. Some travel great distances over water. Losses from choosing this route are probably high. Some Blue-winged Teal, for instance, fly from the northern United States to South America — some 2,500 miles. One immature Blue-winged Teal is recorded as having flown 3,800 miles from the Athabasca Delta in Manitoba, Canada, to Venezuela, in one month.

The average speed at which a duck flies on migration is about 50 miles per hour. This suggests that some non-stop flights over water would take from 40 to 50 hours. Pintails, Lesser Scaup and wigeon bred in Alaska turn up in the Hawaiian islands. Most ducks and geese travel on migration at heights of 1,000 to 3,000 feet, although many go much higher. Sea ducks, such as eiders and scoters, travel much lower, often only a few feet above the water.

Sea ducks are generally chunky birds with thick, impervious down. On the ocean, one can often see them raising themselves in the water and flapping their wings. These birds may spend the whole winter at sea coming to land only to nest. They are killed for food only by native people in the Far North. Their flesh is somewhat unpalatable. Olds-quaws, which are handsome black-and-white sea ducks, winter in both fresh and salt water in Europe, North America and around Japan.

The stifftails are small duck, with short, fanned tails of stiff feathers. They are reddish-colored and have blue bills. They take all their food, primarily vegetable with some animal matter, while swimming along the bottom and sifting it in their bills. In North and South America, this tribe is represented by the Ruddy Duck and the Masked Duck, and in Australia by the Blue-billed Duck.

Among the ducks, the drake remains with the hen only during the egg-laying period, often deserting before the clutch is complete. Thus, the hen must incubate and care for the young alone — the drake having moved off with other males in preparation for the molt. During the molt, the male loses his nuptial plumage, and soon cannot be readily distinguished from the hen. Molting ducks are flightless for a period, usually about 30 days.

The courtship behavior of ducks is not as elaborate, in most cases, as among grebes, but males are assiduous in keeping other males away from their mates. Males do display, however, with movements and posturing that best show their iridescent speculum on the wing. This is particularly true of the dabbling ducks.

White-cheeked or Bahama Pintail (*Anas bahamensis*) Although this bird
appears to be quite pale, most birds of this species are mottled brown above
and below, while only the cheeks and neck are white. It nests from the
Bahamas south through the West Indies and is widespread in South
America to Chile.

Common Eider (*Somateria mollissima*)   The Eider chicks seen here are in a nest of down pulled from the breast of the mother. The collectors of down on the cliffs in Scandinavia now take only part of the nest lining and, as a consequence, do not interfere unduly with the eggs or young.

Left: Black-bellied Whistling Duck (*Dendrocygna autumnalis*)   Formerly known as "Tree ducks," members of this tribe are now called "Whistling ducks." The Black-bellied Whistling Duck perches readily in trees and ranges from Texas to Argentina.

Gadwall (*Anas strepera*)   The Gadwall is widely distributed in North America, Europe and Asia, but is not common. It does not venture into the Arctic, preferring mid-latitude nesting sites. Despite its rather drab appearance here, it is a finely marked, elegant bird, with a white patch on the wing.

Barrow's Goldeneye (*Bucephala islandica*)   Breeding in Iceland, Greenland, Labrador, and in the western part of North America from Alaska to California, this duck does not wander far from its nesting area in winter. It nests in a hollow tree or in cavities in stream banks or, sometimes, under the overhang of boulders.

Right: American Black Duck (*Anas Rubipes*)   A large, dark duck, common in eastern Canada and the United States, the American Black Duck breeds from northern Labrador south to Virginia and Ohio. Seen here in molt, this bird will be unable to fly for about a month. It grows new flight feathers for its autumn migration to southern Canada and the United States.

Blue Duck (*Hymenoliamus malacorhynchos*) New Zealand was once connected to Australia as part of a huge continent, and many bird and insect species are common to both countries. This little duck, however, occurs only in New Zealand.

Bufflehead (*Bucephala albeola*)   The male Bufflehead shown here is in spring plumage. The female is more subdued and has a white patch behind the eye. It nests in holes in trees from Quebec to Alaska and south to northern California.

Common Eider (*Somateria mollissima*) One of the largest of all ducks, the Common Eider can withstand storms and bitterly cold weather with ease. It nests from northern Russia to Ireland and Maine, and winters in the Atlantic and northern Pacific.

American Black Duck (*Anas rubipes*) This is a large duck of the ponds and marshes of eastern North America. It is a dabbler that up-ends while feeding on grasses and other plants below the surface.

Common Goldeneye (*Bucephala clangula*)   The Common Goldeneye breeds in northern forests around the world, building its nest in hollow trees. It is also known as a "whistler" because of the loud whistle made by the wings as it flies.

Harlequin Duck (*Histrionicus histrionicus*)   A beautiful, intricately marked
and colorful duck, the Harlequin nests from eastern Siberia to both coastal
areas of North America. It nests near swift rivers and winters in the ocean,
usually feeding in turbulent water near rocks.

Fulvous Whistling Duck (*Dendrocygna bicolor*)   There are several disjunctive regions where this bird lives: in India and Burma; in the Arabian peninsula; in eastern Africa; in parts of South America, the southern United States, and in Mexico. From these nesting areas it wanders, usually singly, as far north as southern Canada.

Canvasback (*Aythya valisineria*)   Named for its whitish back, the Canvasback nests in prairie potholes of western North America, although it may be seen on migration in the east. It dives for its food, usually in shallow water.

Right: King Eider (*Somateria spectabilis*)   At sea, where it winters as far north as it can find open water, the King Eider is one of the deepest-diving of all ducks. Dives of 180 feet are not uncommon. It feeds almost entirely on animal matter, but females and young eat some buds and leaves when the young are growing.

Left: Canvasback (*Aythya valisineria*)   In dry years the Canvasback, which needs more water than most prairie nesting species in North America, is hard hit. During the dry 1930s the North American population declined dramatically and took many years to recover.

Fulvous Whistling Duck (*Dendrocygna bicolor*)   The relatively small population of this duck in the United States nests, for the most part, on the levees of rice fields in Texas and Louisiana. Unlike most ducks, both parents assist in raising the young. They are nocturnal feeders.

Mallard (*Anas platyrhynchos*)   Here we see the rather drab hen with young.
It is usual for 10 or more eggs to be laid, of which some do not hatch, and
more are lost before the young birds reach the flying stage. Only the large
clutches allow the species to survive.

Ring-necked Duck (*Aythya collaris*)   The female seen here is very similar to the male during the mid-stage of the prenuptial molt. It is also quite similar to the scaups, although slightly smaller, and with a rounder head. On the wing it darts about, rather like a teal.

Mallard (*Anas platyrhynchos*) The bird in the left foreground has its wings set in the downward curve for landing. On taking off from the water Mallards leap straight into the air and are flying immediately.

Comb Duck (*Sarkidiornis melanotos*) A native of northern South America, Africa and Asia, the Comb Duck resembles the Muscovy Duck which, however, has a black head. This bird up-ends, dives and grazes for its food, mostly grain and shoots, but sometimes frogs and insects.

Right: Mandarin Duck (*Aix gelericulata*) This gorgeous bird is a native of the Far East, China, Manchuria, Taiwan and Japan. It is a favorite in zoos all over the world because of its spectacular markings and color.

Preceding pages: Oldsquaw (*Clangula hyemalis*) A resident of both hemispheres, the Oldsquaw winters in open water, both fresh and salt. It is a diver, feeding on small fish and crustacea. In the spring it migrates northward, nesting as far north as the land goes.

Wood Duck (*Aix sponsa*) Considered by many the most beautiful of all ducks, the Wood Duck nests in holes in trees, and in nesting boxes if they are available. It may often be seen perched high in trees.

Musk Duck (*Biziura lobata*)   On a pond in Australia or Tasmania, its home, the Musk Duck is often hard to recognize as a bird. It flaps about, looking more like an active turtle. It is fairly common in swamps, lakes and rivers.

New Zealand Shelduck (*Tadorna variegata*)   Widely distributed on both islands of New Zealand, the New Zealand Shelduck nests near ponds, either on the ground or in hollow trees.

Black-bellied Whistling Duck (*Dendrocygna autumnalis*)   In flight whistling ducks flap their wings relatively slowly looking more like geese than ducks, the legs trailing behind the tail. They then whistle frequently. Some whistling ducks congregate in large flocks, though the Black-bellied is seldom seen in groups of more than a few birds.

Northern Shoveler (*Anas clypeata*)   The markings on this North American
duck are similar to those of the Mallard. The Shoveler is named for its flat,
over-sized bill. It is a dabbling duck.

Left: Northern Pintail (*Anas acuta*) The Northern Pintail is probably the second most abundant duck in North America, after the Mallard, and has the widest distribution worldwide of any of the waterfowl. The photograph does not show the long pointed tail, nor the elegant pointed stripe running down the back of the neck.

Torrent Duck (*Merganetta armata*) The Torrent Duck shown here is in a typical setting — a racing river where it can maintain position in a roaring current. It seldom flies. It occurs from Columbia to Terra del Fuego only at elevations above 6,000 feet.

Water Whistling Duck (*Dendrocygna arcuata*)   The Water Whistling Duck is widely distributed throughout the southwest Pacific as far as Australia. This bird was photographed at Cairns in the northeast corner of Australia. It prefers lakes and lagoons where it dives for its food, usually to about 10 feet. It also dabbles, taking water lily seed and buds.

Ring-necked Duck (*Aythya collaris*)   The male Ring-necked Duck shown here is in full nuptial plumage. The name is inappropriate, for the brown ring on the neck is scarcely discernable, even at close range. This species nests to about 60 degrees north latitude in North America, and winters around the Caribbean.

Northern Pintail (*Anas acuta*)   In North America vast numbers of Pintails nest on the prairies, and the range extends north to the Arctic Ocean. Most North American birds winter in the western Caribbean.

Ruddy Duck (*Oxyura jamaicensis*)   The Ruddy Duck is a North American member of the Stifftail group, so known because of its fanned spiky tail feathers. It dives to the bottom and feeds by sifting animal and vegetable matter through its wide bill.

Left: Tufted Duck (*Aythya fuligula*)   Similar in appearance to the scaups, the Tufted Duck nests throughout Europe, including Iceland, close to lakes and ponds. This is a sociable bird, often joining domestic flocks in parks. Partially migratory, some individuals move south to Africa and Asia.

Smew (*Mergus albellus*)   A mostly-white duck of the "sawbill" group, the Smew nests in the extreme north of Europe and Russia. It migrates to most of central Europe where it winters in rivers and lakes and along the coasts. It nests in hollow trees.

Redhead (*Aythya americana*)   This picture shows the contrast between the strongly-marked male Redhead in nuptial plumage and the rather subdued female. Most Redheads pair in the autumn, remain together during the winter and until the nest is full. The male then departs. This is a North American bird nesting almost entirely in the central plains.

Right: Redhead (*Aythya americana*)   The young of Redheads suffer severe mortality, usually about 80 percent, due to predation and hunting. The population ranges between 600,000 and 900,000 birds depending on breeding conditions in the prairies.

American Wigeon (*Anas americana*)   The principal nesting area of the
American Wigeon is in the pothole country of Saskatchewan and Alberta,
although some birds go as far north as the Arctic Ocean. They migrate
outward and south to the western United States, the Atlantic seaboard, and
the Caribbean.

White-faced Whistling Duck (*Dendrocygna viduata*)   The White-faced Whistling duck is now reported to be very rare in Costa Rica and Panama, and is more common in the tropical parts of South America. It also occurs in Madagascar and some parts of Africa. It is often seen with groups of Black-bellied Whistling Ducks.

Left: Common Merganser (*Mergus merganser*)   A bird with Holarctic distribution in fairly temperate latitudes north of the equator, the Common Merganser, or Sawbill, is a diver, living entirely on small fish and other animal matter. Those shown here are juveniles which have the same markings as the adult females.

Hooded Merganser (*Mergus cucullatus*)   The Hooded Merganser is the only merganser indigenous to North America. The whole population does not exceed 100,000 birds. They nest in tree cavities where hatchlings remain for about a day before heading for the water.

Red-breasted Merganser (*Mergus serrator*)   All mergansers have the ability to
float low in the water like the male Red-breasted Merganser shown here. A
bird of the Northern Hemisphere around the world, it nests in northern
forests and tundra, and winters mostly in salt water.

American Wigeon (*Anas americana*)   The two male American Wigeons shown here are in full spring plumage. One appears to be driving the other off, perhaps to keep it away from its mate. Territorial protection is strong in nesting ducks.

Yellow-billed Duck (*Anas undulata*)   Quite a large duck, resident only in
Africa from Angola to Ethiopia and south to South Africa, the Yellow-billed
Duck is uncommon and local. It is decreasing in numbers throughout its
range where it lives in fresh water lakes, marshes and pools. It is a dabbler,
up-ending for its food, which consists mostly of seeds and shoots.

Red-crested Pochard (*Netta rufina*)   The Red-crested Pochard breeds intermittently in Europe and central Asia on reedy fresh-water lakes and lagoons. It is seldom seen on salt water. After nesting the male loses his handsome appearance and resembles the rather drab female.

Left: European Wigeon (*Anas penelope*)   The European Wigeon is not unlike the American Wigeon, but has a yellow forehead — the American's is white. It nests from Iceland, Scotland and northern Europe to Asia. It winters mostly in salt water and feeds in shallows and mud flats. Occasional birds stray to North America.

European Wigeon (*Anas penelope*)   The European Wigeon shown here is a female. It resembles the male, but is smaller, has a more rounded head, and a rosier coloring.

Rosy-billed Pochard (*Netta peposaca*)   A South American species, the Rosy-billed Pochard lives from southern Brazil through Uruguay, Paraguay, Argentina to Chile. Note the pronounced nob at the base of the bill and the fiery red eye.

Auckland Island Teal (*Anas aucklandica*) The Auckland Island Teal is also known as the Auckland Island Flightless Duck. This drab brown bird is a native of New Zealand and occurs nowhere else.

Lesser Scaup (*Aythya affinis*) A North American species, the Lesser Scaup population varies between five and 10 million birds. It nests from the central plains and California north to the Bering Sea, with the greatest concentration in the Northwest Territories.

Green-winged Teal (*Anas crecca carolinensis*) The average weight of the Green-winged Teal is about 12 ounces. It nests from the Aleutian Islands, the tundra, the prairies to Quebec and, rarely, the northwestern United States. The male seen here is in breeding plumage.

Ringed Teal (*Anas leucorphrys*)   The Ringed Teal lives from the Matto Grosso in Brazil, south through Uruguay, Paraguay, Bolivia and Argentina. The back of the female is similar to that of the male seen here, but the top of the head is brown and there is a line below the eye on the pale cheeks.

Cape Wigeon (*Anas capensis*)   Generally pale in appearance, the Cape
Wigeon lives in Africa, with the greatest concentration in the soda and
brackish lakes of the Rift Valley. Its principal distinguishing feature is the
bright pink bill.

Chestnut Teal (*Anas castanea*)   The Chestnut Teal lives only in Tasmania and Australia where it frequents both fresh and brackish marshes and ponds. It is a cavity-nesting bird that will use nesting boxes readily.

Cinnamon Teal (*Anas cyanoptera*) There are five races of Cinnamon Teal of which four live in South America as far south as Argentina, and the other nests in the western United States and southern British Columbia. The male, seen here, is vividly colored.

Garganey Teal (*Anas querquedula*) The Garganey Teal has a wide distribution from southeast England, across central Europe, Africa, Asia and Indonesia. It is a migrant in the southern part of this range. The female does not have the blue side patch of the male, seen here, and its eye stripe is not as pronounced.

Left: Chestnut Teal (*Anas castanea*) A pair of Chestnut Teal may have two or even three clutches, each consisting of about nine or 10 eggs, in the course of their long breeding season.

Baikal Teal (*Anas formosa*)   The Baikal Teal is native to the taiga of northern
and northeastern Siberia. It has been seen occasionally in Britain and
western Europe, but normally migrates south through Manchuria and Korea
to Japan and southeastern China, sometimes reaching northern India and
Siam.

Blue-winged Teal (*Anas discors*)   The Blue-winged Teal breeds mainly in the pothole country of the North American prairies. Nests are made in long grass as much as a mile from water. The five million or so teal of this species migrate to the southern United States, the Caribbean, and South America.

Lesser Scaup (*Aythya affinis*)   Breeding only in North America, from Alaska to northern Ontario and south to the central prairies, the Lesser Scaup is the most numerous North American diving duck with a population that ranges between five and nine million. It prefers to nest near potholes and lakes at least 10 feet deep.

Surf Scoter (*Melanitta perspicillata*)   A North American species that nests in the northern forested country from Alaska to Quebec. It winters on both oceans as far south as Baja California in the west and Florida in the east. Migration is mainly by sea, although some birds are seen on the Great Lakes in winter.

Greater Scaup (*Aythya marila*)   Compare the white body feathers of this bird
with the rather darker Lesser Scaup shown on page 128. The Greater Scaup
nests in tundra and boreal forests around the northern edges of the
Northern Hemisphere. In North America it breeds only in western Alaska
and near the mouth of the Mackenzie River.

GREBES AND CORMORANTS

Double-crested Cormorant (*Phalacrocorax auritus*) There are 20 species of
cormorant living in all parts of the temperate and tropical world where
there are fish to eat. The Double-crested is common in North America from
Alaska south in summer; it winters in Honduras.

Strictly speaking, grebes and cormorants do not fall into the family of waterfowl, but they share the same habitat and are often seen together in both fresh and salt water. It is for this reason, and for purposes of comparison, that we include a description of them here.

The grebes are a family of 20 species of waterbirds divided into six *genera*. They occur on all continents, except Antarctica, as far north as the Arctic Ocean, and as far south as the tips of the southern continents. All species nest on fresh water, on lakes, ponds, slow-flowing rivers and marshes. Outside of the nesting season, some long-necked and elegant Western Grebes of the Pacific coast of North America, for example, feed in salt water.

Many people, who have never noticed a grebe in the wild have seen them on film, for their elaborate courtship display is a favorite subject of nature programs. There one sees the grebe raise itself, leaving only the stern in the water, and paddle furiously along in an upright position. With the exception of the Pied-billed, grebes have sharp, longish bills, and relatively long necks. Grebes' toes are not webbed, but have flexible lobes which add propulsion and direction while swimming. The ankles and toes are so jointed that they can turn in any direction. All grebes are almost entirely carnivorous: they feed on insects, crustacea and some molluscs which they take, for the most part, under water. Grebes are superbly adapted to life in the water. They are buoyant, but have the capacity to expel the air from their feathers, by compacting them and emptying their air sacs. This allows them to float low in the water, when they choose, or to sink below the surface. Their 20,000 or so feathers are impervious to water.

The legs of grebes are located so far back on the body that they are virtually incapable of walking, or even of standing upright. As a consequence, they nest in soggy masses of floating vegetation, usually concealed by rushes or grass, and anchored to them. The female lays from two to six eggs, which she incubates from three weeks to a month. When hatched, the chicks ride about clinging to the back of the parent, and remain there when the parent dives.

Several species, including the Slavonian or Horned and Black-necked or Eared Grebes, have elaborate crests which may extend under the chin. These are raised during courtship with headshaking and the presentation of a bundle of weeds.

The northern nesting species, including the Horned and Red-necked, undertake long flights on migration. Since the tail is no more than a tuft of small feathers, grebes do not maneuver well. During the nesting season, they seldom take to the air. When they do, they require a long, paddling run for take-off. A few South American species have lost the ability to fly and are, as a consequence, limited to the areas in which they live. Should their habitat change, either through natural or imposed conditions, they are threatened. One, the Colombian Grebe, is probably now extinct and another, the Atitlan, which breeds only on the lake of that name in Guatemala, is threatened by the possible development of a hydroelectric site. When in danger, grebes do not fly, but either dive or sink, and then swim to the protection of the reeds.

Three species, the Horned or Slavonian, the Eared or Black-necked, and the Red-necked, are widely distributed on both sides of the Atlantic. The Least lives from the southern reaches of Texas and Mexico to Argentina, and is common throughout the West Indies. The Great Crested and Little Grebe range from Europe and Africa to Australasia. The grebe most commonly seen in the ponds and marshes of the North American prairies is the Pied-billed, a small stubby-billed bird, known for its slurred whistling notes. The range of brays, chatterings, squeals, grunts and croaks produced by grebes is astonishing, especially in the pre-dawn, when the marsh might otherwise be quite quiet. In the north, Horned or Red-necked grebes are most common.

The 29 species of cormorants are closely related to the pelicans, gannets, tropicbirds, frigatebirds and darters. All have mostly drab black or brown feathers, but some have white on their underparts, and some color on facial patches. The Romans named them *corvus marinus* or, in English "sea raven." This passed through the French as *cor marin*, hence in English to "cormorant."

Cormorants dive for their food from the surface. They push themselves upward with their feet and arch gracefully into the water where they chase their prey. They are wonderfully agile under water: they use their powerful legs for propulsion, while their wings remain tightly by their sides. They feed on small fish at various depths, but it is likely that bottom-feeding fish make up the bulk of the diet for most cormorant species. Cormorants are capable of remaining submerged for a matter of minutes, and of reaching depths of about 200 feet. Most, however, feed in relatively shallow water, fairly close to shore.

These birds have huge appetites. In feeding, they convert protein into nitrates and phosphates in prodigious quantities, enriching the quality of their feeding grounds. Most species have a beneficial effect in that they feed on small fish of no commercial value. Off the coasts of Peru and Chile, however, millions of Guanay Cormorants compete with fishermen for the anchovy catch. It is the Guanays that are most responsible for the flourishing industry which converts the huge quantities of dried guano collected from the islands into fertilizer.

Cormorants, or Shags as some species are called, nest in colonies, sometimes consisting of only a few pairs, but more often numbering in the hundreds. They seek areas, often islands, that afford protection from predators. Some colonies are shared with other seabirds; in Australia and New Zealand several species of cormorant often nest together. Nests must be in a windy place or at the edge of a cliff, for these birds are incapable of walking without tripping, let alone running for take-off. At a crowded site, these birds are unstable, both on landing, and when they are at the nest. Each species has developed signals to indicate its intentions to other nesters. When a bird is about to leave the nest, it opens its mouth to show that its plans are not aggressive. Olivaceous and Double-crested cormorants, which sometimes nest in trees, have great problems landing safely.

When the young of cormorants hatch they are, unlike those of waterfowl, blind and naked. In about two weeks, they are covered with thick down, and in a further five or six weeks, they can fly. During this period, each parent makes many trips to the nest with food.

The feathers of cormorants are permeable, so the skin becomes wet when they dive. Consequently, the birds have to dry their wings after a number of dives. Cormorants can often be seen with wings out-stretched in the sun. Even the Galapagos Cormorant, which long ago lost the power to fly, stretches its rudimentary wings. This habit may also have a temperature-control function. Their dark feathers absorb heat from the sun which must, on occasion, be dispelled by panting. The air passes through the throat pouch, which is rich in blood vessels, and cools the bird.

Cormorants are like pelicans in that all four toes are connected by a web. With ducks and geese, only three toes are connected. Again, unlike waterfowl that have the capacity to store fat in their bodies as insulation and energy for long journeys, cormorants are lean. This limits their range to water that is reasonably temperate.

Several species, including the Olivaceous and Double-crested cormorants, nest both on fresh and salt water but some, including the White-necked Cormorant of Africa, appear to live entirely on fresh water. New colonies appear and others are deserted, particularly on island lakes. One colony of Double-crested Cormorants at Lake of the Woods in western Ontario, is more than one thousand miles from salt water and has been colonized during the past few years where there was none before.

In flight, cormorants can be distinguished from ducks by a slower lumbering wingbeat, and by the hump-backed appearance caused by carrying the long neck slightly lower than the line of the back.

Left: Pied Cormorant (*Phalacrocorax varius*) Known in Australia and New Zealand, where it lives, as the Yellow-faced Cormorant, the Pied Cormorant has a white throat, chest and belly. It nests in colonies in flooded areas, preferring to locate directly over the water.

Eared Grebe (*Podiceps nigricollis*) The Eared Grebe, known in Europe as the Black-necked, is the smallest of the 20 grebe species. Note the chick peeping out from the back. Although the young can swim, they often ride and dive clinging to the mother's back.

Pied-billed Grebe (*Podilymbus podiceps*)   Restricted to the Western Hemisphere, the Pied-billed Grebe lives from the prairie provinces of Canada, south to southern Argentina. It nests in pairs, building a floating nest of rank vegetation. The young leave the nest within hours of hatching. Note the stout short bill.

Right: Horned Grebe (*Podiceps auritus*)   The Horned, or Slavonian Grebe, as it is known in Europe, is Holarctic. It breeds in northern Europe and Iceland and in North America from southern Alaska, south to the central prairies of the United States. It is not a colonial nester and one usually finds only one pair on each pond.

Galapagos Cormorant (*Nannopterum harrisi*) Also known as the Flightless Cormorant, it lives only in the Galapagos where, after thousands of years of freedom from predators, it lost the need to fly. Its wings are vestigial, ragged things. With the introduction of rats and dogs, this cormorant is now in danger of extinction.

Eared Grebe (*Podiceps nigricollis*)   The sharp bill of the Eared Grebe appears to be tilted upward because of the slope of the lower mandible. In full breeding plumage the throat is black and the fan of feathers behind the eye is golden.

Following page: Red-necked Grebe (*Podiceps griseigena*)   Holarctic, the Red-necked Grebe nests north of the Great Lakes, across western Canada and Alaska, northern Asia and eastern Europe. The male bird is shown here incubating. The Eared Grebe nests on fresh water but winters close to shore, mostly in salt water.

INDEX TO PHOTOGRAPHS

Bluebill, *see* Lesser Scaup
Bufflehead, 79

Canvasback, 84, 86
Cormorant
 Double-crested, 131
 Flightless, *see* Galapagos
 Galapagos, 140
 Pied, 136
 Yellow-faced, *see* Pied

Duck
 American Black, 77, 80
 Australian Wood, 67
 Black-bellied Whistling, 74, 96
 Blue, 78
 Comb, 90
 Fulvous Whistling, 83, 87
 Harlequin, 82
 Mandarin, 91
 Musk, 95
 Ring-necked, 89, 101
 Ruddy, 103
 Torrent, 99
 Tufted, 104
 Water Whistling, 100
 White-faced Whistling, 109
 Yellow-billed, 114
 Wood, 94

Eider
 Common, 73, 80
 King, 85

Gadwall, 75
Goldeneye
 Barrow's, 76
 Common, 81

Goose
 Barheaded, 35
 Barnacle, 41, 58

Brant, 42
Canada, 2, 44, 45
Cape Barren, 43, 48
Egyptian, 47
Emperor, 52
Greylag, 51
Knob-billed, *see* Comb Duck
Magellan, 40, 51, 66
Magpie, 53
Nene, 56
Orinoco, 54
Pacific White-fronted, 55
Pink-footed, 57
Red-breasted, 59
Ross's, 60
Snow, 46, 49, 61, 64
Swan, 65
Upland, *see* Magellan
White-fronted, 50, 62
Grebe
 Black-necked, *see* Eared
 Eared, 137, 141
 Horned, 139
 Pied-billed, 138
 Red-necked, 142
 Slavonian, *see* Horned

Mallard, 9, 88, 90
Merganser
 Common, 110
 Hooded, 111
 Red-breasted, 112

Oldsquaw, 92-93

Pintail
 Bahama, *see* White-cheeked
 Northern, 98, 102
 White-cheeked, 72
Pochard
 Red-crested, 115
 Rosy-billed, 118

Redhead, 106, 107

Shelduck, 63
 African, 38
 New Zealand, 95
 Paradise, *see* New Zealand
 Ruddy, 39
Scaup
 Greater, 8, 130
 Lesser, 120, 128
Scoter, Surf, 129
Shoveler, Northern, 97
Smew, 105
Swan
 Black, 31, 32, 33
 Black-necked, 30
 Coscoroba, 17
 Mute, 23, 24, 27, 29
 Trumpeter, 4-5, 22, 28
 Tundra, 21, 26, 34
 Whistling, *see* Tundra
 Whooper, 16, 25

Teal
 Auckland Island, 119
 Baikal, 126
 Blue-winged, 127
 Chestnut, 123, 124
 Cinnamon, 125
 Garganey, 125
 Green-winged, 120
 Ringed, 121

Wigeon
 American, 108, 113
 Cape, 122
 European, 116, 117

PHOTOGRAPH CREDITS